GLACIERS & GRANITE:
A Guide to Maine's
Landscape and Geology

GLACIERS & GRANITE:
A Guide to Maine's Landscape and Geology

By DAVID L. KENDALL
Illustrated by Marie E. Litterer

Down East Books, Camden, Maine

Copyright © 1987 by David L. Kendall
Illustrations copyright © 1987 by Marie E. Litterer
ISBN 0-89272-230-4
Library of Congress Catalog Card Number 86-72764

Design by Janet Patterson
Composition by Crane Services, West Barnstable, Mass.
Printed at Capital City Press, Inc., Montpelier, Vt.

5 4 3 2

Down East Books
P. O. Box 679
Camden, Maine 04843

Cover Photograph: Lower South Branch Pond, by David Kendall

Contents

Foreword, by Roy L. Farnsworth 7

Acknowledgments 9

Introduction 11

1. The Regions of Maine 13
2. Glaciation 21
3. The Battered Coast 43
4. Mountains 77
5. Water on the Land:
   Weathering, Lakes, and Rivers 87
6. Noticing Rocks and Minerals 113
7. Plate Tectonics 143
8. Maine Through Geologic Time 157
9. Geology in Human Affairs 177
10. Road Logs 189
11. Sites to See 219

Bibliography 228

Glossary 230

Index 237

To Florence Lamphere Kendall,
who, from my earliest memories,
taught me to appreciate scenery.

Foreword

The State of Maine intrigues people with views of a rockbound coast, Mount Katahdin and lesser mountains, the great rivers, and many ponds and lakes. Such scenery is bound to its geologic setting and the processes acting on this and all sections of the earth. Geologists are constantly asked by travelers to explain the rock formations they have seen, or to answer questions as to how or why some feature of the landscape has developed.

The author, with his experience in mining geology and in the field of education in earth sciences, is well qualified to answer many of the questions raised by the curious. This book minimizes the professional language of the geologist and speaks in the language of the layman, presenting basic geologic fact as related to particular geological features of scenic interest. While many geologic features are subtle and visible to only the professional eye, he has chosen those which anyone can observe along the commonly traveled ways of the state.

Scenery is synonymous with the enjoyment of travel, and this book will surely add understanding to the enjoyment of Maine's varied landscape.

Roy L. Farnsworth
Professor of Geology
Bates College, Lewiston, Maine

Acknowledgments

In writing this book I have drawn freely on published geological literature, especially items issued by the Maine Geological Survey and by the Maine Critical Areas Program of the State Planning Office. A list of publications from these two agencies with authors' names appears in the Bibliography. The Geological Society of Maine publishes a series of Bulletins called *Maine Geology*, from which I extracted a description of the two tills at Roque Bluffs by Robert P. Ackert, Jr. in Bulletin No. 2 and information on the Machias-Eastport area from Olcott Gates in Bulletin No. 3. A basic geological textbook I have frequently consulted is *Earth*, by Frank Press and Raymond Siever, published by W. H. Freeman and Company, San Francisco. I have also profited from many personal discussions with geologists throughout the state, most of them members of the Geological Society of Maine and the Maine Mineral Resources Association, although in most cases it would be impossible to identify their contributions precisely.

I am indebted to Archie W. Berry, of the University of Maine, Farmington, who read the entire manuscript and made a number of valuable suggestions, particularly with respect to technical geological matters, and to William F. Meyer, Jr., who read several of the chapters and offered excellent suggestions for making the book more useful for the nontechnical reader/traveler. Errors, of course, remain my own responsibility.

Introduction

The purpose of this guide is to help those who are looking for comprehensible answers to the questions, "What happened here? How did the land get this way?" Some may use this book as an informal text on Maine geology, reading through from front to back. It is also a field guide, and can be used like any nature guide, by leafing through to find answers to particular questions about specific sites.

The landscape of Maine is not a random, accidental jumble of hills and valleys, rivers, and coastlines. Landscape is the result of processes we can see today—weathering, erosion, deposition—that have acted over immensely long periods of time on bedrock and loose surficial materials of a variety of compositions and structures. Other processes have played a part in the past, though they are not significant at present—earthquakes, volcanism, glacial sculpting. The land, responding to these forces, takes on a shape that reflects the nature of the underlying rocks, just as a building reflects its frame.

Many people find their interest in geology aroused when they come upon a new vista and notice it with fresh eyes. A coast with rocky headlands separated by a smooth, curving beach, a peak with sweeping vistas of scattered lakes and protruding mountains, or even a deep roadcut exposing contorted and veined bedrock—one of these could trigger the curiosity that leads to landscape appreciation.

Any perceptive person can enjoy the Maine landscape; you do not have to know anything about its geological structure or derivation. It might even be argued that to know too much about the details could impair your appreciation. On the other hand, the more we know about art, music, and poetry, the more we enjoy them, and it is the same with landscape.

Rocks tell their own story, but they reveal their secrets most reluctantly—in tiny hints and puzzling riddles. No less than medicine, geology is interdisciplinary, combining the insights of chemistry, physics, biology, and all the specialties in between, to unravel the message in the rocks. In this book we describe, in an understandable way, the important geological processes that have taken place throughout geologic history and thus equip you, the amateur observer, with the facts necessary for a satisfying appreciation of the scene before you.

We begin with a description of the principal regions of Maine (Chapter 1). Next, some major geologic principles are illustrated with examples drawn from the wondrously varied Maine scenery (Chapters 2 through 6). Then we examine what is is known of the geologic history of the state (Chapters 7 and 8), and the impact of Maine's geology on its people (Chapter 9). Finally, Road Logs (Chapter 10) call attention to interesting features along selected roads that are frequently traveled and present good cross-sections of the regions.

The scenic features described in this book are readily accessible. Many are found in state parks or are standard hiking destinations and easily located. Roadcuts can usually be examined safely on foot, if desired, except along Interstate 95 and the Maine Turnpike, where stopping, except for emergencies, is prohibited (however, these two highways have many large and interesting cuts that are instructive even without stopping, especially if you have read ahead in the Road Logs and are prepared to watch for them).

Maine has been described as a state too large to explore fully in one lifetime, but small enough to try. This guide makes no pretense to completeness; no book could describe all that is to be seen. We can only suggest the stories behind Maine scenery and hope that they will help you view it with new enjoyment and understanding.

1
The Regions of Maine

The wide variety of Maine's scenery is due to its geology; the nature and structure of the underlying rocks have determined how physical and chemical forces carved the landscape. Weathering softens some kinds of rock more than others, preparing it for sculpting and removal. Freezing water in the cracks of broken rock forces them apart, crumbling the outcrops. Even resistant rocks eventually succumb to the pull of gravity and slabs are torn from craggy peaks, leaving cliffs with piles of broken rock at their bases. Meandering rivers cut into their banks, carrying away soft sediments only to build sandbars with the same material farther downstream. The ocean relentlessly beats at the rocky coast, searching out any zone of weakness to feed the ceaseless mill of waves grinding and smoothing the shoreline. The unsubtle force of a mighty ice sheet grinding down from the north between one hundred thousand and twelve thousand years ago was the latest major influence on the land, but steady, persistent shaping, though not always apparent, continues. The result of all this is a mosaic of landscape patterns, not everywhere tamed and gentle, but everywhere interesting and inviting exploration.

From the air, or on a good topographic map, several distinct regions of Maine are obvious: sandy flatlands in the southwest, the ragged coastline, a central upland back from the coast, wide, rolling farmland in the northeast corner, and a major mountain upland that occupies nearly half of the state along the northwest side. Each region reveals a different story to the curious observer.

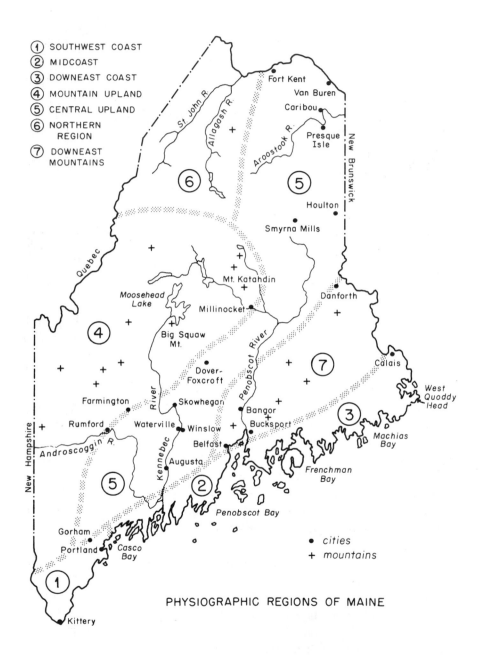

① SOUTHWEST COAST
② MIDCOAST
③ DOWNEAST COAST
④ MOUNTAIN UPLAND
⑤ CENTRAL UPLAND
⑥ NORTHERN
   REGION
⑦ DOWNEAST
   MOUNTAINS

• cities
+ mountains

PHYSIOGRAPHIC REGIONS OF MAINE

Southwest Coast

The Atlantic coastal plain, broad and clearly defined in many states to the south, narrows in New England and comes to an end near Portland. **York County** has the only typical coastal plain in Maine. For a number of miles inland, the land is almost flat, with only an occasional higher rise like **Mount Agamenticus,** for sailors a significant landmark in an otherwise featureless skyline.

From **Kittery** to **Portland** the coastline is scalloped, with broad sandy beaches between wide-spaced, prominent headlands: **Cape Neddick, Bald Head Cliff, Cape Arundel, Biddeford Point,** and others. For thousands of years, vast amounts of sand and gravel were spread over the land and dumped into the ocean by the advancing glacier. Raging torrents of meltwater pouring from the wasting glacier later spread even more sediment across the plain.

The sea is smoothing and straightening the coastline by cutting into the headlands, reworking the stones and pebbles into finer material, and winnowing out the softer, less resistant minerals. Currents and waves spread the sand into broad beaches between the headlands: **York, Ogunquit, Wells**, and **Old Orchard.** Wind heaps the sand into dunes, which become natural shock absorbers for the fury of the stormy surf. It is a coastline that teems with life. The beach has a well-known appeal for people, and the marshes and wetlands are the nurseries for hundreds of varieties of wild plant and animal life.

Midcoast

Northeastward from **Portland** and **Casco Bay,** the Midcoast is radically different from the coastal plain. Here the sea reaches far inland along drowned valleys that form narrow winding bays, separated by rocky peninsulas that end in points with picturesque lighthouses, like **Pemaquid** and **Marshall Point,** looking out to the open Atlantic.

In contrast to the Southwest Coast, where the bedrock lies parallel to the beaches, along the Midcoast the layers of bedrock are sharply warped in long, upright folds striking inland. The valleys have been eroded in softer layers in the downwarped portions of the folds, while the ridges are preserved by more resistant bedrock layers on the crests. The long, steep-sided bays make excellent cruising and moorings for sailboaters, shelter from the worst storms of the sea. Beaches are few and small, mostly found in coves, with the notable exception of magnificent **Popham Beach** near the mouth of the Kennebec River, which furnishes the necessary sand.

Downeast Coast

East of **Penobscot Bay** the coast, though no less irregular, takes on a different character. Bays are wider and there is a maze of islands, some large enough to have year-round communities with roads and automobiles. The bedrock is different. It is granite, great tonnages of which were quarried in the post–Civil War building boom. Some granite is still quarried on order. Low mountains and knobs of granite scrubbed round by the glacier break up the skyline. This part of the coast, with its broad, island-dotted reaches of **Frenchman, Blue Hill, Pleasant and Machias bays,** is of outstanding scenic beauty.

The coastline from Machias Bay to **West Quoddy Head** is fairly straight with few inlets. One is at **Cutler,** where the narrow bay forces a twenty-eight-foot range between high and low tides. From the high cliffs at **West Quoddy Head** you can see the cliffs of Grand Manan Island, Canada, across nine miles of channel. This part of the coast is less developed, and the settlements are mostly still picturesque fishing villages.

Mountain Upland

Mountains fascinate nearly everyone. It is exhilarating to toil up an ever-steepening slope, through woods and scrubby vegetation, and emerge above timberline with a vast landscape stretching below you. Even those who do not climb are struck by the sight of a range of mountains, their rounded backs like a parade of elephants on the skyline. Our view from the air cannot miss the Mountain Upland striking northeasterly from the New Hampshire line nearly across the state. From ground level the change is equally pronounced.

The Mountain Upland rises rather abruptly along a line striking northeast through **Rumford, Farmington, Dover-Foxcroft,** and **Millinocket.** Early railroad surveys showed a pronounced change in grade as they crossed this line, and even today this is apparent as you drive northwest along any of the cross-cutting highways. From **Boarstone Mountain** near Monson, for example, with mountains at your back and on both left and right, the view of the wide Central Upland to the south shows clearly that you are on the edge of the Mountain Upland.

The **Kennebec River**, draining **Moosehead Lake**, roughly divides the mountain area into a northern section dominated by **Mount Katahdin**, and a southern section from **Mount Bigelow** to **Old Speck** on the New Hampshire line.

It is a surprise to climb the steep slopes to the top of Mount Katahdin and to discover for the first time **The Tablelands**, a broad, tundra landscape on the shoulder of the mountain, stretching for a mile or more in an open, gentle slope from Baxter Peak northwest to the forbidding, spruce-forested Klondike. You feel released after the strenuous climb, often aided by handholds, and envy the ravens soaring easily over the alpine meadowland. To the west you can see that the tops of the highest mountains all rise to about the same elevation. Similar rolling uplands near the summits of other New England mountains, notably in the Presidential Range of New Hampshire, indicate that at one time, perhaps fifty million years ago, a smooth, rolling land existed where mountains are today. Only small fragments of this old landscape remain. In one early publication the Mountain Upland was termed the Moosehead Plateau. The term plateau, however, connotes a region of flat-lying bedrock, broadly lifted en masse without much disturbance, and it could be misleading if applied to this region of many peaks of strongly contorted bedrock.

The western Mountain Upland is a jumble of peaks from Old Speck at Grafton Notch to Mount Bigelow (both included in Maine Public Reserve Lands). Few summits rise to 4,000 feet but it is a rugged land of huge lakes and outstanding mountain scenery. Wild streams cascade down steep narrow valleys, spilling over falls and carrying loads of sand and gravel, pebbles and cobbles, to be spread over the landscape where the streams meet the broader valleys of the Central Upland.

Central Upland

Several very large folds, their crests and troughs trending northeast, rippled the crust under Maine like giant swells on a smooth ocean. The Central Upland lies on one of these, a broad trough with many smaller crests and troughs included within the general downwarp. The land is rolling, not flat, but in elevation it rises very little; from about 200 feet at **Gorham** in the southwest, to only 400 feet near **Mattawamkeag,** more than 150 miles northeast.

The southern part of the Central Upland was the dumpsite of the glacier, which brought vast thicknesses of ground-up rock scraped from the land to the north, and left it in low, streamlined hills. These in turn were washed by vast quantities of meltwater from the wasting ice, leaving wide expanses of sand. The sand was whipped up into dunes by the wind, unimpeded by vegetation in that harsh arctic climate, forming the so-called desert of Maine.

Farther north, from **Augusta** to **Bangor,** the open, rolling land with its loamy soil is more amenable to farming. Here the smooth ridges and hills provide wide, pleasant views, while east of Bangor farmland gives way to forest and lakes. Just north of **Smyrna Mills** and **Houlton** streams flow north to the **Aroostook River.** This land along Maine's eastern boundary, the home of the famous Aroostook County potato, is open and well-settled. It contains some of the best farming soils in the state due to the limy nature of the underlying rocks, from which the soils were derived.

Northern Region

A region of rolling hills, the watershed of the **St. John and Allagash rivers,** is separated from the Central Upland in Aroostook County by a range of low mountains west of Route 11. This range, marked by **Gardner and Deboullie mountains,** stretches 50 miles south to **Willard and Reed mountains,** where streams flowing to the Aroostook River are divided from those entering the watershed of the East Branch of the Penobscot River. The divide marks the southern margin of the region.

A peculiarity of the Northern Region can be seen on a map. The tributaries to the **St. John and Allagash rivers** tend to be parallel and enter their respective rivers at more or less right angles, in the manner of a trellis. This pattern of drainage developed on bedrock that is uniform in nature and of fairly gentle slope. Moreover, the bedrock in this region of Maine is some of the least altered by the disruptive effects of mountain building and intruding molten rock from below. The rocks are so little altered that in many places fossils, comparatively rare in Maine, can be found.

Most of the region is covered by a thick mantle of glacial rubble;

bedrock is not abundantly exposed. Scratches on bedrock indicate that in this region ice flowed northwest rather than the usual southerly trend. The explanation of this rather surprising fact is that during the late phases of the ice age a remnant cap of ice existed over the mountains of Maine for some time after the **St. Lawrence River** valley had been freed of its ice. Gravity pulled this ice northwest toward the open St. Lawrence River.

Northern Maine is thickly forested, and for over 150 years large timber and paper companies have harvested lumber and pulpwood here. Farms are few and scattered and generally trace their origin back to lumbering days when food was grown for the men and their livestock. That this lack of agriculture is more a result of the pattern of land use than of any geologic limitation is suggested by the fact that just over the Canadian boundary, where the geology is essentially the same, farms and cleared lands are widespread.

Downeast Mountains

From a point between **Waterville** and **Belfast,** a wedge of land stretches northeastward 125 miles to **Danforth** and **Calais** on the New Brunswick border. This belt, the Downeast Mountains, separates the Central Upland from the Downeast Coast. Beneath this land lie large irregular masses of granite, many of which have been eroded flat, but here and there prominent rounded peaks, some more than fourteen hundred feet high, rise from the forested land. From **Lucerne,** south of **Brewer** on U.S. Route 1A, there is a fine view of the southern peaks. In the northern part there are glimpses of widely separated mountains like **Lead, Passadumkeag,** and **Musquash,** rising to twelve or fourteen hundred feet above the low and boggy land.

The landscape of Maine is a sculpture produced from varied stone by rivers and oceans, by rain and wind and glacial ice, working continually for 100 million years. Rough calculations suggest that New England should have been reduced to a flat lowland in only fifteen to twenty million years. Obviously, the present landscape is no flat plain; there must have been uplift of the crust during the 100-million-year interval. This uplift is believed to have taken place in a geologically short span of time some twenty to twenty-five million years ago. Uplift rejuvenated the rivers, causing them to run faster and to erode at a faster rate. The flat land, cut into by the rejuvenated rivers, was carved into a network of sharp valleys whose sides merged, leaving little of the the old plain. Today there is only a suggestion of it in the even tops of the long ridges in central Maine.

Dissection of the landscape by rivers and streams continued until the arrival of the Ice Age, one to two million years ago, with its multiple continental ice sheets advancing and retreating. The landscape of Maine prior to the advance of the ice, in most respects, was probably similar to what it is now. In spite of the fact that the ice attained a thickness of several thousand feet, completely burying even the highest peaks, the base of the glacier probably followed the original drainage pattern carved into the bedrock. Glaciation changed the surface topography, gouging valleys deeper, rounding off hills and mountain peaks, and damming streams to create lakes and bogs, but the general shape of the land had already been determined by the nature of the bedrock. The positions of mountain ranges and uplands, the surrounding lowlands, and the major stream patterns, were probably much as we see them today.

2
Glaciation

Stop along the side of the road in central Maine on a hilltop with a commanding view. Valleys and ridges roll away to blue mountains on the skyline many miles away. All of the scenery has been affected by glaciation. The mountain tops have been rounded and grooved, and streams are still cutting down between ridges. Many valleys have been plugged up with sand and gravel, disrupting the drainage and forming lakes and ponds and bogs. The land has been left with a blanket of loose, stony debris that is slowly being converted to soil. The glacier has been gone only about twelve thousand years, so soils are thin and young.

The preglacial landscape of Maine probably resembled the present landscape of the southern Appalachians, beyond the reach of the great ice sheet. Maine's mountains, too, had been subjected to millions of years of weathering and erosion, softening the profiles and smoothing the slopes. Glaciation probably did not greatly change their form but the deeply weathered rock and soil was scoured away, leaving the harder, fresher rock that we find today.

The study of glacial geology is especially appealing because it is enjoyed, and easily grasped, in an outdoor laboratory of spectacular scenery. Moreover, most of the processes we envision in Maine as the actions of a great ice sheet can, in fact, be observed taking place today on a smaller scale in British Columbia, Alaska, Greenland, Antarctica, and other places where glaciers are still found. It is not hard to find contemporary evidence for our interpretation of the landscape.

Alpine glaciers had been studied in Europe for a long time

before it was recognized that landscape many miles from the mountains also showed features known to be associated with glaciation: polished and grooved rocks, piles of debris left when the ice melted away, boulders far from their bedrock origin, and vast amounts of sand and gravel spread over the land by meltwater from the ice. One of the great breakthroughs of geology occurred about 150 years ago when geologists first recognized that great ice sheets of almost unimaginable size and power had once covered not just the mountains but vast areas of land. *Continental glaciation*, like many other great concepts and inventions, is now taken as established fact.

The Work of Glaciers

Two different glaciation processes combine to affect our landscape. One of these can be thought of as *destructive:* rock is plucked from its bed and dragged along, grinding and scarring the overridden rock. The other process, resulting in new landforms—rolling and rounded hills of gravel and sand, long narrow "horsebacks" of gravel

Use of Theory in Science

For some people the word "theory" is almost derogatory. "That's just theory!" they say, implying that an idea is impractical, visionary, or even suspect. Very different is the scientists' use of theory, frequently misunderstood by the public.

To a scientist, a theory is a unifying principle, the very framework on which scientific understanding is built. Without a theory to organize and integrate them, the facts yielded by scientific research are little more than a miscellaneous collection. But beyond organizing existing information, a theory permits prediction into the unknown, showing where research is likely to produce new knowledge. Theories are never complete; they are always being modified and improved as new information accumulates. It is as though the foundation of a building is constantly strengthened and deepened, permitting larger and more elaborate construction to be added to the top.

For a scientist, theories are not fantasies or tentative guesses. Those are called hypotheses, and they are very useful for guiding further research or experimentation. Hypotheses flow from theories, and confirmed hypotheses add to the structure of the theory.

stretching across lowlands, and the flat lakebeds from ice-dammed rivers—can be considered *constructive*.

The Glacier Destroys. If you rub an ice cube against a rock you will see quickly which wins the abrasion test; the ice crumbles and has very little effect on the rock. Yet we are told that glacial ice scratched and grooved the bedrock in "striations" sometimes more than an inch deep. The real story is that not ice, but rock, frozen into the base of the glacier like a very coarse sandpaper, did the cutting. The immense weight of great thicknesses of glacial ice exerted tremendous force against the bedrock. As the glacier moved, a few feet a year, the sharp corners of the embedded rocks (picked up from overridden knobs and projections) gouged and chiseled their grooves.

Where the soil cover has been stripped away from the bedrock surface it is possible to see the effects of glacial grinding and polishing. In many roadcuts along Interstate 95 and other newer high-

Nearly 150 years ago geologists noted that great thicknesses of loose rock debris, huge isolated boulders, and deep grooves and scratches cut into smoothed knobs of bedrock far from the mountains could not be attributed to the action of rivers but instead were similar to features found near glaciers in the mountains. Gradually the idea emerged that glaciers, obviously responsible for the effects seen in the mountain valleys, must also have covered the land many miles beyond the mountains, transporting boulders and carving the land before they disappeared in meltwater. Thus was born the Theory of Continental Glaciation, an excellent example of the founding, development, and confirmation of a scientific theory.

Continental glaciation, now an established fact, is no longer referred to as a theory, yet the idea is an abstraction. The theory served the purpose of correlating the myriad factual obvservations of geologists all over the world into a coherent story. It continues to suggest new ideas to pursue, new places to look, new problems to solve, right up to the present day. This is what a theory is supposed to do. There is nothing so practical as a good theory.

Glacial scratches and polish in Lucerne granite.

Glacial polish, Routes 6 & 15, near Monson.

ways, the top of the cut is bare, exposing the undulating, remarkably smooth surface, visible even from a moving car. Along the coast in some places, storm waves have stripped away the glacial debris from the bedrock, leaving grooved and scratched surfaces exposed at low tide.

Grooves and scratches in bedrock record the direction of the glacier's motion. Scratches left by the glacier are remarkably parallel over distances of many feet, and this distinguishes them from ordinary scrapes and scratches made on bedrock by plows and bulldozers. Glacial scratches are also uniformly weathered, whereas recent marks generally cut through the weathered surface, exposing fresh rock. In Maine most grooves and scratches trend southeast, but in the Northern Region interesting scratches indicate that ice movement there was northwesterly into the St. Lawrence Valley. Apparently during the waning stages of glaciation the St. Lawrence River was open and into it the ice-capped mountains along the present-day Canadian boundary poured their icy flows. Sea-level glaciers are prone to breakup by storm waves, and milder weather at the lower altitudes causes them to retreat, opening up the valleys faster. The mountain glaciers no doubt persisted a few centuries longer.

Many mountains in Maine have a sloping north side but are craggy and broken on the south-facing side. This shape was caused by the moving ice, which rode up the north slope, grinding and smoothing it, but plucked away the rock on the "downstream" side, leaving a steep cliff. The direction of ice movement is clearly shown in the resulting mountain profile. Some offshore islands (for example, the Porcupines, near Mount Desert Island) show the same glacially shaped profile, which is not surprising since the islands are themselves the tops of submerged mountains.

Although today's warmer climate has eliminated alpine glaciers from Maine, the effects of former glaciation are quite evident on the sides of many of Maine's mountains, most notably **Mount Katahdin.** Comparing the shape of the **Great Basin** and the adjoining **South and North Basins** with similar rock basins still occupied by glaciers in the Rocky Mountains, it is easy to visualize the ice not long gone from the side of Katahdin. These steep-walled amphitheaters, called *cirques*, look like bites out of an apple.

Close-spaced cracks in the rock promote the development of

Mount Kineo, from Rockwood. The cliff profile is a good example of glacial plucking.

Mount Katahdin, showing the glacial cirque of North Basin.

cirques. Freezing water expands and, if confined in a crack, can exert enough pressure to break the rock. More water enters, and the cycle of freezing-thawing eventually reduces even the hardest rock to rubble. Where the glacier is in contact with the mountainside, freezing and thawing take place most of the year. Thus, a glacier gradually bites its way up the mountain slope, carrying away the broken rock. When it finally melts, it leaves a craggy-walled, flat-bottomed, half-bowl gouge in the mountain like the basins on Mount Katahdin. The **Knife-edge** between Pamola Peak and South Peak is the southern wall of South Basin, marking where the cirque is breaking through to the other side of the mountain.

It is common to find a lake, called a *tarn*, in the bottom of a glacial cirque, like **Chimney Pond** in the South Basin of Mount Katahdin. The greatest weight, and thus the deepest gouging, was concentrated in the center of the basin. A lip of rock together with a pile of rock rubble left at the mouth of the cirque holds back water and creates the tarn. The **Basin Ponds,** to the northeast, have a different origin. They formed behind a dam of loose rock debris, called a *moraine*, left by the glaciers that carved the cirques.

Other mountains with cirques are **Crocker Mountain** in the Carrabassett region, and mountains in **Grafton Notch State Park** near the Maine–New Hampshire border, north of Newry.

Rivers and streams, always seeking the lowest possible elevation, cut gullies and valleys that are V-shaped in cross-section. Glaciers, on the other hand, fill their valleys with ice wall-to-wall. Grinding and plucking continues wherever the ice is in contact with rock, and the result is the carving of the sides as well as the bottom of the valley. When the ice finally melts away, the landscape is left with a U-shaped valley. Grafton Notch State Park occupies such a glacier-sculpted valley.

Not only are glaciated valleys broader, they are straighter and have gentler curves than river valleys. **Mount Desert Island** displays several U-shaped valleys, almost perfectly parallel and trending a bit east of south. **Somes Sound,** nearly dividing the island in two, is of particular interest because it is a *fjord*, a valley cut much deeper than sea level by a glacier that extended an unknown distance out to sea. The valley was later filled by the sea when the meltwater from the wasting ice raised sea level to its present elevation. With

Chimney Pond is a tarn at the foot of Mount Katahdin. In the background, the Basin Ponds were formed by a moraine dam. (Photo by Martin Womer.)

the exception of the Hudson River estuary, no other fjord exists on the East Coast.

The Glacier Builds. Glaciers build as well as carve. With the debris from their sculpting they heap up hills and fill in hollows. They spread a veneer of crushed rock over the land. Water from the melting ice sorts sand and gravel. Huge lakes of muddy water, dammed temporarily by ice blockades, gently settle a mantle of silt and clay over their beds.

Broken rock material of every size and description, which has been picked up and carried along by the ice, is eventually dumped and distributed by the ice and meltwater. Deposits of this rock debris, called *glacial drift*, take many forms, some of which are simply unsorted piles. At some time in its history a glacier's forward motion may be just matched by the melting taking place at the downhill end. The forward motion of the ice has not stopped but an equilibrium between melting and advancing has been established. The glacier, like a great conveyor belt, carries rock along and releases it at the melting glacial front, where it accumulates in a pile at right angles to the progress of the glacier. This pile, marking the line of equilibrium, is called a *moraine;* it will persist as a low ridge of land after final retreat of the ice. Moraines are common in Maine, especially within a few miles of the coast, and form ridges that may be ten to fifty feet wide, as much as one hundred feet high, and extend for a mile or more. Because they form across the end of a lobe or tongue of ice, they tend to run in an easterly direction.

Meltwater coming from a wasting glacier is always milky with ground-up rock flour, and it may also carry a tremendous load of sand and gravel. Many gravel pits in Maine show the effects of meltwater distributing and sorting rocks, sand, and clay into layers of similar sizes, often in alternating layers of coarse and fine sediments. The layers reveal something of the history of the meltwater streams: boulders and cobbles indicate turbulent, violent flows of great volume, while sand and silt indicate quieter, possibly deeper water. Modern glaciers end at broad banks of sand and gravel crisscrossed by shallow streams weaving braidlike patterns over the flats, so we infer that the vast sand and gravel deposits of southern Maine are a legacy from the wasting continental ice sheet.

The finest silt and clay was carried into the sea where it settled out to form a deep layer of soft, uniform sediment. This is easily seen from Interstate 295 in **Portland** at low tide in the **Fore River,**

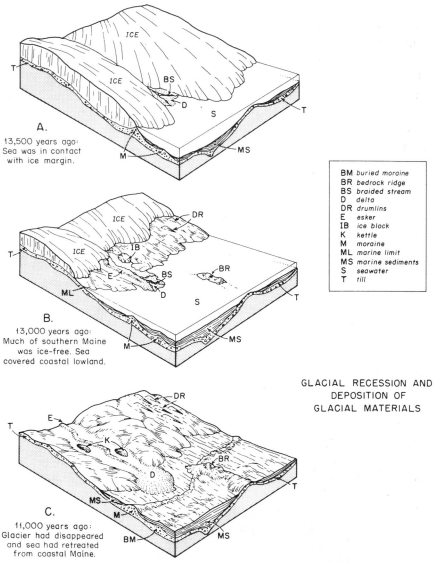

A.
13,500 years ago:
Sea was in contact
with ice margin.

BM	buried moraine
BR	bedrock ridge
BS	braided stream
D	delta
DR	drumlins
E	esker
IB	ice block
K	kettle
M	moraine
ML	marine limit
MS	marine sediments
S	seawater
T	till

B.
13,000 years ago:
Much of southern Maine
was ice-free. Sea
covered coastal lowland.

GLACIAL RECESSION AND
DEPOSITION OF
GLACIAL MATERIALS

C.
11,000 years ago:
Glacier had disappeared
and sea had retreated
from coastal Maine.

Landforms left by the retreating glacier. (After Tucker, in Thompson and Borns, eds., Surficial Geologic Map of Maine, *Maine Geological Survey, 1985)*

Back Cove, and **Presumpscot River** estuaries, as well as many other coastal sites, the well-known "clam flats." Marine silt, identified by local concentrations of sea shells, is found as high as 400 feet above present sea level and as far inland as **Medway.** This silt shows the extent of the sea at its maximum inundation of the coast. Silt, slightly coarser than clay, is not always stable, even on very gentle slopes. Several disastrous landslides, most recently in **Gorham** and **Rockland,** occurred when large areas of silt suddenly slumped down, carrying along buildings and large trees.

When meltback of the glacier exceeds the forward motion, the glacier is said to "retreat." As the glacier wastes away, all of the rock debris it had been carrying drops out and is left like a blanket covering the ground. The debris, called *till*, is a mixture (in widely varying proportions) of sand, silt and clay, and rock fragments up to large boulders. It is not bedded or sorted because water had little opportunity to distribute it, and for the same reason the fragments tend to be angular, not rounded. Because of the admixture of clay, cutbanks of till stand at a steep angle. Some till at the base of the glacier was subject to great compaction by the weight of the overlying ice. This *hardpan* layer is difficult to excavate and is almost impermeable to percolating water, sometimes creating problems for construction engineers and for homeowners who require septic systems.

Glacial till forms a lumpy, rolling, hummocky landscape with abundant boulders and stones showing through in fields and pastures. A common landform built of till is the *drumlin*, a hill shaped like the bowl of an upside-down spoon. It is formed of especially sticky clay till that was smeared rather than picked up by the ice. The blunter, steeper end is upstream and it tails off in the direction the glacier traveled.

Drumlins typically are longer than they are high or wide, forming pronounced hills running from a hundred to a few thousand feet long and rising fifty to one hundred feet above the general level. They often occur in groups, and from the air or on a topographic map they look like so many gigantic whales with their heads pointing upstream. Drumlins are abundant in the southern and southwestern portions of the state, streaming in a southerly direction. They are readily seen from the air but are difficult to recognize on the ground because they are large enough to be considered just part of the rolling terrain, but not large enough to stand out as a low mountain. A good example is **Great Hill** near Eliot, which is being excavated for fill. The cut face shows the considerable proportion of clay and the extreme variety of larger, unsorted particles, from sand to boulders.

A conspicuous linear ridge of gravel and sand, with steep sides and narrow top, often stretching for miles, is known in Maine as a "horseback." These have an interesting origin. As the ice sheet was melting, great torrents of water carrying vast loads of sand and gravel flowed in long narrow tunnels under the ice. As the climate warmed and melting slowed, the volume of water and its velocity slackened, decreasing the stream's ability to carry sediment. As a result the sand and gravel plugged up the tunnel. When the ice finally melted away, a ridge of water-washed sediment, called an *esker*, remained where the tunnel had been. Eskers are especially obvious in boggy country, where they may provide the only easy pathway. Many old roads in Maine follow the crests of eskers. A northeast-trending belt across central Maine, 100 miles north to south, contains many fine examples of eskers mostly paralleling the southerly pattern of modern rivers and streams. For reasons geologists do not understand, few eskers are found northwest of a line from Moosehead Lake to Presque Isle.

An esker well known to Maine geologists is the **Enfield Horseback,** a sinuous, forested, and steep-sided ridge about fifty feet high. It carries a road on its narrow crest from Enfield some eight miles south to Scotts Corners. The road, about two miles east of U.S. Route 2, makes the esker easily accessible. Even easier to examine is the **Whalesback** near Aurora, which is traversed for a short part of its length by Route 9. (One of the Road Logs in chapter 11 describes it in more detail. As you travel these horseback roads, try to picture the tunnel with its raging torrent of meltwater carrying the sand and gravel you are driving over, while overhead lie thousands of feet of ice.)

These are but segments of a very extensive esker system that stretches almost continuously from Mount Katahdin to the sea. Eskers provide an easily worked source of clean sand and gravel fill for construction projects, and have been exploited in many places around the state. Gravel pits in eskers are good places to pick up samples of rocks of many different types, collected for you over a wide area by the glacier.

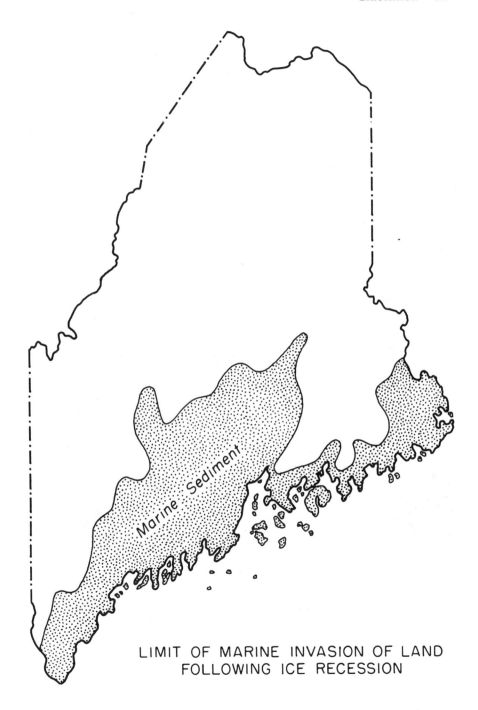

Marine Sediment

LIMIT OF MARINE INVASION OF LAND
FOLLOWING ICE RECESSION

Frequently, large boulders of a type of rock different from the underlying bedrock are found in the landscape in positions that cannot be explained as the result of ordinary transport by water.

Cross sections of an esker, the Enfield Horseback.

View to the northeast from the Whalesback, Aurora.

The famous **Balanced Rock** on **South Bubble** in Acadia National Park is a spectacular example of such an *erratic*, as is **Daggett Rock** near Phillips on Route 4 north of Farmington. Picked up and carried along by the glacier, they were left, erratically, where we find them.

The huge volumes of meltwater pouring off the ice sheet had considerable effect on the land. In some places channels cut by raging torrents are now found high and dry, recognizable to an educated eye. Rock debris from the ice sheet was easily carried by these fast-flowing steams. The streams slowed as they approached sea level and more gentle slopes, and the debris, sorted out by size, settled to form the widespread deposits of stratified sand and gravel now opened up as gravel pits throughout Maine. Because these rocks have been tumbled and thrown about by water they are smooth and rounded, some nearly spherical. The finer sand formed deltas near the shorelines of lakes and bays, while silt and clay settled out in the quiet deeper water. Much silt and clay was carried farther to form thick mud beds on the sea floor.

As the lakes dried up, the sand was exposed to fierce northwest winds, which piled the sand into dunes as much as twenty feet high and, in some cases, miles long. In this bitter climate there was little

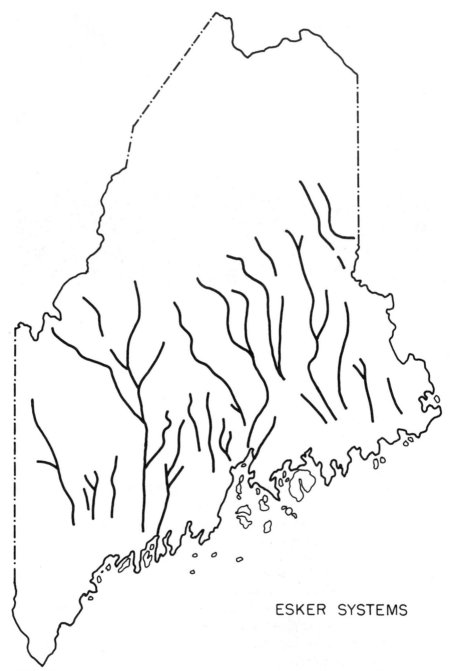

ESKER SYSTEMS

(After Borns, et al., Eskers in Maine, Critical Areas Program Planning Report 67, 1979.)

vegetation to hold the sand. Only as the climate moderated did vegetation creep in and stabilize the dunes under a thin blanket of developing soil. Pine trees thrive on this well-drained soil. This is a fragile soil cover, and with the coming of settlers, cultivation disturbed it in many places, creating opportunities for the wind to reactivate the drifting. "Blowouts" appear when the wind is able to

An erratic boulder at the Enfield Horseback, Aurora.

Granite erratic boulder underlain by slaty, fine-grained metamorphic rock, St. Albans.

"Fossil" sand dune at Anson.

get at the underlying sand where the vegetation and soil have been removed, and the drifting sand dune migrates, sometimes burying forests that stand in its way. The Desert of Maine, a commercial attraction near **Freeport,** and similar landscape along Route 133 near **Wayne,** are good examples.

The Land Rebounds

At its maximum extent, forty thousand years ago, the great ice sheet probably extended to Georges Bank, 180 miles east of the present southern New England coastline. The weight of more than ten thousand feet of ice was immense; so great, in fact, that the crust of the earth actually bent down beneath the load. During the time of maximum ice, much water had been extracted from the sea and retained in the ice sheet. This withdrawal, of course, lowered the level of the sea, perhaps as much as 400 feet. When the ice front began to recede twenty thousand years ago, the position of the shoreline at any time was a function not only of the depression of the land but also of the level of the sea itself. As the ice melted, water rushed back into the sea, and the crust, relieved of its burden, began to rebound. By about fourteen thousand years ago the ice front was probably at a position just beyond the present coastline.

Uplift was a slower process than melting, however, and the sea invaded far inland from the present shoreline. Marine fossils embedded in silt and clay show that sea water thirteen thousand years ago lapped into the major river valleys as far upstream as Livermore Falls on the Androscoggin, Medway on the Penobscot, and Bingham on the Kennebec River, locations presently about four hundred feet above sea level.

Many moraines show evidence of submarine origin. Apparently the ocean washed against the edge of the floating glacier. As the ice melted, the rock debris it contained dropped into the sea, combining with sand and gravel washed into the sea by streams flowing from inland heights beneath the ice. Elsewhere, cobbles and boulders mixed with fine silt and clay suggest that floating masses of ice, broken loose from the glacier's face, drifted out to sea and melted, dropping their loads of rock to the sea floor.

Faster rising of the land finally overcame the effects of rising sea level, and by twelve thousand years ago the coast was drained, exposing the near-shore sea floor. Deltas that had been built by debris-laden streams flowing into the sea are now high and dry many miles from the present coast. **Pineo Ridge,** about five miles northeast of Cherryfield, is a fine example of a delta built where the ocean lapped against the melting glacier. This flat surface, some twenty-five square miles, is largely in blueberry cultivation and shows a steep northern edge where the delta was in contact with the ice. The melting ice and collapsing delta margin left a hummocky topography. A prominent cliff can be seen on the seaward (south) face of the delta, cut in the soft sediments by waves during the time the land was emerging from the sea. On the south edge, torrents of meltwater cut channels, some as much as five feet deep and thirty feet wide, in the emerging delta.

The climate was arctic and although the higher mountain peaks were free of the continental ice sheet by this time, permanent snowbanks on their northern and eastern sides led to the development of alpine glaciers. Along the coast, icebergs "calved" into the sea as they do today from glaciers in Greenland. Some of these apparently stranded in shallow water and were buried in the accumulating sediment. Final melting of the icebergs left *kettles*, steep-walled pits in the sand ranging up to several hundred feet in diameter and several tens of feet deep. Kettle lakes are common in the sandy Downeast Mountain region.

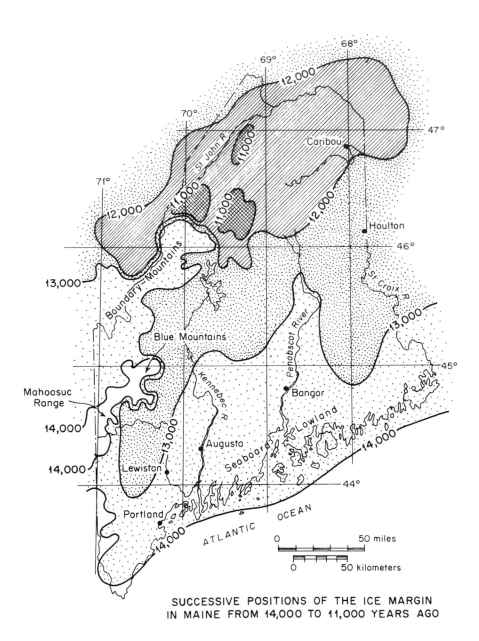

SUCCESSIVE POSITIONS OF THE ICE MARGIN
IN MAINE FROM 14,000 TO 11,000 YEARS AGO

(*After Thompson and Borns, eds.*, Surficial Geologic Map of Maine,
Maine Geological Survey, 1985.)

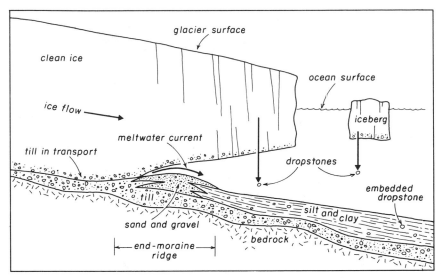

Cross-section of glacier where it meets the sea. Many end moraines in coastal Maine probably formed from deposits of sand and gravel carried by meltwater currents emerging from beneath the glacier along the grounding line. Sand and gravel in the seaward part of the moraine is interstratified with silt and clay; till in the central and landward parts of the moraine is deposited by minor readvances of the ice. (Redrawn from model developed by H.W. Borns, Jr., in W.B. Thompson, Surficial Geology Handbook for Coastal Maine, *Maine Geological Survey, 1979.)*

As the ice melted, uplift continued and the ocean receded further to leave the ragged coastline of today, with its many bays and estuaries separated by fingerlike peninsulas. By eleven thousand years ago the last of the ice caps melted from northern Maine, and the alpine glaciers finally melted away from the cirques they had cut on Mount Katahdin.

There is evidence that now the land is sinking along the Maine coast near York and even more noticeably near Eastport, for reasons not understood. We are also seeing a worldwide rise in sea level as the polar ice caps melt. These changes are only fractions of inches per year, but the fractions do add up. Apparently, the balance between sea and land levels creating our present coastline is only temporary, geologically speaking.

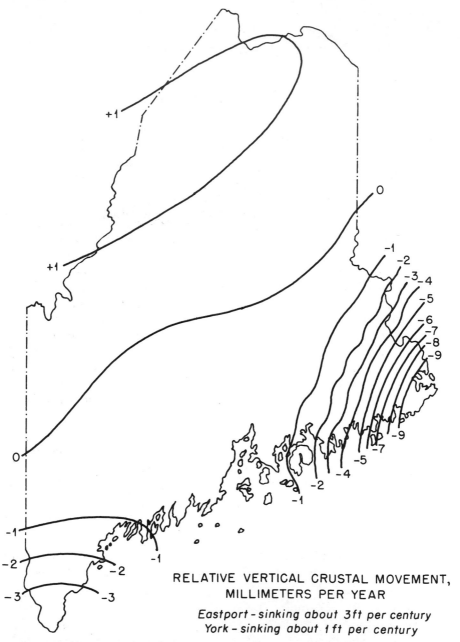

RELATIVE VERTICAL CRUSTAL MOVEMENT,
MILLIMETERS PER YEAR

Eastport - sinking about 3ft per century
York - sinking about 1 ft per century

(After Tyler and Ladd, "Vertical Crustal Movement in Maine," Maine Geological Survey Open File Report 80-34,1980.)

3
The Battered Coast

From the well-known "rockbound coast," with its cliffs and head-lands and offshore islands of solid rock, to graceful curving sandy beaches, creeks and inlets, and broad salt marshes, the variety of coastal landscapes in Maine is remarkable. It is said that Maine's coastline measures three thousand miles, taking in all the bays and estuaries. Currents and waves and raging storms steadily change the shape; headlands are broken down, gravel is reduced to sand, and sand is shifted back and forth. Sediment brought to the sea by the larger rivers is sorted and distributed. It is a landscape of endless fascination under constantly changing conditions of weather and light.

Formation of a Beach

Long swells in the ocean make moving parallel lines as they gradually approach the shore. They look like a low roll of moving water, but the bobbing gulls, rising and then dropping again as the swell moves past, prove that it is the form of the swell, not the water itself, that is moving. As it approaches shallower water the swell runs aground. Friction with the bottom causes the lower part to slow up, and the swell changes into a steepening wave that topples over in a great shower of foam and rush of water.

The splashing water and the bursting bubbles hurl salt spray into the air, creating the haze visible lengthwise along the beach. The salt spray plays an essential role in the production of rainfall, providing the condensation nuclei for coalescing raindrops. Salt is a tiny but important part of the earth-water system.

After a wave breaks, the motion of the water changes from the

43

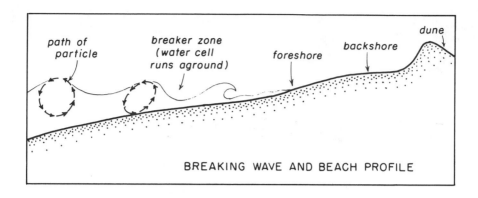

path of
particle

breaker zone
(water cell
runs aground)

foreshore

backshore

dune

BREAKING WAVE AND BEACH PROFILE

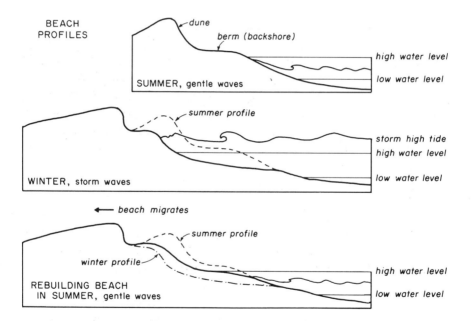

BEACH
PROFILES

dune

berm (backshore)

high water level

low water level

SUMMER, gentle waves

summer profile

storm high tide

high water level

low water level

WINTER, storm waves

← beach migrates

summer profile

winter profile

high water level

low water level

REBUILDING BEACH
IN SUMMER, gentle waves

circular oscillation, demonstrated by the bobbing sea gull, to a horizontal rush as the foaming water moves landward from the surf zone. It is this energetic rush that moves the sand. Waves can either build or erode beaches depending on how steep the wave is when it breaks; steep waves tend to erode beaches, while more gentle waves build them.

In heavy weather steep waves wash farther up the beach and the returning water moves faster, carrying sand away with it. Erosion of the beach and the seaward transport of beach sand result in the building of underwater *sandbars* at about the point where the swells are breaking. This sand will reverse its motion under the influence of milder waves and once again move landward. Milder waves tend to wash sand up the beach face, and since the returning flow is gentler, the water deposits the sand rather than carrying it away.

Waves ordinarily strike the beach at a slight angle, one end coming ashore before the rest of the wave. The water runs diagonally up the beach and washes back down straight, following a zig-zag path along the beach and setting up a longshore current. In times of moderate wave action this current causes a steady drift of sand along the beach. During periods of high winds and stormy surf the longshore current can be quite strong, enough to knock bathers off their feet and carry them along. At these times boulders and cobbles and great tonnages of sand are moved along the beach. The longshore current tends to smooth the coastline by filling in small bays with sand and even choking off the mouths of rivers.

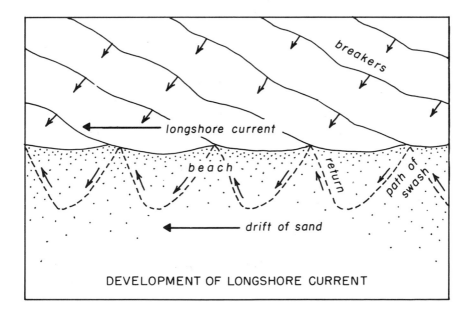

DEVELOPMENT OF LONGSHORE CURRENT

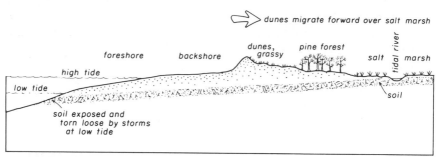

Beach/dune/marsh profile.

The natural shape of a sandy shoreline consists of a *beachfront* facing the ocean, backed by *sand dunes,* and behind them *salt marshes.*

The profile of the beachfront itself has two distinct sections. The *foreshore* is the gently sloping area where waves break, wash up, and then, their energy spent, run back to the sea. High tide pushes the foreshore farther inland but the profile is not greatly changed. The *backshore* is formed seaward of the dunes during storms when sand is thrown higher and farther up on the beach than during normal weather. It resembles a raised bench and may be nearly flat. Many beaches in Maine are backed by stony ridges and berms landward of the sandy beach. These are built by storm waves, which have enough energy to move and deposit cobbles and pebbles. To some extent these stony bastions protect the upper beach from ordinary erosion.

All of the rocky headlands from Kittery to West Quoddy Head are battered by the relentlessly eroding sea and left ragged, cut up by small coves. Often in these little coves are *pocket beaches,* arcs of sand with a high percentage of pebbles and cobbles derived from the destruction of the rocky headlands. The surging waves constantly rattle the pebbles and stones back and forth, a great mill grinding sand. Comparatively little of the sand on Maine's beaches, however, is the result of local grinding of coastal rocks by wave action. Most of it is derived from glacial debris.

Dunes

Sand from both the backshore and the overwash is subject to the action of the prevailing winds and is heaped up into drifting dunes. Dunes tend to be steep on the seaward side and more gently sloping on the back. Certain grasses and perennial plants are adapted to the harsh environment of the dune and are able to live on the sand by sending long roots down as much as six feet. Unless dunes are anchored by vegetation they move inland and smother the forest or marsh they encounter.

Where dunes have been excavated for their sand, beds can be seen dipping at various angles, crossing and recrossing each other. This is caused by shifting winds drifting the sand this way and that. The pattern is recognizable in inland dunes dating back to the Ice Age and is also found in fossil dunes preserved as sandstone in other parts of the country.

Really furious storms may hurl water through breaches in the dunes, in a violent overwash that carries sand to the low area behind the dunes. Northwest winds, strongest in the fall and winter, rework sand deposited in the backdune area by storm overwash, creating dunes that migrate seaward. Northeast winds, although less common, are frequently strong and associated with storms. Because they bring rain, these winds move very little of the heavy, wet sand, but they also create high-energy waves, which are responsible for beach erosion.

During storms the dunes become the land's primary bulwark of defense. Storm waves wash up to the base of the dunes and sometimes crash against the dunes themselves. At this time the value of sand as a natural barrier to destruction is readily seen. The force of the storm waves is spent on the yielding sand, which moves but also absorbs the energy of the waves. Nevertheless, a single winter storm of great power can undo the work of many months of beach building.

Landward from the dunes is a salt marsh, a very special place because it is the nursery for a great many species of fish and marine life and supplies a considerable amount of plant food to the marine environment as tides ebb and flow. Larger plants, including pine trees and shrubs, can grow on the protected landward side of the dune, and a sod of salt-tolerant marsh grasses develops where the dune meets the marsh. **Popham Beach State Park** is a splendid place to see an undisturbed sand beach displaying all these features.

Source of the Sand

Maine was covered by an ice sheet that until some 28,000 years ago extended out to sea all the way to the continental edge, beyond Georges Bank and Nantucket. The ice sheet scoured the top of Maine and removed most of the ground-up rock and soil, dumping it into the ocean far beyond the present coastline. Even as the ice front retreated, however, glacial action continued. Most of the glacial till and outwash deposits found on land in Maine are dated from this period of retreat of the continental ice sheet. Most of the beaches are, therefore, the product of erosion and sorting and reworking of glacial debris along the shoreline, both above and below sea level.

While glacial debris comes in all sizes, from silt and clay to cobbles and boulders, only sand grains accumulate and build into beaches. Finer particles are washed away to settle out in deep, quiet water, while coarser cobbles and boulders are not moved at all. Under a lens, beach sand looks like a collection of tiny jewels of many different kinds. Close inspection of beach sand with a simple magnifier can be a delight, and the nature of the sand can give some indication of its history.

Constant abrading and winnowing of sand grains by the waves tends to eliminate softer minerals. A beach like **Ogunquit** with a high proportion of fine, clean quartz sand (the hardest common mineral) reflects a long period of erosion and transport of sediment. If the source of the sand is weathered granite, heavier minerals such as garnets may be abundant enough to be concentrated in layers by the sorting action of the waves. The sand in some places on **Popham Beach** takes on a pinkish color due to the high proportion of garnet. The sand also glitters with mica flakes. Although soft, the flat mica particles stay in suspension in the water, which delays but does not avoid their eventual pulverizing. An unusual occurence is at **Sand Beach** in Acadia National Park where the sand, which has a greenish tint at close range, is more than 50 percent shell fragments, including broken spines of sea urchins.

The natural profile has been destroyed along many Maine beaches, particularly in the heavily populated southern region, by development of roads and building sites to accommodate summer visitors. The dunes have been built upon or flattened to open up the view, and much of the backdune marshy area has been filled, so do not

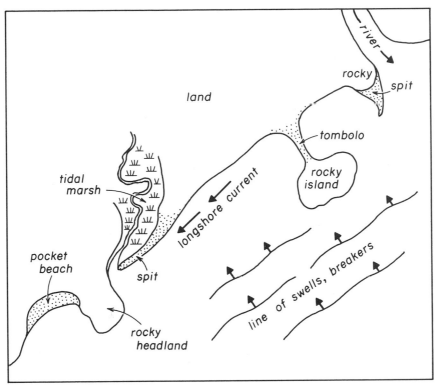

Four types of sand beach.

expect to find these features everywhere. Seawalls have been erected
in some places in an effort to protect shoreline property from the
sea's stormy onslaughts. The natural form of a beach is dynamic and
ever-shifting, however, and efforts to control it generally tend to
create other problems. Seawalls alter the gentle slope of the beach.
Waves that normally would wear themselves out washing up this
slope now crash with full force against a rigid wall, creating great
turbulence and strong eroding currents that carry off the sand and
eventually undermine the seawall.

Characteristics of the Coast

The coast of Maine can be divided physiographically into several
parts. The Southwest Coast from Kittery to Cape Elizabeth is noted
for two large beach sytems: Ogunquit-Wells and Old Orchard. Sep-

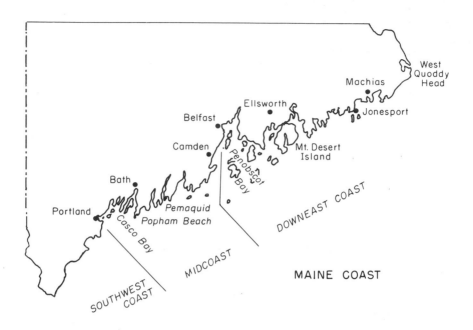

MAINE COAST

arating these is the ragged headland of Cape Porpoise. The Midcoast, north of Portland and Casco Bay to Owls Head on the west shore of Penobscot Bay, is known for its long bays and narrow peninsulas tipped with lighthouses as at Pemaquid. The Downeast Coast, Penobscot Bay to West Quoddy Head, the far southeastern corner of Maine, is a complex of large islands and broad bays, the best known of which are probably Mount Desert Island and Frenchman Bay. The last twenty-mile stretch of this coastline is remarkably straight, with few bays or harbors, and vertical cliffs more than 150 feet high at Quoddy Head State Park. Each section is described in more detail below.

The Southwest Coast. Between Kittery and Portland there are five principal headlands: **Kittery, Cape Neddick, Cape Porpoise, Biddeford Pool,** and **Cape Elizabeth.** Between these headlands are sweeping sandy beaches, including two especially large ones, **Ogunquit-Wells** beaches and **Ferry–Old Orchard** beaches, each more than eight miles long. There are also sizable sand beaches between smaller headlands—such as **Long Beach** south of Cape Neddick, and **Goose Rocks Beach** north of Kennebunkport—as well as numerous smaller beaches named on road maps.

From Kittery to Ogunquit the coast is rocky and beaches are few and small. The headlands are striped with thin-bedded rocks standing vertical or at a steep angle. These rocks, among the oldest in Maine, were deposited as layers of volcanic ash and sediment in a shallow sea more than 400 million years ago. **Cape Neddick,** however, is an exception. This rounded point, and **The Nubble,** an island with a lighthouse just a few feet offshore, are an unusual rock known as gabbro. Like granite, gabbro crystallized from molten material many miles deep in the earth, but it has a different chemistry. The pluglike shape of the gabbro mass is responsible for the distinctive round outline of the point and The Nubble.

North of **Cape Neddick Harbor** stretch almost continuous cliffs and a prominent headland, **Bald Head.** A public path atop the cliffs between Perkins Cove and Ogunquit, called **Marginal Way,** provides unmatched views of the rocky scenery and the surging sea sweeping in and out of ragged crevices and chasms below. From the northern end of the path you can see the sands of **Ogunquit Beach.**

The beach from Ogunquit to Kennebunkport is interrupted by **Moody Point,** which divides the longshore currents that nourish the Moody-Ogunquit beaches to the south and Wells–Drake Island beaches to the north with sand derived from submerged glacial deposits.

At **Ogunquit** the south-flowing longshore current carrying its load of well-washed quartz sand, encountered deeper, quieter water where the Ogunquit River meets the sea, and the current slowed. The sand settled out, and gradually a point, called a *spit*, developed. This spit has now extended more then a mile and a half south of the original mouth of the river, creating a sandy barrier that almost cuts it off. The **Ogunquit-Moody Beach** is the best example of a *barrier spit* in Maine. The road south from Moody Beach village ends at a wastewater treatment plant, but the spit continues a mile or more. Midway, a footbridge connects the spit to the town of Ogunquit, and a road at the south end provides easy public access to this broad, very gently sloping beach. The sand is very fine and more than 90 percent quartz grains, most of which are clear and glassy, but enough are iron-stained to make the dry sand a light tan color.

Looking from Ogunquit Beach toward heavily developed Moody Beach.

Barrier spits sometimes encroach from both sides of a river's outlet, as at Wells Beach and Drake's Island beach, to create *tidal salt marshes* between the beach and the land. These marshes are extremely important in the ecology of the coast, and without the protection from stormy seas that the barriers provide, the marsh areas could not exist.

At Wells the longshore current, moving north, built a spit across the mouth of the **Webhannett River.** The river was forced to flow north before entering the sea, creating a tidal marsh between the spit and the mainland. (A road crosses this marsh on an artificial causeway to Wells Beach community.) The spit threatened to cut off Webhannet River and the harbor. This natural process interferes with the desires of men, so jetties (close-spaced dikes at right angles to the beach) have been built to channel the currents flowing into the ocean. The water moves sufficiently fast to keep the break in the beach open and deep enough for boats to enter and leave the harbor. Sand is accumulating against the south side of the jetty as the longshore current encounters this obstruction and slows, dropping its load. The beach is widening, a natural dune may be building, and beach vegetation is beginning to take hold, but there is little

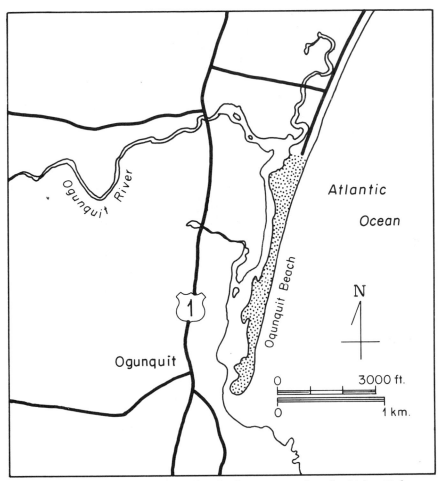

Ogunquit is Maine's best example of a barrier spit beach. (After Nelson and Fink, Geological and Botanical Features of Sand Beach Systems in Maine, *State Planning Office, 1980.)*

evidence of the original beach and dune topography in this densely built area other than the raised elevation of the houses built on top of the old dunes. Any landscape that is not covered with mowed lawns is paved. Public access to the beach is provided by walkways from the road every block.

The Maine coast experiences three to five major storms a year, striking from the northeast and east, and sometimes accompanied by a surge of sea water several feet above the expected high water. Major storms last long enough to encompass more than one high tide and are generally large enough to affect a substantial length of the coast. Violent storms eroding deeply at **Wells Beach** have revealed details of the recent (geologically speaking) history of the beach. Beneath the sand is a layer of peat in which tree stumps are embedded, and underlying this is marine clay and silt, evidence of an old tidal salt marsh.

These layers tell a story of rising sea level and westward migrating shorelines. Arthur M. Hussey II, of Bowdoin College, who has studied this portion of the coast, explains that shortly after the front of the ice sheet retreated from the coast 13,000 years ago, clay and silt brought to the sea by meltwater settled out of the murky water. No doubt **Moody Point** and the adjacent rocky projections were about a mile offshore at this time. The land, in response to the removal of the great weight of ice, rose faster than did sea level, and by three thousand years ago, when rebound had ceased, the shoreline was considerably below present sea level.

The glaciers continued to melt even after the land had finished rebounding, so sea level began to rise rapidly. Barrier beaches developed, anchored to the islands, and lagoons and marshes with a floor of peat formed behind them. Eventually the marshy land filled in enough that pine trees, which require drier soil, could grow there. At that time (about three thousand years ago, as determined by radiocarbon dating of the pine stumps) sea level was probably eleven to thirteen feet lower than at present, according to Dr. Hussey. When sea level rose once again, a few centuries later, the shoreline again migrated landward, burying the marsh and pine forest under sand and creating the beach we have today.

Sea level along the Maine coast continues to rise as the land sinks and the polar ice caps melt, at rates from ten inches per century near Portland to as many as fourteen inches per century in Eastport. This is a very rapid change, geologically speaking, and it is producing worrisome effects on the shoreline and coastal settlements.

There is only limited public access to the arc of beach from **Drake Island** to **Kennebunk Beach.** At the latter, the sea-facing slope of **Great Hill** exposes a cross-section of stratified glacial drift, beds of sand and gravel topped by a layer of sand. Glacial deposits

Rounding and weathering of jointed granite.

like this are the source of sand for many beaches. The **Kennebunk Beaches** are small and enclosed by rocky points. The shoreline road is built on a seawall but winter storms frequently tear it up. A drive around **Cape Arundel** offers views looking west to the beaches of Kennebunk.

Cape Porpoise and the numerous islands off Cape Porpoise Harbor and Goose Rocks Beach are granite, the southernmost granite along the coast. You will notice the rounded shapes of the weathered rocky knobs, as compared to the jagged and angular layered rocks of Kittery and Bald Head, for example.

Incoming waves from the ocean tend to wrap around rocky headlands, creating turbulent currents behind the jutting rock. Many headlands, and some islands, are draped with sandy beaches where sand-laden currents have been interrupted. Waves striking the headlands break off pieces of the rock, creating sea cliffs along the shore, especially if the rock has lines of weakness such as joints and fractures. The bedrock in front of the cliff is planed flat by waves grinding with the debris plucked from the cliff. This wave-cut bench inclines gently toward the sea, and the upper reaches are usually exposed at low tide. The bench tends to dissipate the energy of incoming waves and thereby limits the shoreward retreat of the sea cliff. Cliff-and-bench shoreline topography is common along the rocky Maine coast, presenting fine vantage points.

Biddeford Pool, the town, is built on a rocky headland. To the north lies the pool itself, a tidal basin that is nearly drained at low water and almost closed by a mile-long spit of sand supplied by the **Saco River.** The Pool is cut off on the south by a sweeping beach that stretches southwest more than two miles to the next promontory, **Fortunes Rocks.**

The geologic features displayed at Biddeford Pool and the **East Point Sanctuary** make this an excellent spot to visit. The quartzites and slates forming the headland originally were sandstones and limy shales deposited in horizontal bands. The beds are now vertical or steeply dipping, and in a few places you can see that they were contorted into folds by immense forces. Basalt, a dark greenish-black rock that weathers chocolate-brown, was injected when molten into cracks measuring up to four feet wide. The basalt weathers more readily than the harder quartzites. In some places the sea has loosened blocks of basalt and removed them, leaving a steep-walled narrow trench in the bedrock.

Faults—cracks along which blocks of rock broke and slid during earthquakes millions of years ago—cut across East Point in various places. They are recognizable by crushed rock along their courses, and by *slickensides*, the polished faces along which the blocks slid. It is fascinating to climb around eroded dikes and into cuts where fault-weakened rock has been removed by stormy seas, allowing you to see these features in three dimensions.

Milky-white quartz veins and veinlets cutting through the whole series of rocks are much in evidence. The coarse-grained quartz was crystallized from a fluid that apparently did not completely fill the voids. Some cavities are filled with jagged quartz crystals, and such pointed crystals can only form where there is space for them to grow. They are interesting to examine closely.

East Point in the recent past was covered by a layer of glacial debris perhaps ten feet thick, but the encroaching sea is removing it. Most of the little coves along the point are paved with pebbles and boulders but very little sand. The finer material of the glacial till has been washed away to be added to the broad beaches accumulating to the south. Among the pebbles and cobbles are a few that clearly are not related to the bedrock of the point. These were picked up somewhere to the north and carried along by the glacier, then released from the glacial overburden of the point by the eroding waves.

On the northeast side of Saco River begins a great beach stretching more than six miles from **Camp Ellis** and **Ferry Beach State Park** to **Old Orchard Beach** and on to the Scarborough River. Much of the southern portion, including the state park, is in a nearly natural condition but the northern part is densely built up and almost totally altered.

Similar to Biddeford Pool and East Point in many respects, although on a smaller scale, is **Prouts Neck.** The rocky promontory is draped with two sandy beaches, **Western Beach** on the south and **Scarborough Beach** to the north. Sand is being swept northward along Old Orchard Beach, cutting off a river and creating a salt marsh and bay, until it reaches **Pine Point.** Here the Scarborough

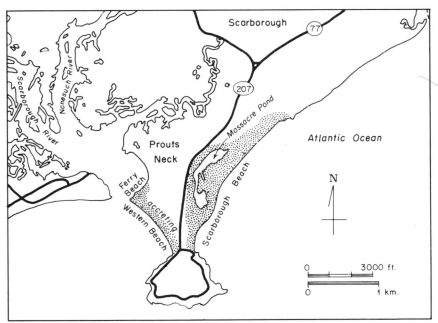

Prouts Neck and Scarborough Beach. (After Nelson and Fink, Geological and Botanical Features of Sand Beach Systems in Maine, *State Planning Office, 1980.)*

River is strong enough to keep a channel open but the sand is transported across to Western Beach, where it is accumulating against the headland of Prouts Neck. To the north and analogous to the pool at Biddeford Pool is **Massacre Pond,** fresh water now, but perhaps a salt marsh lagoon before being cut off completely from the ocean.

Cape Elizabeth, jutting out to sea, protects the shoreline to the southwest from the strong winter winds from the east and northeast. **Crescent Beach,** a pocket beach and a state park, is nestled in a cove west of the cape. It extends about ¾ mile between two rocky points. Only the western end is exposed to the open ocean, and here the beach is widest and the frontal dune is highest. The sand, comparatively coarse and poorly sorted, probably represents onshore transport of sea-floor glacial deposits. At the eastern end there is much less sand, and it is finer, suggesting deposition by eastward-moving longshore currents and wind.

The Cape Elizabeth shoreline is rocky cliffs all the way from **Two Lights State Park** to **Portland Harbor.** The rocks are thin-bedded quartzite and slate, the same kind of rock exposed at most headlands from Kittery to Penobscot Bay (capes Neddick and Porpoise are exceptions already mentioned). Portland Head Light marks the northern end of this portion of Maine's battered coast.

The Midcoast. The character of the Maine coast changes drastically northeast of Portland. Compared to the Southwest Coast's smooth, broad beaches separated by bulky headlands, the coast from Casco Bay to Penobscot Bay is very ragged indeed. U.S. Highway 1 strikes a reasonably straight line between Brunswick and Rockland, lying about as close to the coast as practicable with a minimum number of bridges. Even so, it crosses tidal estuaries at **Bath, Wiscasset,** and **Newcastle-Damariscotta.** Deep cuts in the rock along the highway between **Woolwich** and **Wiscasset** expose rusty and weathered layered rocks, together with irregular masses of coarse granite intruded into the folded layers. This same series of rocks is displayed everywhere on the Midcoast. From the highway, narrow peninsulas, some as long as fifteen miles, stretch southward to end in rocky points looking out to the open ocean.

The peninsulas and their intervening bays are remarkably straight and parallel, a coast of flooded river valleys. About 400 million years ago immense forces deep inside the earth pushed westward, rumpling layers of sediment on the ocean floor into vertical folds, much as would happen if you slid your hand over the dinner table, pushing the tablecloth ahead. In addition, masses of granite were injected, molten, into the crumpled layers. This folded bedrock much later was carved by rivers—the **Kennebec, Sheepscot, Damariscotta, St. George,** and others—making their way to the sea. In general, the valleys followed downfolds and the ridges were the crests of the folds. Although buried under ice, this land was not greatly altered by the continental glacier, except by a veneer of glacial till that covers everything.

When the sea rose following the melting of the ice, the valleys were flooded, creating long, narrow bays separated by equally narrow peninsulas. Some, like **Harpswell Neck,** are many miles long and less than a mile wide. Other peninsulas are crossed by short channels that break the peninsula into islands, like **Bailey and Orrs islands,** and **Arrowsic and Georgetown islands.** Many other peninsulas, like **Friendship** and **St. George,** end in a string of small islands, the nearly submerged tops of ridges. The Midcoast region is the scene of much boat traffic, both commercial and recreational. Lighthouses have been built on the ends of some of the peninsulas, and two, **Pemaquid and Marshall Point lights,** are accessible by road. Others are on islands just offshore.

Beaches on the Midcoast are few but they include the best examples of natural beach left in Maine. The Kennebec River flows into the sea at **Fort Popham,** built on a projection of coarse granite that has narrowed the mouth of the river. It disgorges a tremendous volume of sand, building a large submarine delta, which in turn provides the material for the largest beach in the Midcoast region. Complex currents of river and tide have distributed the delta sand south of the fort along **Coast Guard Beach.** To the west, **Hunnewell and Popham beaches** form a continuous strand extending for more than two miles. Private development limits access to Coast Guard and Hunnewell beaches, but Popham Beach is accessible to the public at **Popham Beach State Park.** It extends to the Morse River, whose currents add to the mix of beach-shaping forces. This broad, south-facing beach is very flat and at low tide is hundreds of feet wide. Complex currents sort the particles and leave ripple marks in

the fine, reddish brown sand. Garnets and heavier minerals concentrated by the oscillating water give a purplish tint to the ripple
marks. This is river sand that has not yet been subjected to extensive

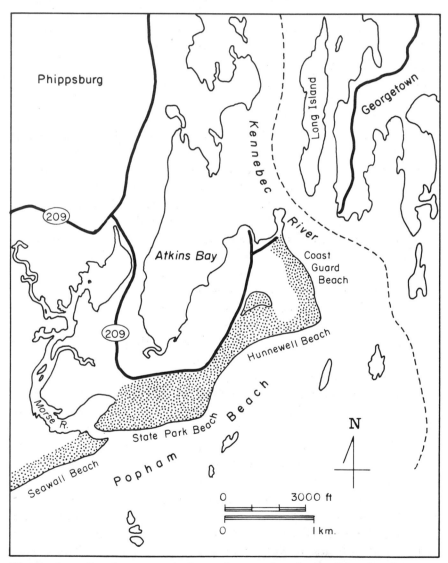

The Popham Beach system. (After Nelson and Fink, Geological and
Botanical Features of Sand Beach Systems in Maine, *State Planning
Office, 1980.)*

milling by the ocean, accounting for the variety of rock and mineral grains.

Two rocky islands, **Wood and Fox islands,** are tied to the mainland by sand bars called *tombolos.* The result of swirling currents eddying around the islands, tombolos often begin as two sand cusps, built out from the mainland and from the shoreward end of the island, that eventually meet to make a continuous landbridge. The tombolo connecting Wood Island to the east end of Hunnewell Beach is awash at high tide, and is sometimes breached by storm-raised longshore currents. Except during the highest high tides, one can walk on the tombolo from Popham Beach to Fox Island.

Between Morse River and Sprague River to the west, **Seawall Beach** stretches for about a mile. Together with Popham Beach, this is the longest stretch of unaltered barrier beach in Maine. Seawall Beach is under the control of the Nature Conservancy and is reserved as a research area, so public access is limited.

Southwest winds have built dunes all along these beaches. At Popham Beach a pine forest growing on the backs of old dunes is separated from the beach by a series of grass-covered dunes reflecting older beachfront positions. Hunnewell Beach historically experiences the greatest storm destruction of beachfront property in Maine, but the value of the protection provided by dunes is recognized, and efforts to preserve them are evident. Paths crossing the dunes are few and in many places are replaced by boardwalks.

Highway 127, on the way to **Reid State Park,** crosses several interesting rock-lined tidal inlets trending north-south, like most of the "grain" of the midcoast. At Reid State Park the straight, rather steep **Mile Beach** connects **Griffith Head,** a high knob of coarse-grained white granite, with **Todd's Head,** about three-quarters of a mile southwest. Griffith Head is deeply eroded by the sea, which has removed every soft zone or layer it can reach. The footing is rough but secure as a result. On the west flank of the granite knob are exposures of rusty weathering layers, the thinly banded country rock into which the coarse white granite was intruded. The sand at Mile Beach is noticeably coarser than at Popham and accounts for the steeper beach face; water can drain through the coarse material more readily so waves can pile it steeper. A spit projecting southwesterly from Todd's Head across the mouth of Little River is creating **Half Mile Beach.** From the shape of the spit it is clear that longshore currents are carrying sand to the southwest. This sand is finer, moreover, indicating that it has been carried farther than the sand of Mile Beach. A high, relatively narrow dune ridge runs parallel to the beach. These are the northernmost dunes in Maine.

Pemaquid Point is one of the most picturesque places on the Maine coast. In addition to its photogenic lighthouse the point offers fascinating and artistic shapes carved by the sea from the thin-layered bedrock. Variations in the hardness of the layers is brought out by the crashing waves, which remove every grain as soon as it is loosened from the decomposing rock. The original layers of sand and mud, more then 400 million years old, were heated and recrystallized, folded and tipped vertical. During the process they were also invaded by molten rock (seen today as the thick, white masses of coarse-grained granite) more or less following the layering. A peculiar bunching and thinning of these masses along their length has been termed *boudinage*, French for sausage. Remnants of the darker rock plastered to the white have been etched out in fantastic shapes that have caught the eye of many photographers.

On the western flank of Pemaquid Point, when the tide is low and the sea is relatively quiet, you can hear smooth and nearly spherical boulders rolling back and forth like so many bowling balls, pushed by the restless sea. They are rolling in channels measuring a few inches to a foot or so wide, formed in the tightly folded bedrock.

Marshall Point, near Port Clyde on the end of St. George peninsula, is carved from a gray granite. Here a very interesting pattern, like bricks in thick mortar, has developed where molten granite invaded a dark greenish rock, breaking it into rectangular blocks.

From Marshall Point the coast strikes northeast to form the west side of **Penobscot Bay.** Geologically, the coastline from Marshall Point all the way to Bucksport is essentially the same; that is, the rocks are metamorphic layers with only minor bodies of granite. For this reason, this part of the coast is included here in the Midcoast Region.

Owls Head Light, built on a point of rusty weathering rock, offers a fine view of west Penobscot Bay.

Mount Battie in **Camden Hills State Park** provides a magnificent view of Camden Harbor and Penobscot Bay. The mountain, accessible by road, is a knob of metamorphosed conglomerate, a

Contorted schists at Pemaquid Point.

Rounded boulders in grooves of folded, eroded schist at Pemaquid Point.

former bed of sand, stones, and gravel with rounded stones up to six inches in diameter. The rock is well exposed at the top of the mountain, especially at the lookout to the east. Weathering has had little effect on the rocks in the thirteen thousand years since they were uncovered by the melting ice sheet. The glacier scrubbed clean any weathered rock debris that once might have existed. This happened so recently, geologically speaking, that since then the resistant, nearly insoluble rock has decomposed only along cracks into which moisture and plant roots can penetrate. Where the mat of vegetation is pulled away, the rock is hard and clean except for superficial staining.

The Downeast Coast. East of Penobscot Bay, the coast once again changes character. While the Midcoast Region is fringed with long, narrow peninsulas and coves, the Downeast Coast is marked by broad bays and large islands. In **Penobscot Bay** more than eight miles of open water separate Rockport and North Haven Island, and there are many open reaches of several miles in **Blue Hill, Frenchman, Englishman, and Machias bays.** Many of the islands, though ragged like **Vinalhaven,** are roughly circular, not linear, in outline.

As usual, differences in landscape can be attributed to the underlying geology. During the formation of this portion of North America's coast, large pluglike masses of granite intruded into beds of volcanic and sedimentary rock. The largest of these granite bodies, and best known because of Acadia National Park, is **Mount Desert Island.** Here erosion has carved **Cadillac Mountain,** the highest prominence on the east coast of the United States. Other large islands that are mostly granite are **Vinalhaven, Deer Isle, Swans Island,** and **Isle Au Haut,** and there are many smaller ones.

Granite was quarried in huge tonnages from this area during the last century and is still being quarried at **Stonington.** The principal operating quarry is just offshore on **Crotch Island,** but one accessible by road is **Settlement Quarry** in Webb Cove, off the Oceanville Road. This stone is of exceptional quality and was used in the Kennedy Memorial in Boston Harbor.

Large quarries operated on Vinalhaven, Dix, Hurricane, and many other islands. Although the stonecutters' homes and villages are gone, the quarries, now filled with water, are still to be seen.

At a number of them, unfinished columns, cornices, and paving blocks lie where they were left when the granite building boom ended seventy-five years ago.

While granite predominates in this area, dark volcanic beds are abundant enough to make a contrast. On the northern part of **Deer Isle,** and across Eggemoggin Reach in **Sedgwick,** the bedrock is dull grey lava flows. Most of **North Haven Island** is also made from volcanic rocks. In many locations from Cape Rosier on Penobscot Bay to Blue Hill on the east side of the same peninsula, the very hard and dense, almost flinty, rocks contain mineral deposits in sufficient concentration to have sparked a mining boom in the late nineteenth century. Sporadic mining of copper, lead, and zinc lasted well into this century. Indeed, the last mine shut down as recently as 1977.

Around the northern ends of **Blue Hill and Frenchman bays,** and many smaller bays in the area, are comparatively drab fine-grained rocks of a type and age similar to the rocks of Cape Elizabeth. A few mineral prospects were located in these rocks also.

An unsurpassed view of this coast is obtained from **Caterpillar Hill** on Routes 175-15, a mile and a half north of Sargentville. A panoramic sweep of 180 degrees stretches from the Camden Hills on the west to Mount Desert Island on the east. Before you, seemingly at your feet, is the Deer Isle suspension bridge, deceptively tiny from here, while beyond lie the many islands of Penobscot and Blue Hill bays.

Between Great Spruce Head and Butter Island, is a group of islands called the **Barred Islands.** They are named for the graceful tombolo of sand that links the two northern islands. At the water's edge on one of these is an excellent exposure of *pillow lavas,* so-called because the rounded blobs of lava, a foot or more in diameter, resemble plump pillows. From a little distance the pillows appear to be as soft and plastic as they were when the molten lava plunged into the sea and was chilled, forming individual balls of lava nestled together in a pile.

Some of the most interesting glacially sculpted scenery of the eastern United Sates is found on **Mount Desert Island. Cadillac Mountain,** easily reached by road, is famous for its coastal vistas of wide bays and rocky headlands, the dark forests of spruce and fir coming down to the water's edge. Rounded mountains of pink and

The tombolo at Barred Islands, Penobscot Bay.

salmon-colored, coarse-grained granite dominate the island. They were ground down by the ice sheet a hundred thousand years ago and are separated by glacially sculpted U-shaped valleys. The surging sea beating against the shoreline is slowly carving the headlands and building pocket beaches from the debris. **Acadia National Park** offers not only beautiful scenery but also an enjoyable opportunity to learn some important geologic principles. In the Visitors Center there are excellent geological displays and publications. In this book we describe some highlights, leaving the details to others.

Mount Desert Island is shaped like a big baseball glove with the fingers and thumb separated by **Somes Sound,** a deep, narrow fjord that nearly cuts the island in two. Acadia National Park takes in most of the eastern part of the island and a large portion of the western part. State Route 3 circumnavigates the fingers (the eastern half) and Route 102 does the same for the other half. The island takes its roughly circular shape from the structure of the granite rock.

There are wide views of Frenchman Bay along Route 3 from **Hull's Cove** to **Bar Harbor.** At low tide the bar, which gives its

Sand Beach at Acadia National Park is a very small barrier beach that also shows characteristics of a pocket beach.

name to the town, is dry. It is actually a gravel tombolo connecting to Bar Island. South of Bar Harbor the road passes **The Tarn,** a small lake in the bottom of the glacially scoured valley between Champlain and Dorr mountains. Route 3 leaves the coastline after rounding Northeast Harbor, but fine views of Somes Sound are found along **Sargent Drive,** a side road leading north from the village of Northeast Harbor.

The **Park Loop Road,** which begins at the Visitors Center, provides a good sample of the features for which Acadia is famous, including rugged coastal vistas, sea-carved **Thunder Hole,** and **Sand Beach,** where the sand is partly shell fragments. Between Schooner Head and Great Head is a scenic overlook and parking area from which you can walk down to the sea cliff and **Anemone Cave,** hollowed out of shattered granite rocks by pounding storm waves. The Loop Road passes through broad-bottomed glacial valleys occupied by **Jordan Pond** and **Eagle Lake.** Perched high on **South Bubble,** and easily visible from the road, is a huge erratic boulder left there by the melting ice sheet. The drive to the top of Cadillac Mountain is rewarded by a wide view of Frenchman Bay, the Atlantic Ocean, and the many islands offshore.

From Somesville, Route 102 passes by **Echo Lake,** long and narrow, in a valley gouged deep by the glacier. About a mile south of Somesville a side road to the east leads to **Hall Quarry,** once a source of high grade granite but now occupied by a boatyard.

Route 102A south of Southeast Harbor circles **Bass Harbor Head.** Storm waves have thrown up a natural barrier of gravel and stones, cutting off a small bay that is now a boggy pond, at **Seawall** picnic and camping areas. Along the shore at the picnic area are dense, hard rocks made of ash and fragmental debris erupted from ancient volcanoes four hundred million years ago. **Bass Harbor Head Light,** on the extreme southern tip of Mount Desert Island, is one of the more photographed lights on the Maine coast.

From Bass Harbor village and Bernard, Route 102 stretches north. Exposed along the north shore of **Seal Cove** are outcrops of broken rock fragments cemented in granite. This is part of the Shatter Zone, formed around the margin of the Cadillac Mountain granite when it intruded into the overlying mass of sediments and volcanic rock. **Seal Cove Pond,** east of the road, is another of the elongated lakes formed in valleys deepened by the great ice sheet. About a mile before reaching Somesville there is a fine view down the length of **Long Lake** with rounded mountains on both sides.

On **Sand Point,** just east of Salisbury Cove village on the northern edge of Mount Desert Island, is an interesting geological feature called **The Ovens,** unfortunately accessible only by boat or (by permission) across private property. These are caves hollowed out of a vertical cliff of fractured volcanic tuff by surging waves. The cliff is seventy-five or more feet high, and the sea laps at its base. For this reason the caves can be visited only at low tide, preferably a morning low tide so the sun will be shining into the caves. To the east, or left as you face the cliff, is a narrow, ten-foot-high sea arch you can walk through.

Tuff is a very hard, dense, light greenish-gray layered rock, resulting from the deposition of volcanic ash. Here the beds incline gently to the north. They have been cut by numerous faults, in some places greatly shattering the beds and permitting groundwater to seep in and loosen angular blocks of all sizes. These blocks have been torn out and removed by storm waves, forming caves. One is

The Ovens, sea caves in volcanic tuff, Mount Desert Island.

Sea arch at Acadia National Park.

Basalt dike in granite at Grindstone Point, Schoodic Peninsula.

at least thirty feet deep and eight feet high. The cliffs are enlivened by colorful yellow and red deposits left by dripping groundwater following the fractures. The cliff is crumbly and should be approached with caution; blocks and slabs can break loose without warning.

On the extreme left the cliff slopes down, and the greenish thin-bedded tuff layers can be seen in contact with the underlying blue-gray, massive, slaty rocks. The contact is emphasized by the color contrast. Contacts between two rocks of different age and origin are ordinarily buried under soil and weathered rock, but here waves have stripped away all debris and have provided an easy lesson in geology.

The pocket beaches between promontories of the cliff are paved with "shingle" of flat, slaty rock; the higher up on the beach, the thinner and more delicate the flakes.

On the east side of Frenchman Bay, **Schoodic Peninsula** is part of Acadia National Park and is notable for the exposure of greenish black basalt dikes, slabs of rock cutting vertically through the fine-grained red granite that makes up the peninsula. Some of the dikes are many feet wide, stretching north-south many hundreds of feet.

The basalt is less resistant to erosion than the granite, and where blocks of basalt have been carried away a vertical trench is left into which the sea surges with a thunderous rush and plumes of spray.

The granite is sliced by horizontal cracks a few feet apart, which dip gently toward the sea. This *sheeting* is caused by the release of pressure on the rock after erosion and removal of the overlying cover. Vertical breaks, called *joints*, combine with the sheeting structure to produce huge slabs, ranging from a few inches to a few feet in thickness. Some of the great slabs have been thrown slightly askew by the immense power of storm waves. At low tide, a wide apron of solid granite is spread out around the peninsula.

The red granite is the same as that of Mount Desert Island and no doubt extends beneath Frenchman Bay. The basalt dikes are younger. If you find a convenient spot to examine them closely you will satisfy yourself of this interpretation. Notice that the edges of the dikes are very fine-grained, indicating that the molten basalt chilled quickly against the cold, older granite. In some places a fracture zone can be found running at a broad angle to the dike, leading us to wonder why the basalt did not fill these fractures too. The answer is apparent: the fractures are continuous through both granite and basalt and thus were formed after the basalt was emplaced.

East of Schoodic Peninsula several other points of igneous rock jut out to sea. **Dyer Neck** and **Petit Manan Point** east of Gouldsboro Bay are granite, but **Ripley Neck, Cape Split** and the **Addison** peninsula, and **Jonesport** are all underlain by *gabbro*, a rock similar to granite in origin but darker (described in Chapter 6). The landscape is little affected by this chemical difference in rock. Offshore, **Beals and Great Wass islands** are part of a mostly submerged granite mass.

The Downeast coast is rough and beaches are few and small, but **Roque Island** in the middle of Englishman Bay is a conspicuous exception. On the north side of the island a gravelly sand beach stretches between the two headlands, **Squire Point** and **Great Head**. On the other side is the mile-long, ocean-facing arc of **Great South Beach.** The beach is protected by islands that lie between it and the open sea, deflecting ocean swells so that only low-energy, generally constructive waves arrive at the beach. The result is a beautiful curving strand of clean quartz sand with few rock particles, derived from glacial drift now almost completely eroded.

Roque Bluffs Beach is about one-half mile of coarse sand, with boulders and cobbles below the low tide level. The beach started as a sand spit spreading west from the mouth of Englishman River. Eventually it met Shoppee Point and cut off a tidal lagoon, which is now a freshwater pond where the State Park has developed swimming facilities. The sand on the beach face is progressively finer and cleaner (that is, more quartz and fewer rock particles) as you move landward, away from the water's edge. This may be due to winnowing by the onshore wind.

A bluff a mile to the east of the beach exposes a scarp of glacial drift, the raw material for the beach. The scarp is the cross-section of a moraine that contains two layers of till separated by a layer of crudely stratified sand and gravel. The tills have a high content (about 40 percent) of silt and clay, which makes them hard and compact, while the intervening layer is almost devoid of clay. The two tills are representative of two different ice advances, separated by an interval of melting during which the boulders, cobbles, and pebbles were sorted and deposited by torrential meltwaters and the fine silt and clay were washed out to sea.

Shoppee Point is made of interbedded fossiliferous sedimentary rocks and volcanic flows, with some good exposures on the west side of lava pillows and blocks caught up in the sediments. Basalt dikes also cut through the rock.

From Cutler to West Quoddy Head the coastline is quite straight, reflecting the **Fundy Fault,** which runs offshore to form the Bay of Fundy. This fault is one of a number of great rifts in the earth's crust related to the breaking off of Europe from North America and the formation of the Atlantic Ocean nearly 200 million years ago.

The easternmost point of the United States, **West Quoddy Head,** is marked by a red-and-white-striped lighthouse built atop a high cliff overlooking **Grand Manan Channel;** across the channel is Grand Manan Island, Canada. The cliffs are volcanic and gabbro rocks with a few basalt dikes. Between rocky promontories are small pocket beaches of cobbles and pebbles of many rock types. Trails along the top of the 150-foot cliffs provide fine views of the sea surging in and out of **Gulliver's Hole,** a narrow chasm where a vertical fault in the

Low tide at Cutler Harbor.

The reversing falls at Pembroke.

rock provides a softer zone that has been partly excavated by the sea. During heavy weather the surf crashing against the rocky cliffs is awesome.

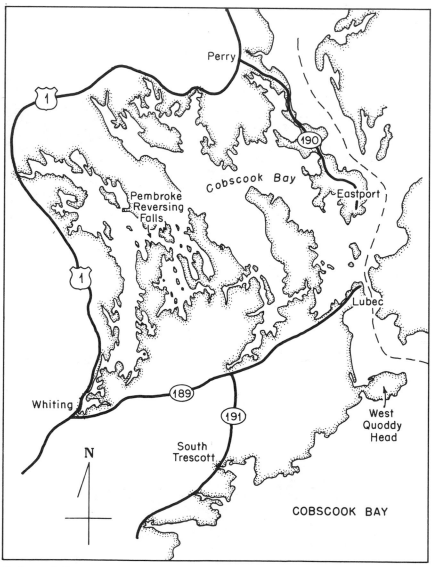

Cobscook Bay

Cobscook Bay, separating Lubec and Eastport, is part of the Passamaquoddy Bay complex, and is noted for its range of as much as twenty-eight feet between high and low tides. The changing of the tide brings great roaring surges of water in and out through shallow, narrow passages. (See Chapter 10 Road Log for U.S. 1 at Pembroke, for directions to an excellent viewing site for one of these "reversing falls.")

Maps of Cobscook Bay show a pronounced arcuate shape to the smaller bays and their peninsulas. This shape of the land reflects the structure of the bedrock. The layers of lava and ash have been warped into a broad arch, eight to ten miles across, which plunges down to the east. Erosion has progressed faster in some beds, and the arcuate pattern of the more resistant beds—the peninsulas—has resulted. In most of New England this kind of feature is apparent only after detailed geological mapping, but here a discerning eye can pick it out even on a road map.

4
Mountains

"The tops of mountains are the unfinished parts of the globe."

—Thoreau

The mountains, the bony spine of Maine, stretch northeast nearly across the state. They are the northern extremity of the Appalachian Mountains, and a backdrop to the gentler landscape of most of the state. Low mountains are found in other parts of the state, as well as beyond into New Brunswick, but the chain of high mountains ends with **Mount Katahdin,** (at 5,267 feet, the highest summit in the state). Few peaks in Maine are higher than four thousand feet although a number reach heights between three thousand and four thousand feet, modest summits even by Eastern standards. What distinguishes mountain landscape, however, is not simply total altitude but rugged local relief—the difference in elevation, and how steep the grade, between valley floor and peak.

Anyway, the true measure of a mountain is not necessarily its elevation but its effect on the viewer. Maine's mountains are equal to any, on this scale. Who does not rouse to the sight of blue mountains on the skyline, placing a comforting limit to the world? If you are a mountain hiker, your excitement increases as you approach, looking for possible routes to the summit, whether or not you intend to climb. You shiver a bit as you contemplate the steepness of the cliffs and the bright scars of slides; they look tempting but you know they are not the easiest way to the top.

Contrary to what we might expect, the backbone of highest mountains does not form a drainage divide; most of the major rivers, the **Androscoggin,** the **Kennebec,** and the **Penobscot,** cut right through the mountains in their southerly course to the ocean. It is only north of Mount Katahdin that a low mountain range blocks the rivers from a direct southerly route to the sea; the **Allagash and St. John rivers** must flow seventy miles northeast from their headwaters to get around the mountain barrier.

Why Are There Mountains?

Landscape appreciators are quite apt to be aware of the geologic underpinnings of landscape when we are in mountain country because much bare rock is in evidence. Cliffs and rock faces often expose different rock types and perhaps some of the internal structure of the rocks; that is, tilted, folded, and broken beds, or perhaps crystalline masses with streaks of light-colored quartz. In weathering, crumbling, mountain terrain it is easy to see that some mountain rocks are more easily eroded than others, creating ravines and gullies but leaving harder knobs protruding. A range of mountains rising above the general level of the land might suggest the question: Why are the mountains where they are?

Examine the geologic map of Maine and you will see a certain correspondence between the location of the mountains and the distribution of rock types. For example, masses of *granite*, a common building stone that crystallized from a molten condition, are most abundant in two general areas: the Downeast Mountain region of eastern Maine and the Mountain Upland, from the New Hampshire border northeast to Mount Katahdin. Some of the largest mountains, **Katahdin** and **Cadillac,** for example, are made of granite.

So, where there is granite there are mountains? Not quite. A closer look shows that there is a large mass of mountains in western Maine, from **Mount Bigelow** to **Mount Blue,** that does not match the pattern of granite on the map. Apparently these mountains are made of something other than granite. Even more damaging to our first impression, where many of the largest patches of granite occur on the map there are lakes: **Sebago** and **Mooselookmeguntic** in western Maine, the large lakes north of Millinocket, and **West Grand Lake** northwest of Calais. Obviously, accounting for Maine's mountains is not simple.

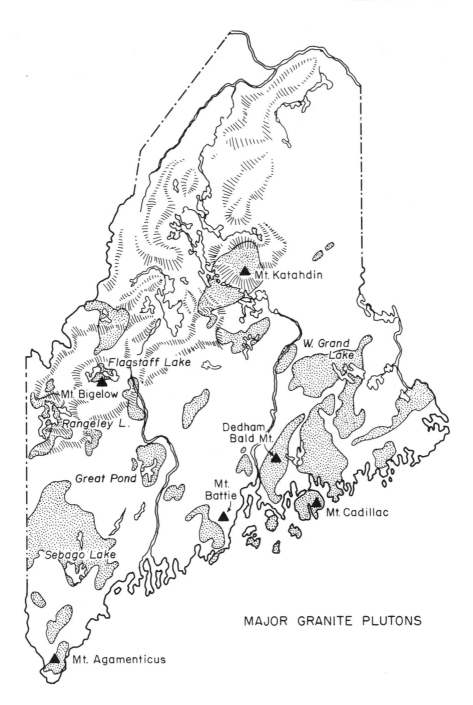

Mt. Katahdin

W. Grand
Lake

Flagstaff Lake

Mt. Bigelow

Rangeley L.

Dedham
Bald Mt.

Great Pond

Mt.
Battie

Mt. Cadillac

Sebago Lake

MAJOR GRANITE PLUTONS

Mt. Agamenticus

Most geologists now believe that mountain building is the result of the collision of great slabs (or *plates*, as they are called) of the earth's crust as they slide over the surface of the globe, an idea described more fully in Chapter 7. As two crustal plates approach each other, the sand and mud that have accumulated, many thousands of feet thick, on the bordering shallow margins of the continents are crumpled and deformed.

Some rocks may be shoved up onto the continents to raise high mountain chains like the Himalayas, which are the result of India pushing into Asia, buckling the crust before it. No doubt this also took place hundreds of millions of years ago in the region we now call the Appalachian Mountains, including some of the mountains of Maine. Some parts of the early Appalachians might well have been as high and rugged as today's Himalayas.

Other portions of the crumpled plate edges are dragged to great depths below the surface, to be partially or even completely melted. The folded rock layers well exposed along Maine's coast from Kittery to Pemaquid Point owe their structure to this process.

Some of the molten rock is returned to the surface as lava. Volcanoes erupt in this zone of continental collision throughout the mountain-building period, spewing great volumes of ash into the air and pouring lava onto the surface. **Mount Kineo** and **Big Spencer Mountain** on the east side of Moosehead Lake, and **Traveler Mountain** north of Mount Katahdin, **Quaggy Joe Mountain** in Aroostook State Park, and sharp-pointed **Haystack Mountain,** dominating the skyline between Presque Isle and Ashland, are all volcanic rock, chemically similar to granite but harder, denser, and much finer grained. These mountains, though carved from lava, are not volcanoes; their original cones, if they ever existed, were long ago planed flat. Later, uplift of the land followed by erosion and sculpting of the less resistant surrounding rock left their steep and prominent outlines.

Mountains of Crystalline Rock. Large amounts of the molten rock do not reach the surface but cool and solidify at great depths, forming great pods and domes of crystalline granite. We would never see these domes but for erosion, which strips off the cover. At **Mount Katahdin,** for example, the cover once may have been nine miles

Mount Kineo

deep. All of this rock, and much of the dome, are eroded away, leaving only a small portion still projecting into the sky.

The continental collisions responsible for Maine's mountains spanned many millions of years, culminating some 200 million years ago. Then followed 135 million years of erosion, and by 65 million years ago the land had been reduced to a plain, as the rolling Tablelands on the shoulders of Katahdin reveal. About 25 million years ago when the eastern part of North America was arched up, the streams quickened, cutting deeper, and erosion began the creation of the present landscape. Finally, scouring by the continental ice sheet, and dumping of the resulting debris, disrupted the natural drainage patterns. The result is a low-relief, lake-dotted upland punctuated by a few peaks that survived the grinding of the ice sheet.

Baxter Peak on Mount Katahdin is 5,267 feet above sea level, just short of a mile. Hikers in the past remedied that "shortcoming" by building a thirteen-foot cairn at the summit. Among New England peaks the elevation is not unique, but Katahdin rises from lowlands on the south and east that are only 400 feet above sea level. Even

The Tablelands of Mount Katahdin.

to the north the surroundings are only about 1,000 feet. The height of the mountain is emphasized by this lack of sloping foothills; it seems to shoot right up, its steep sides scarred with landslides in many places.

Mount Katahdin is akin to an iceberg rising out of the sea. Baxter and the several other peaks that make up the Katahdin massif—Pamola, Hamlin, Howe, Russell, the Turners, and several others—are the last remnants, the crest, barely eight miles in diameter, of a very large mass of eroding granite. Egg-shaped in plan view, this granite pluton extends downward several miles beneath the surface and across the landscape for more than twenty miles to the southwest. Most of this land is occupied by low mountains and large lakes, described by Thoreau as "glittering in the dark forest like pieces of broken mirror scattered across a lawn."

The freshly broken rock of Mount Katahdin is pinkish due to the presence of a pink mineral, feldspar, though most surfaces are weathered gray or covered with gray lichens. The granite weathers and decomposes into blocks along regularly spaced cracks called *joints*. Great slabs, quarried by frost from the mountainside, litter the slope. Some have tumbled to the very foot, where they block

Weathered granite breaks into slabs and blocks, Mount Katahdin.

the swirling rivers. The nature of the rock, pink and coarse-grained, is well displayed along the **West Branch** of the **Penobscot River,** where whitewater charges through chasms and pours over falls in one of the prettiest stretches of wild river in the East.

An elongated dome of coarse granite, from which several small peaks protrude, stretches from Orland, on U.S. Route 1, northeast for thirty-five miles. **Dedham Bald Mountain,** near Route 1A, and **Peaked Mountain,** off Route 9 near Clifton, are easy but rewarding climbs, both part of this large granite body. In York County, **Mount Agamenticus** is at the center of a circular (in plan view) mass of granite six miles in diameter, which like the other granite bodies may extend downward several miles, according to seismic evidence.

Other granite mountains readily accessible to hikers are **Saddleback** and **The Horn,** southeast of Rangely, each a bit over 4,000 feet. North of Rangeley, **West Kennebago Mountain,** about 3,700 feet high, offers a sweeping view from Mount Katahdin to Mount Washington in New Hampshire.

Sugarloaf, a mountain near Carrabassett well known for its recreational development, is formed from a rock that is crystalline, like granite, but of different chemical composition. This is **gabbro,**

and like granite, it was emplaced in the molten state at considerable depth, and there solidified. Gabbro is a darker rock than granite and contains no quartz. (The distinction between granite and gabbro is discussed further in Chapter 6.)

Mountains Made of Other Rocks. When molten rock was emplaced many miles below the surface, it was very hot and under great pressure. This intrusion had a severe effect on the enclosing rocks, baking and altering them. New minerals were formed when the gasses and fluids accompanying the molten rock reacted with chemical elements in the surrounding rocks. The principal result, as far as landscape is concerned, was the hardening of these contact rocks. What had been relatively soft rock—mudstone, shale, and sandstone, for example—became very dense and durable slate and coarse-grained, garnet-bearing schists and gneisses, more resistant to the ravages of erosion than the crystalline rocks they surround. **Big Squaw Mountain,** near Greenville, and **Mount Bigelow, Mount Blue,** and many other high peaks in the western part of the Mountain Upland owe their origin to this difference in hardness of the bedrock.

Finally, features like **Mount Battie** and **Mount Megunticook** in the Camden Hills of the Midcoast Region, are not made of either crystalline rocks or hard contact rock. They are knobs of very hard rocks, originally sand and gravel on the continental shelves, that were caught between the colliding continents. The sediments were subjected to great heat and pressure deep within the crust, though not enough to melt them; the original pebbles and gravel can still be seen, embedded in a sugary-looking, finely crystalline matrix that reveals their history. These rocks that have been changed in form are called metamorphic. The continental ice sheet, grinding down from the north at least four times in the last one million years, rounded the tops and plucked rocks from south-facing cliffs to make the Camden Hills.

Because of their combination of altitude and geographic latitude, many of Maine's peaks have a timberline, an elevation above which the arctic climatic conditions are too rough for any but the most hardy (often dwarfed and gnarled) plants to grow. This occurs

Mount Bigelow, from Stratton.

at something just less than 4,000 feet, and adds to the enjoyment
of mountain hikers, for many mountain summits thus provide an
unobstructed view over the land. The bare knobs on **Mount Desert
Island** are due, on the other hand, to a disastrous fire in 1947 that
burned the forest from practically the whole island. Stripped of this
protective vegetation, much of the soil eroded away. The mountain
vegetation is starting to reclothe the slopes but it will take a long
time.

Maine's mountains, then, are not so much heaped up as they
are carved from the earth's crumpled crust. Every raindrop, every
rill, every rushing stream gaining power as it plunges down the
slope, does its part to shape the land. At first this produces rugged
terrain because rocks vary in their resistance, but eventually all rocks
succumb. Gradually the skyline is softened as peaks are worn away
and valleys and lowlands are filled. If not interrupted, erosion and
deposition of the sediment will finally reduce the land to a plain.

Bit by bit the stuff of the continent is carried to the sea, to be
deposited as sediment, compacted and cemented into rock, and
ultimately uplifted once again to form new land. Whether the new

land will be an uplifted plateau of undisturbed rock layers, or complicated mountains formed from layers of rock thrust over one another in great folds and faults and cut through by molten rock from
the depths of the earth, depends on many geologic circumstances.
These circumstances are the subject of later chapters.

5
Water on the Land: Weathering, Lakes, and Rivers

The carving of landscape begins with weathering, the process by which minerals are decomposed by water. All minerals have at least some solubility in water, and because rocks are mixtures of minerals in a variety of proportions and textures, it is more useful to speak of the weathering of minerals than of rocks. Rocks of the same type—the granite family, for example—may display quite different rates of weathering because of slight differences in mineral composition. Moreover, the texture of the rock (that is, the size of its mineral grains) is important in determining how fast it will weather because weathering begins along grain boundaries. Generally, fine-grained rocks weather and decompose more slowly.

Crumbling Rocks

In weathering the most important chemical reaction is hydrolysis, where water acts as a chemical. The water molecules participate in a chemical reaction, not merely acting as a solvent like tea dissolving sugar. The decomposition of feldspar, a mineral that accounts for 30 percent of all minerals exposed to weathering, results in the formation of **clay,** a hydrated mineral. Partly weathered feldspar, although still hard, takes on a white, chalky look. The process also increases the volume and breaks down the mineral's structure. This expansion of volume, and the stress it puts on mineral grains, is of great importance in the weathering of rock.

Crumbling of coarse-grained granite like that of **Mount Katahdin** is due more to hydrolysis of feldspar than to any other action.

Weathering granite boulders at Enfield Horseback.

Close-up of weathering granite.

Granite in all stages of decomposition can be found on the summit and slopes of the mountain. On close examination you can see the effects of water seeping along grain boundaries, releasing grains and crumbling the rock. In some places, rotten rock can be pulled away by hand. Deeply weathered granite is exposed on the sides of gullied trails, and in many places the gravels underfoot are sharp and angular; they are largely released feldspar grains that are still hard enough to resist abrasion.

Many rounded knobs of granite display *exfoliation*, the spalling off of thin concentric shells of weathered rock. This happens at all scales, ranging from hand specimens to whole mountainsides, such as **Peaked Mountain,** east of Eddington on Route 9. Another example is **Dedham Bald Mountain**, south of Route 1A, where the soil cover on the road to the fire tower has been stripped away, exposing a pavement of rock. In many places the apparently solid, coarse-grained granite actually sounds "drummy" beneath your boot. Exfoliation is loosening large slabs of the rock that one day will be spalled off and find their way to the bottom of the mountain.

Oxidation, the combining of oxygen with elements in the minerals, is responsible for much of the color change in weathering rocks. Simple rust, iron oxide, is a good example because iron-bearing minerals are common in Maine rocks. Roadcuts in many places expose small veins of **pyrite,** iron sulfide, which turn the rocks yellow and reddish brown as they oxidize. Much granite, like that of **Cadillac Mountain** on Mount Desert Island and nearby **Schoodic Point** is naturally red, however, and surface weathering has had nothing do with it; fresh rock from deep inside the outcrop is just as red.

Weathering penetrates only to shallow depths in most Maine rocks. In unglaciated parts of the country, the Southern Appalachians, for example, weathered rock extends as much as one hundred feet below the surface. If such thicknesses ever existed in Maine they were scrubbed away by the ice sheet. It has been only ten thousand years since the last of the continental ice melted away, not time enough to develop more than a few inches of weathered rock.

Limestone and marble, in which the principal minerals are carbonates, are weathered by simply dissolving in rainwater. Rain contains enough carbon dioxide from the atmosphere to be very slightly acidic. As minerals go, carbonates are quite soluble in water, and over geologic time rain effectively dissolves the rock. Only small areas in Maine are underlain by carbonate rocks, notably parts of **Knox County** and eastern **Aroostook County.**

It is interesting to observe the different rates of weathering on gravestones in old cemeteries. Slate is very fine-grained, and slabs two hundred years old still show lettering and carving in sharp detail, while marble slabs only a few decades old may already be nearly obliterated. In our time gases added to the atomosphere by smoke-stack industries have increased the acidity of rainwater, greatly accelerating the decomposition of limestone.

Bare mountain summits weather away much more slowly than do the forested slopes. Where vegetation covers the rock, the root mat tends to hold moisture in contact with the rock and adds organic acids, which increase the rate of decomposition. Nevertheless, the development of soil from rock is a slow process as humans reckon time, and the process can be interrupted by natural or manmade disasters. Catastrophic fires or landslides may remove the weathered cover, exposing bedrock in wounds that are very slow to heal. Many mountains like **Cadillac** owe their open, rocky summits to fire rather than altitude.

The power of expanding ice to break bottles and plumbing is well known, so it is not surprising that this effect is also important geologically. Freezing and thawing of water in cracks and crevices, repeated many thousands of times, eventually weakens the rock. Arctic conditions exist on the tops of most of the higher mountains, and here physical breaking by ice may be more important than chemical decomposition by liquid water. On **Mount Bigelow,** for example, fine-grained rocks, which decompose very slowly, are broken into blocks, slabs, and fragments of all sizes by the action of freezing water. The result of the freeze-thaw process can be seen also in roadcuts, particularly those in slate and other thin-bedded rock. In many places the slaty rock is split into knifelike slivers and shards. During the spring when melting temperatures in the day are followed by freezing at night, rock is loosened and dislodged, often onto the highway below.

An interesting feature related to frost action on loose stones is found on the **Tablelands of Mount Katahdin,** those gently sloping shoulders well above timberline. North of Baxter Peak and just below the summit, a "stream" of boulders about forty feet long is slowly making its way down. Freezing water beneath the stones expands, lifting them slightly. Because of the slope, when the ice melts, the stones are lowered back into place a bit farther downhill. This action repeated thousands of times gradually produces a stream of stones. The outer edges are thinner, and in some places the stream actually flows around obstructing boulders, indicating that the movement is real, but slow almost beyond our ability to measure. Elsewhere, loose rock has been formed into rings and networks by much the same mechanism, though they are not readily seen from eye level. Heaving soil in the center of the ring pushes the rocks radially outward. Rings from adjacent centers combine to form networks.

Mass Movements: Rocks and Gravity

Beneath most steep rock cliffs is a pile of broken angular blocks called *talus*. Good examples are on the southern slope of **Barren Mountain,** near Monson (inaccurately named Barren Slide) and in Acadia National Park at the base of **Champlain Mountain,** along Route 3. A distinction can be drawn between a rock fall and a rock slide. A rock fall differs from a rock slide in at least two respects:

Talus slopes below cliffs on Barren Mountain, from Boarstone Mountain.

(1) it forms by the gradual accumulation of rocks from above as they are loosened, more or less, one by one; (2) there are very few small particles mingled with the large blocks. Rock slides, on the other hand, involve large masses of rock and soil, and move en masse down the slope, sometimes very rapidly and for considerable distances.

Talus, also called "scree" in mountaineering literature, characteristically forms a slope of about thirty to thirty-five degrees, the angle of repose for loose material. This angle is changed very little by the size of the pile or the diameter of the fragments. Because there is very little fine material to embed the larger rocks, the slope is likely to be unstable. Many of the rocks are balanced precariously, and even though it might have been many years since the rocks fell from the cliff, a slight disturbance could set them in motion again. For this reason climbing a talus slope can be dangerous, particularly near the upper, steeper, parts. A fine cliff and talus slope, with blocks up to twenty feet in diameter, formed on **Horse Mountain** in the northeast corner of Baxter State Park. They are visible from the road along Grand Lake Mattagamon.

Rock slides add to the scenery of mountains and seem to emphasize their steepness and rugged character. One of the better known in Maine is **Abol Slide** on Mount Katahdin, a scar on the south slope that extends for a mile or more from the edge of the Tableland to the foot of the mountain. It is visible from a great distance and was probably used in the earliest ascents. As climbing routes, slides can be deceptive; although they appear to offer the quickest route to the top, they are also the steepest and never the easiest trails on the mountain.

A number of other slides are visible on the west side of Mount Katahdin. **O-J-I Mountain** gets its name from slides that at one time seemed to form these letters, although more recent slides have largely destroyed the pattern. Many other rock slides can be seen on the steep slopes of other peaks in this rapidly weathering granite mass.

Landslides ordinarily have a high proportion of fine material, and the whole mass comes down in a single flow that may last minutes or days. While there may be a steep scar at the top where the land broke away, there is not usually a rocky cliff. Landslides sometimes occur after the soil has been saturated with water, permitting the soil to slide on a slope that when dry is stable. In 1973 a landslide occurred in **Rockland,** involving large blocks of clay several feet across and many feet long. Sizable trees went with the slide and were left tilted back twenty to twenty-five degrees.

At **Gorham** in September 1983, nearly seven acres of land slid into the Stroudwater River and Indian Creek, taking a house, several vehicles, and a number of large trees with it. It all happened in just a few moments. This is gently sloping land, not what you might expect for landslide country , but the soil is deep clay deposited in the sea from glacial meltwater, and it is crossed by streams with banks twenty to twenty-five feet high. The slide took place on the nose of a peninsulalike bank, surrounded on three sides by the streams. It had been an unusually dry summer so rainfall had nothing to do with it. What triggered the slide is not known, but great blocks slipped intact along a break-away plane about forty feet below the surface. An area 450 feet wide was involved in the sliding. Most blocks slid about fifteen to twenty feet, leaving arcuate scars totaling several hundred feet long. Landslides like this are not frequent in Maine but they all seem to involve the glacial marine clay. They generally occur where a bank has been undercut by a stream or the ocean, though their effect is far greater than that from simple bank caving.

Water in the Ground

Maine receives about forty inches of rainfall, distributed fairly evenly throughout the year, and for this reason the state is well covered with vegetation. The natural cover is forest; farmers keep fields free of brush only by constant effort.

About 50 percent of the precipitation, including melted snow, runs directly into rivers and streams and finally back to the ocean. Between 30 and 40 percent either evaporates upon falling or is taken up by plants and transpired back into the atmosphere. The remaining 10 to 20 percent soaks into the ground to become what is known as *groundwater*.

Water soaking into the soil moves through the pore spaces between soil particles. It is pulled down by gravity until it reaches a level that is already soaked with water. The top of this zone of saturated soil is called the *water table*. The water table is closer to the surface in lowlands; a well on a hill must be drilled deeper than

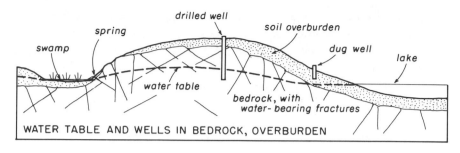

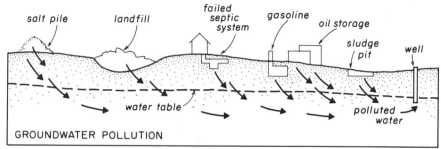

Groundwater and the water table. (After Caswell, Groundwater Handbook, 1979.)

one in a valley to find water. Moreover, the elevation of the water table varies with the season. During warm, dry periods the water table falls as less water is added than is evaporated and transpired by growing plants. Wells that are barely deep enough in a wet period are likely to fail during a dry spell. Most rural people depend upon shallow wells dug in the glacial overburden, bedrock wells, or springs for their water supply.

Groundwater can penetrate where the bedrock has been fractured, filling the cracks. Wells in many parts of Maine are drilled into rock in the justified expectation that the hole will intersect enough water-filled cracks to furnish a water supply. It is difficult to predict where these cracks will be found, but geologists analyzing aerial photos often can spot linear patterns that indicate fracture zones, thus raising the odds in favor of finding water.

Springs occur where groundwater has been conducted to the surface, perhaps by cracks in the bedrock. For this reason cliff faces and roadcuts often are wet—and covered with beautiful icicles in winter. In glacial soils a layer of impermeable silt and clay may prevent the normal downward migration of water, forcing it to flow along the layer of clay until it reaches the surface of the land. In some glacial soils a layer of compacted and nearly impervious material, called *hardpan*, will stop water from penetrating deeper. If that layer should be intersected in a roadcut or excavation the water will seep out, sometimes in considerable volume during wet seasons. Although large springs are not common in Maine, some flow at rates of several hundred gallons per minute.

Much of the state is covered with glacial sands and gravels. Because of their high porosity these make excellent *aquifers*, or water-bearing layers. Water readily moves through the large spaces in these materials and may accumulate in great volume. Wells in some locations, driven into thick beds of sandy glacial material, yield hundreds of gallons per minute.

Yields from bedrock wells average less than 10 gallons per minute, plenty for most domestic and farm purposes, but some wide fracture zones supply water up to 150 gallons per minute. Wells at **Stonington** maintain a steady yield of more than 100 gallons per minute, a very high yield for granite bedrock wells. This water, moreover, is remarkably pure and has no radon gas, which is sometimes a contaminant of wells drilled in granite.

Groundwater Pollution. The percolation of groundwater through soil and sand and gravel goes a long way toward purifying it. Contamination in the form of harmful bacteria and viruses occurs where groundwater drains through farm wastes but these are rather quickly neutralized by organisms in the soil. Filtration removes practically all of the solid suspended matter. Dissolved substances, however, are not removed by these natural means. Soluble substances such as nitrates and phosphates from fertilizers and sewage, introduced to groundwater by human activities, remain in solution. When they find their way to lakes and streams, unwanted growth of aquatic plant life is the result.

More serious is the presence of toxic wastes, including pesticides, many of which are man-made and do not decompose naturally. Landfills and refuse dumps exposed to rain develop a toxic leachate that may find its way into aquifers and, farther along, into water supplies used by humans. Leaking underground storage tanks are allowing oil and gasoline to enter aquifers in some locations in Maine.

Salt supplies used on highways in the winter, if not protected from rainfall, can leach into the groundwater. Pollution of groundwater is a serious problem because groundwater flows only a few feet per day, and once polluted an aquifer is virtually impossible to purify. Consideration of the geological setting is necessary when designing disposal and storage sites.

Lakes

Lakes form in valleys or lowlands where the water table meets the land surface. Although surface runoff adds considerable water to lakes during wet periods, it is the steady supply of groundwater percolating in through their sides and bottoms that permits larger lakes to maintain their levels during dry seasons.

Maine is famous for its many beautiful lakes, although driving in summer along the tree-lined roads and highways you may be unaware of their numbers until the road tops a rise. Some of Maine's largest lakes are tucked between mountains: **Mooselookmeguntic, Rangeley, Flagstaff, Moosehead, Chesuncook,** and **Chamberlain,** for example. Other very large lakes such as **Sebago, Great Pond** (Belgrade), **West Grand Lake,** and the series of lakes on the New Brunswick border known as the **Chiputneticook Lakes,** lie in lowlands. The mountain lakes tend to be bordered by rocky shores and steep mountain sides that make striking scenic views. The lowland lakes, on the other hand, largely developed in glacial outwash, are known for their beautiful sandy beaches.

How Lakes Form. Lakes are created by some natural or man-made feature that holds back the water in its journey to the sea. Where there is a lake or pond, the groundwater intersects the surface of the ground and is impeded, at least temporarily, in its ceaseless quest for a lower elevation. Lakes are temporary geological features, some lasting a few centuries, others perhaps a few thousand years, but it is their fate to disappear. Some lakes are fed in large measure by groundwater, and if their drainage basin is large they tend to maintain a fairly constant level all year. Others, like mountain lakes, are fed largely by surface runoff from rain and melting snow, and fluctuate in level according to the season.

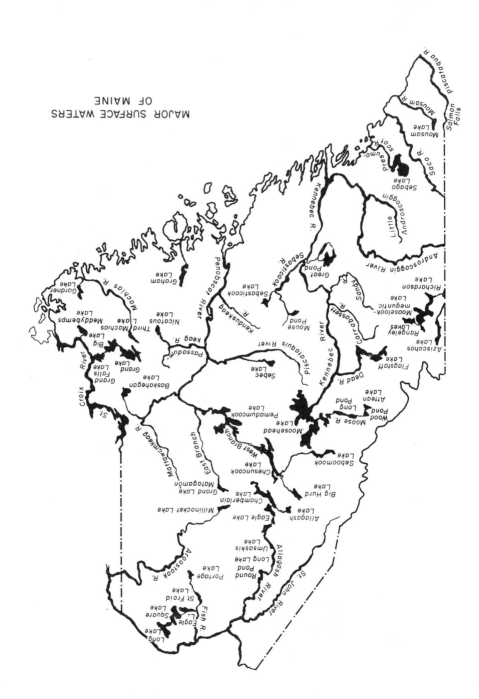

MAJOR SURFACE WATERS
OF MAINE

A number of mountains hold small high-altitude lakes, tiny gems reflecting their rock settings. Mount Bigelow, with its **Horns Pond,** and **Tumbledown Pond** between Tumbledown and Little Jackson mountains are examples. A few mountains enclose within their rocky slopes a special kind of lake called a *tarn.* **Chimney Pond** in the South Basin of Mount Katahdin, and several ponds in the North and Northwest basins belong to this category. Tarns occupy the floor of cirques scooped out of solid mountain rock by alpine glaciers. Rain and meltwater from winter snow are held in by rock ridges or moraines left by the glaciers.

Some lakes, like **Sebago,** were formed where streams are dammed by sand and gravel. The **Crooked River,** flowing south from Bethel, carried vast quantities of sand from the melting glacier and distributed much of it on a wide floodplain, through which it followed a shifting, braided course. After the ice had melted and the great floods of water subsided, the river cut into its floodplain, carrying much sand to Sebago Lake, where a delta was built more than a half mile into the lake. Waves and currents are distributing this sand along the lakeshore, forming the broad beaches for which the park is well known.

A large proportion, perhaps most, of Maine's lakes have been raised and enlarged by damming their outlet streams. Indeed, many lakes without the dam would be little more than a wide spot in the river; "deadwater" it was called in the past. One by-product of the raising of lake levels was "dri-ki," the vast piles of stumps and logs created by flooding the edge of the forest. Eventually the drowned trees broke loose from the lake bed, floated to the surface, and drifted to the lee side of the lake. In some places this created not only a navigational hazard but also a ragged, impenetrable barrier many hundreds of feet wide between the shore and open water. Newer lakes, **Flagstaff,** for example, have had the shoreline cleared of trees before the dam was closed, greatly reducing the hazard and the unsightly mess.

How Lakes Disappear. The streams that help fill the lake also lead to its demise by depositing sediment in the lake. It is common to find a sandy *delta* at the mouth of a stream feeding into quiet lake waters. Over the years the delta will grow, steadily filling the

Lake Onawa delta, from Boarstone Mountain.

lake. A good example is at **Sebago Lake,** already described. On a smaller scale, a delta has formed at the upper end of **Lake Onawa,** near Monson. There is a splendid view of it from Boarstone Mountain, and you can see that **Long Pond Stream** has already filled in at least a half mile of the northwest arm of the lake.

The encroachment of vegetation from their shores is another hazard to the existence of shallow lakes. Marsh vegetation, including shrubs and trees, grows onto the shore, creating soil and eventually filling in the lake.

In some places peat-forming moss fills in the depression, younger plants growing on top of older, gradually mounding up until the center of the *peat bog* is as much as twenty feet higher than the margins. A moatlike ring, often with standing water, surrounds the bog. Peat plants depend entirely on rain water for nourishment.

There are more than 700,000 acres of peat bogs in Maine. Interstate 95 crosses **Alton Bog,** a good example, about twelve miles north of Bangor. There are many more north of Bangor, for example, **Sunkhaze and Crystal bogs,** and along the Downeast Coast near Columbia Falls lies the **Great Heath.** Some of these bogs have a commercial value. Peat is mostly harvested for horticultural pur-

poses, but recently there have been studies of the economics of producing fuel pellets from it.

Many of the large, flat sandy areas in the lowlands of southern Maine were once the floors of lakes fed by streams from the melting ice sheet. Once their ice dams melted, the lakes quickly drained, leaving layers of silt and clay as the principal evidence of their former existence. In other places a constriction of bedrock in the river channel prevents free flow, backing up water to form a lake. **Snow Falls** gorge on the Little Androscoggin River in West Paris is such a place, and there are many more to be found when you learn to recognize them. All dams finally erode, the water flows away and the lake disappears, but the flat bottomland is its memorial.

Lakes and bogs are sensitive to conditions in their surrounding watersheds, which contribute runoff and groundwater to the lake. In the Mountain Upland lakes generally are small because there is rapid runoff of precipitation from the steep slopes and little soil to hold groundwater. The water level in these lakes falls quickly during dry periods, and streams draining the lakes have wide seasonal fluctuations in volume. Lakes in the Central and Downeast Mountain regions, on the other hand, are developed in thick deposits of glacial overburden with abundant supplies of groundwater. This leads to larger lakes with more constant levels, and the draining rivers consequently show less seasonal variation.

Most soils in Maine were derived from nearly insoluble rocks and consequently are thin. Natural rainfall is slightly acidic, and there is little in the rocks and soils to neutralize it, but plants and animals in the natural ecosystem have adjusted to this slightly acidic environment over the millions of years they were evolving. Today's pollution of the atmosphere by acid-forming gases, however, increases the acidity of rainwater far beyond the neutralizing ability of the soil and threatens to upset the natural balance. Rainfall, and therefore runoff and lake water, of unnaturally high acidity is evidently having harmful effects on the biology of Maine, damaging forest trees and raising the acidity of lakes and streams to a level that inhibits the reproduction of aquatic life.

Streams and Rivers

Mountain streams, like the **Carrabassett River,** are fed almost entirely by runoff. Without large lakes to help stabilize the flow they

tend to be very responsive to the weather, rising quickly after rain-storms. Canoeists in mountainous country need to be aware that rapids that appear quite manageable under normal flow conditions can become raging masses of white water during rainy periods, and then subside again fairly quickly. Mountain streams can also be bone-dry in the summer, for lack of adequate nourishment.

In mountainous areas where slopes are steep, streams are small in volume but their currents are fast. Fast-flowing streams cut deeply into their beds and can move large cobbles and boulders, tumbling them along the bottom during periods of high water. As stream flow slackens, larger rocks quickly settle; stream beds where the landscape is rugged are strewn with rounded rocks and boulders.

Streams flowing off the steep mountains of western Maine tend to radiate outward from the peaks in all directions. A different pattern occurs in the gentler topography of northern Maine, drained by the **Saint John and Allagash rivers.** Small, parallel tributary streams flow into the rivers at right angles, forming a pattern resembling a trellis. Both these patterns, *radial* and *trellis*, are related to the nature and the structure of the underlying bedrock. The radial pattern is formed on prominent resistant rocks that have no persistent grain or linear structure to govern stream flow. These moun-

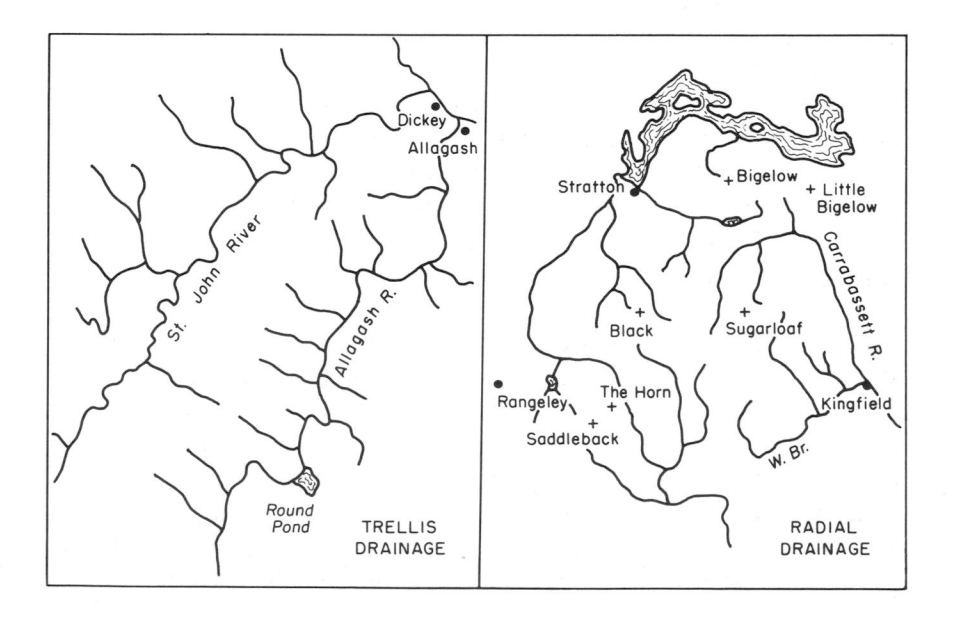

tains erode into rugged and diverse topography as the streams, encountering rocks of many types, flow in all directions from the heights, seeking the path of least resistance to lower elevations. The trellis pattern in northern Aroostook County developed on more uniform rocks hardly affected by the hardening processes of mountain-building. Streams flowing over these rocks are unimpeded by differences of rock type and flow in relatively straight lines to the main rivers. These in turn follow long, gentle northeast-trending folds in the bedrock.

Streams in flat land overflow their banks at times of high water, currents quickly subside, and much sediment is dropped. In this way a floodplain builds up, which later in the season will be rich, flat bottomland well suited for farming.

Most of a stream's work is done during periods of flooding and high water, but erosion of the streambed and its banks goes on constantly. Streams on flat land tend to meander in wide curves that migrate laterally across the floodplain. The **Saco River,** especially in the upper part from Fryeburg to Hiram, is an outstanding example of a meandering river.

Just as you are pushed against the car door when the vehicle goes around a curve, the momentum of the flowing water tends to hurl it against the outside of a curve. This causes the stream to undercut the outer banks of a curve and to carry the sand and fine material downstream. On the inside of the curve the current is slower and the stream must drop some of its load. A sandbar builds up, trailing off downstream. The looping channels, migrating sideways, sometimes intersect. When this happens the river is likely to cut across the loop, abandoning part of its former course and shortening its ceaseless quest for lower elevations. The abandoned channel is known as an *oxbow*. A fine example is found on the upper reaches of the **Aroostook River** about eighteen miles, by road, south of Ashland. The **Sandy** and the **Saco** rivers also display these features as they wind over sandy floodplains. Roads parallel to the streams, for example, Route 113 along the Saco and Route 134 along the Sandy, offer a chance to study the process in detail. Streams of all sizes, whether a river in its floodplain or a rivulet draining a tidal flat, follow the same physical laws. Meander patterns develop wherever the gradient (the slope of the streambed) is very low.

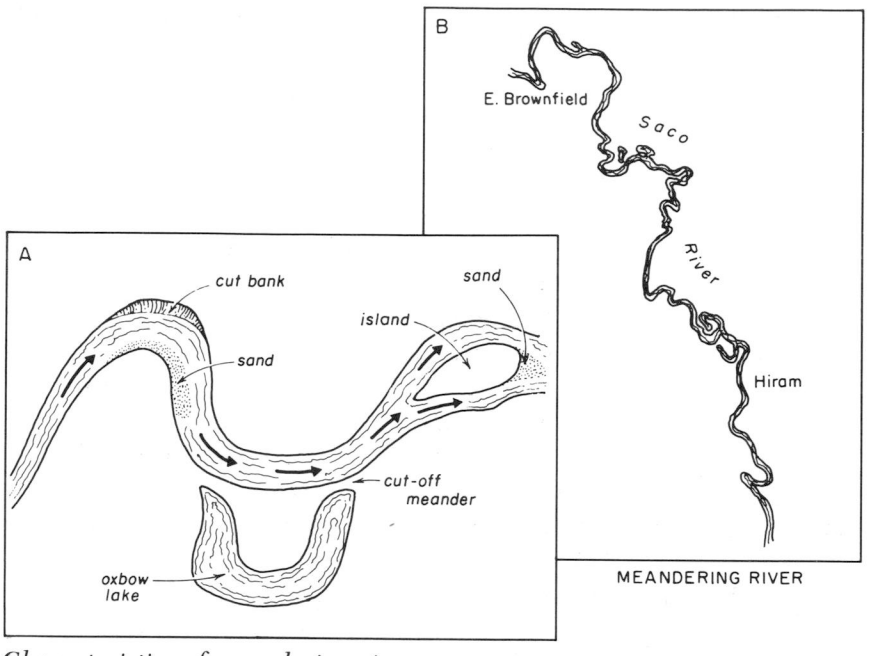

Characteristics of meandering rivers.

An abandoned meander can be seen to left of present river channel, Kennebec River above Anson.

The Major Rivers. An early hydrographic survey of Maine, in 1869, noted that the natural arrangement of south-flowing rivers and northeast-trending bedrock promotes the formation of waterfalls, and therefore abundant sites for waterpower. Development of Maine was tied closely to the availability of waterpower, and settlement followed the rivers inland from the coast. Most of the inland cities are on sites of former waterfalls. Travel, including by rail, was largely controlled by the river valleys. Not until modern highways were constructed did development become oriented northeast-southwest.

The **Aroostook, Fish, and Allagash rivers** all join the **St. John River** in draining northernmost Maine. They are the only major rivers in Maine that flow northeasterly. The Aroostook and Allagash originate in the Mount Katahdin region, while the Fish drains a series of large lakes: Eagle, Square, and Long. The Allagash River, roughly parallel to the upper reaches of the St. John, is well known because of its designation as a Wilderness Waterway. It is a popular canoe route, about half of which is on long, narrow lakes.

The **Penobscot River** and its tributaries drain a large portion of northern Maine. There are two branches, East and West. The **West Branch** rises north of Moosehead Lake and drains two large lakes, Seboomook and Chesuncook. The influence of Mount Katahdin on the West Branch was recorded at the turn of the century by Fannie Hardy Eckstorm: "Katahdin rules over all that West Branch country, a calm despot. Mute, massive, immense, hard-featured, broad-shouldered, nowhere can you get in that country where the broad forehead of Katahdin is not turned upon you. Snow and rain it sends to that region; it floods the river from its flanks; its back cuts off the north wind, making the valley hot; the road of the farmer it has closed, and the way of the lumberman it makes unduly difficult, by sowing the whole country with millions of tons of granite chipped from its sides....Katahdin makes all that region what it is." (from Penobscot Man, 1904. Used by permission of Juniper Press, Bangor, Me.).

The **East Branch** drains Grand Lake Mattagamon, and the slopes and smaller lakes east of Mount Katahdin. In the mountains the slopes are steep and currents are fast. Both branches are noted for their challenging whitewater. During some wild years in Maine's early history, water from **Telos Lake** northwest of Mount Katahdin, which would naturally flow down the Allagash River and into Canada,

was diverted by a cut through solid rock into **Webster Stream** to permit driving logs from north of Katahdin down the East Branch, thus avoiding a Canadian duty on the logs.

The branches emerge from the mountains and join at Medway. The land below is markedly flatter and the river spreads over a wide floodplain. Beyond Mattawamkeag the river meanders through shifting loops and oxbow lakes in the floodplain. The river is joined by the Mattawamkeag, Piscataquis, Pasadumkeag and Kenduskeag rivers before meeting tidewater at Bangor, the upper reaches of a long, sinuous estuary that becomes Penobscot Bay. About two miles north of Milford the river actually splits. One branch, bearing west around Old Town, takes on a life of its own and is called the **Stillwater River.** It rejoins the Penobscot below Orono. There are good roads with fine views on both sides of the river all the way from Bangor to Medway (Route 116 on the west bank or U.S. 2 on the east).

The **Kennebec River** starts by draining Moosehead Lake and receives major contributions from the Dead, Carrabassett, Sandy, and Sebasticook rivers before flowing into the sea at Fort Popham. It is famous as part of Benedict Arnold's route to Quebec during the Revolution, and it is prominent in Maine's logging history. U.S. Highway 201 largely follows the river and provides many fine views. There is still an untamed stretch, the gorge below Indian Pond, only a few miles from the river's source, but numerous dams control the river from The Forks on down. Madison-Anson, Norridgewock, Skowhegan, Waterville-Winslow, and Augusta are sites of dams on former falls. Downstream from Augusta the river valley is open to the sea, and there is a tide in the river channel.

The **Androscoggin River** begins by draining Umbagog Lake and flows almost straight south for thirty miles to Gorham, New Hampshire, where it turns sharply east. The river occupies a rather narrow valley where it enters Maine near Gilead. At Rumford there must have been spectacular falls in earlier years, because the change in elevation is 175 feet in about a mile, but the falls have been obliterated by two dams. Rumford-Mexico, Livermore Falls–Chisholm, Lewiston-Auburn, and Topsham-Brunswick are twin cities built at sites of major waterfalls that supplied power in the nineteenth century. The Androscoggin joins the Kennebec at Merrymeeting Bay north of Bath.

The **Saco River** originates in the White Mountains of New

Hampshire and enters Maine at Fryeburg. It is best known for its meandering course and sandy beaches, which are a great attraction to canoeists looking for an easy paddle in summer. The river flows between Saco and Biddeford just before delivering its great load of sand to the ocean for distribution to Ferry and Hills beaches.

The **Ossipee River,** also rising in New Hampshire, is paralleled by Route 25, a scenic drive. It has a steeper gradient and is faster, and its valley is narrower than that of the Saco, which it joins at Cornish.

The long rivers that drain the Mountain upland—the Saco, Androscoggin, Kennebec, and Penobscot—seem to have an aversion to granitic areas, low though they are and occupied by short streams and lakes. The Androscoggin River, for example, goes out of its way to avoid the huge granite mass overlain by Sebago, Long, and other large lakes. The Kennebec River appears to pick its way carefully around the granite of Great Pond in Belgrade, taking a sharp north-easterly turn at Norridgewock and then turning southerly once more at Skowhegan. It squeezes carefully between two granite bodies at Augusta. The Penobscot River swings west below Mattawamkeag, skirting large lakes in granite terrain of Hancock County. We might expect a river to get its start by simply connecting these low areas. Evidently that did not happen. Instead, the long rivers are found in areas of hard, fine-grained rock. Why this should be so is not yet understood by geologists.

Another peculiarity of stream behavior is found in western Maine. The town of Bethel is located at a sharp bend of the **Androscoggin River,** which at that point is sizable. Near Bethel are several small streams flowing north into the Androscoggin. The **Crooked River,** on the other hand, begins by draining Songo Pond, not more than a mile or two from the Androscoggin River, and flows south. Songo Pond actually lies between two of the north-flowing Androscoggin tributaries, Mill Brook and Pleasant River, whose headwaters are well to the south. That the Crooked did not flow north into the Androscoggin is the result of the glacier disrupting the general north-ward flow pattern and forcing Songo Pond to drain southward. The Crooked River flows south through sandy land in a remarkably me-andering path, over forty miles if the course were straight, to join the Songo River just before it empties into Sebago Lake at Sebago State Park.

Waterfalls

As a stream cuts its channel deeper it is likely to encounter rocks with differing degrees of resistance to erosion. The softer parts erode more easily but harder layers tend to remain, impeding the stream and creating waterfalls. In many places a stream flowing over fairly uniform rock finds a softer portion of the rock or perhaps a crack or other zone of weakness, and carves itself a narrow channel known as a *gorge*. Gorges contain cascades of tumbling water but they differ from waterfalls in being essentially linear, steep-walled features. Falls are short, with a vertical or near-vertical drop of the water. In Maine the two terms are often used interchangeably, though.

Waterfalls on Granite. It is not practical, of course, to try to describe every waterfall in Maine, but an understanding of the geologic processes that form them will increase your appreciation of any waterfall. One way to categorize waterfalls is by the bedrock structures that formed them. For example, streams flowing over granite with evenly spaced cracks, called *joints,* tend to pluck out blocks of rock, creating steplike falls. **Swift River Falls,** at a rest area on Route 17 about six miles north of Mexico, is a good example. There are two drops for a total of about seventy-six feet. The granite has also been sculpted by the flowing water into a variety of interesting shapes.

Step Falls, about four miles downstream (southeast) of Grafton Notch State Park and easily accessible from Route 26, is also formed on jointed granite. It is a long series of cascades with a total fall of over 150 feet.

Big Ambejackmockamus Falls on the West Branch of the Penobscot River, four miles below Ripogenus Dam, is easily accessible by a short walk from the road. The river plunges over jointed pink granite rocks in several falls of fifteen feet or more.

Waterfalls on Thin-Bedded Rock. Many falls occur where slaty, resistant rock is crossed by a stream. About nine miles north of Monson, the Elliotsville Road crosses **Big Wilson Stream** at the site of a pretty waterfall. The total fall is not great but the stream here is wide and the water pours over the vertical slate rock in several small drops. Blocks of slate have been carried away, leaving deep

1. Swift River Falls
2. Step Falls
3. Big Ambejackmockamus Falls
4. Big Wilson Stream Falls
5. Little Wilson Falls
6. Smalls Falls
7. Moxie Falls
8. Allagash Falls
9. Grand Pitch
10. Grindstone Falls
11. Ripogenus Gorge
12. Kennebec Gorge
13. Gulf Hagas
14. Screw Auger Gorge
15. Snow Falls Gorge
16. North Anson
    Gorge
17. Rumford Falls
    and Gorge

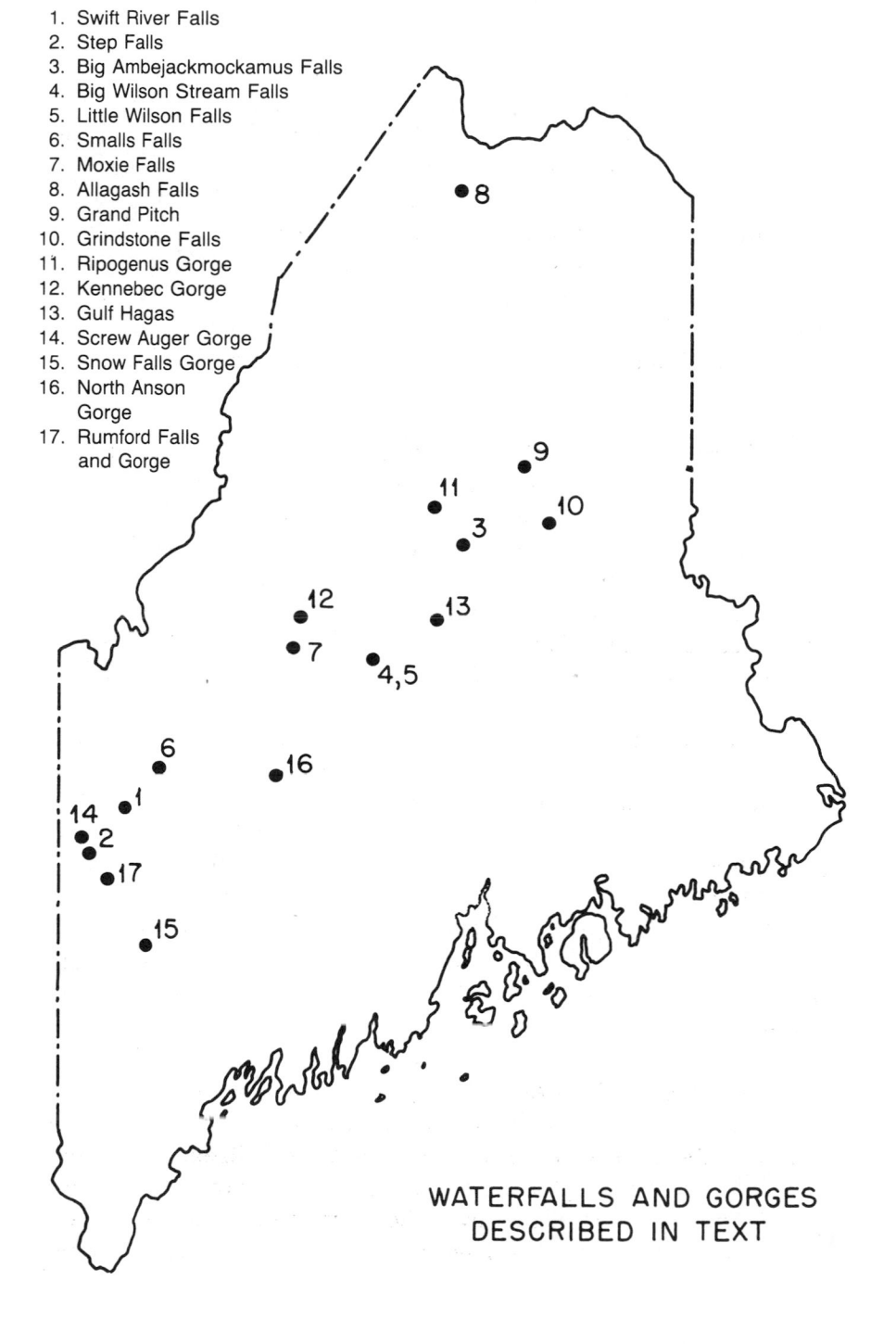

WATERFALLS AND GORGES
DESCRIBED IN TEXT

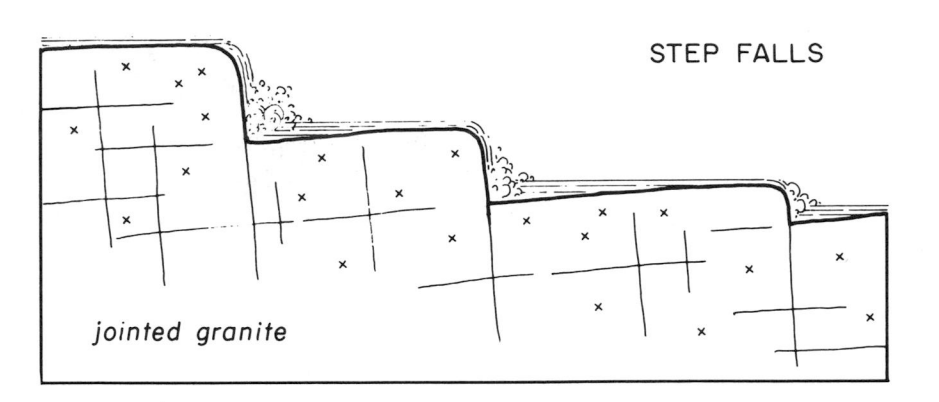

STEP FALLS

jointed granite

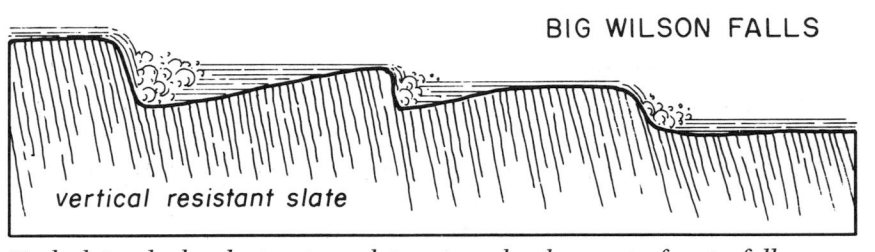

BIG WILSON FALLS

vertical resistant slate

Underlying bedrock structure determines development of waterfalls.

pools between the falls. The Appalachian Trail crosses here, and the pools are a welcome swimming spot for hikers on a hot summer day. **Little Wilson Falls,** about two miles up the side tributary of Little Wilson Stream, occupies a very narrow declivity in vertical slate. Its plunge of more than seventy-five feet is impressive. Farther down, on Big Wilson Stream, is **Tobey Falls** near Willimantic, a set of falls with an overall drop of seventy-five feet. They also are developed on vertical slate, and the water has sculpted a number of interesting potholes and channels. **Smalls Falls** on the Sandy River is a popular picnic spot off Route 4, north of Madrid. Here also, a series of falls and pools developed on vertical, thin-bedded rocks that strike across the river. Two streams come together here, and there are fine waterfalls on both.

Moxie Falls is about 2½ miles northeast of The Forks, where Moxie Stream enters the Kennebec River. This is one of the most beautiful waterfalls in New England. Moxie Stream narrows to less than twenty feet and then plunges in a thundering roar over a vertical

sixty-foot cliff into a pool below. Upstream from the falls small-scale folding is easily examined in the slaty rocks of the stream bed.

Allagash Falls, on the Allagash River, is accessible only by canoe, and it is an impressive sight. Approaching from upstream you hear the roar of plunging water and see mist rising from the falls as you come around the last bend. The river makes this wide swing just before it narrows sharply and forces its entire volume over a twenty-foot drop into a deep pool.

Grand Pitch on the East Branch of the Penobscot River is another beautiful falls accessible only to canoeists. The river takes a twenty-foot drop over the falls, which is at right angles to the trend of the thin-bedded, vertical bedrock. This falls was a major obstacle to the log drives of the past and is a source of many river-driving tales.

Grindstone Falls is also on the East Branch, but it is readily viewed from Route 11 at a roadside rest area about nine miles north of Medway. The river crosses vertical, resistant slaty rock over a small vertical drop, followed by a long stretch of rapids downstream.

Gorges

Gorges are usually found in rugged landscape and typically have steep, rocky walls where fast-flowing water has found a zone of weakness in the bedrock. The cascading stream follows this zone for some distance, widening and deepening it, creating scenes of great beauty.

Ripogenus Gorge on the West Branch of the Penobscot River, near the southwest corner of Baxter State Park, is more than a mile in length. Its upper reaches are developed in sedimentary beds broken by several faults at various angles. Limy pods and fossils have dissolved out of the shaly rock, leaving a rough, pockmarked surface. In its lower portion the gorge enters pink granite, part of the Mount Katahdin massif. The granite walls are vertical, and here the river fills the gorge wall-to-wall with roaring, churning white water. The cliffs above provide a good view of rafters in their large rubber boats, riding over the standing waves.

Rafters only are treated to the sight of another major gorge, that of the **Kennebec River** between Indian Pond and The Forks. It is a magnificent twelve-mile V-shaped canyon with steep walls rising more than 250 feet above the bottom. The most spectacular

part of the gorge is the first few miles below the dam (built in 1955) at the end of Indian Pond. Water is controlled by the dam, and when it is flowing, it is awesome. There are places where twelve-person rafts have been flipped by the standing waves. This portion of the Kennebec River is parallel to the general northeast trend of the bedrock and may have been determined by less resistant layers of rock.

Gulf Hagas, about sixteen miles northwest of Brownville Junction, is occupied by a modest stream but it is a very impressive gorge. For four miles the river plunges through a narrow cleft cut in resistant slaty rocks, over a number of vertical falls, some as much as fifty feet. In all, the river drops more than four hundred feet.

There are many other less spectacular but far more accessible gorges in Maine. Grafton Notch State Park's **Screw Auger Gorge,** is about a hundred feet long but only ten feet wide and perhaps twenty feet deep—really just a deep crevice. The stream drops over several small falls in the gorge and has carved interesting half-round chambers and potholes in the solid black-and-white granite. There are also some masses of very coarse pegmatite, a variety of granite, in which large flakes of mica sparkle in the sun.

Snow Falls Gorge, a rest area on Route 26 about two miles south of West Paris, is another narrow granite chasm with several

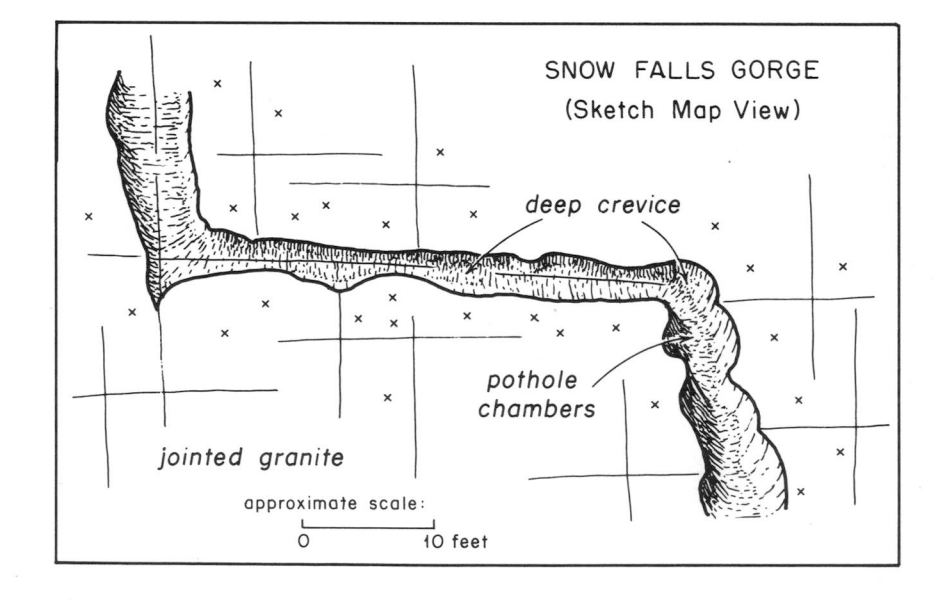

SNOW FALLS GORGE
(Sketch Map View)

deep crevice

pothole
chambers

jointed granite

approximate scale:

0   10 feet

falls and carved sides. The abandoned foundation of a mill and a raceway still remain on the west bank. This falls formed at a constriction in the valley caused by the granite mass. Upstream, the valley of the Little Androscoggin River is much wider.

North Anson Gorge on the Carrabassett River is conveniently studied from the Route 201A bridge and from Route 16 in the village. This gorge is not in rugged terrain and its walls are not steep, but the river follows a twisting and tumultuous path through the ledges and outcrops before entering the wide floodplain of the Kennebec River.

The rivers of Maine are a precious resource with many values, some of which compete. In 1974 the state legislature enacted Shoreland Zoning, which protects a 250-foot border along "Significant River Segments" from degradation by uncontrolled development. The intention is to conserve and enhance water quality and natural beauty. Defined "segments" include parts of many of the most scenic rivers, though not the West Branch of the Penobscot.

6
Noticing Rocks and Minerals

Rocks come in all colors and sizes; some we find handsome, some ugly. Some are hard, others soft; some heavy, and some lighter. Each rock by its mineral content and its texture—whether crystalline or granular, coarse or fine—and by its structure—massive, bedded, folded—tells where it came from, what conditions were like there, how long ago it took its present form, and much more. The clues to events that took place long before the final shaping of the landscape are contained in rocks.

It is not a simple history, and we cannot begin to unravel it until we can tell one rock from another. It is as important for a geologist to know rocks and minerals as it is for a biologist to know plants and animals; these are the starting points of the science.

Minerals are to rocks as bricks are to a wall; minerals combined together make rocks. They are natural chemical substances for which formulas can be written, sometimes simple, like SiO_2 for quartz, but often complex and involving a number of elements, like $KAl_2(AlSi_3)O_{10}(OH)_2$ for mica. Minerals are a subject unto themselves, which we leave to a later section.

Rocks are mixtures of minerals, and the proportions of these mixtures can vary considerably. Nevertheless, rocks can be classified into major groups and then into families within which the members have similar mineral composition. The major rock types are *igneous* (rocks that were once molten), *sedimentary* (rocks of consolidated sediment), and *metamorphic* (rocks changed by heat and pressure).

Igneous Rocks

The first group gets its name from the Latin, *ignis*, for fire, a reference to the fact that these rocks crystallized from a molten magma, deep inside the earth.

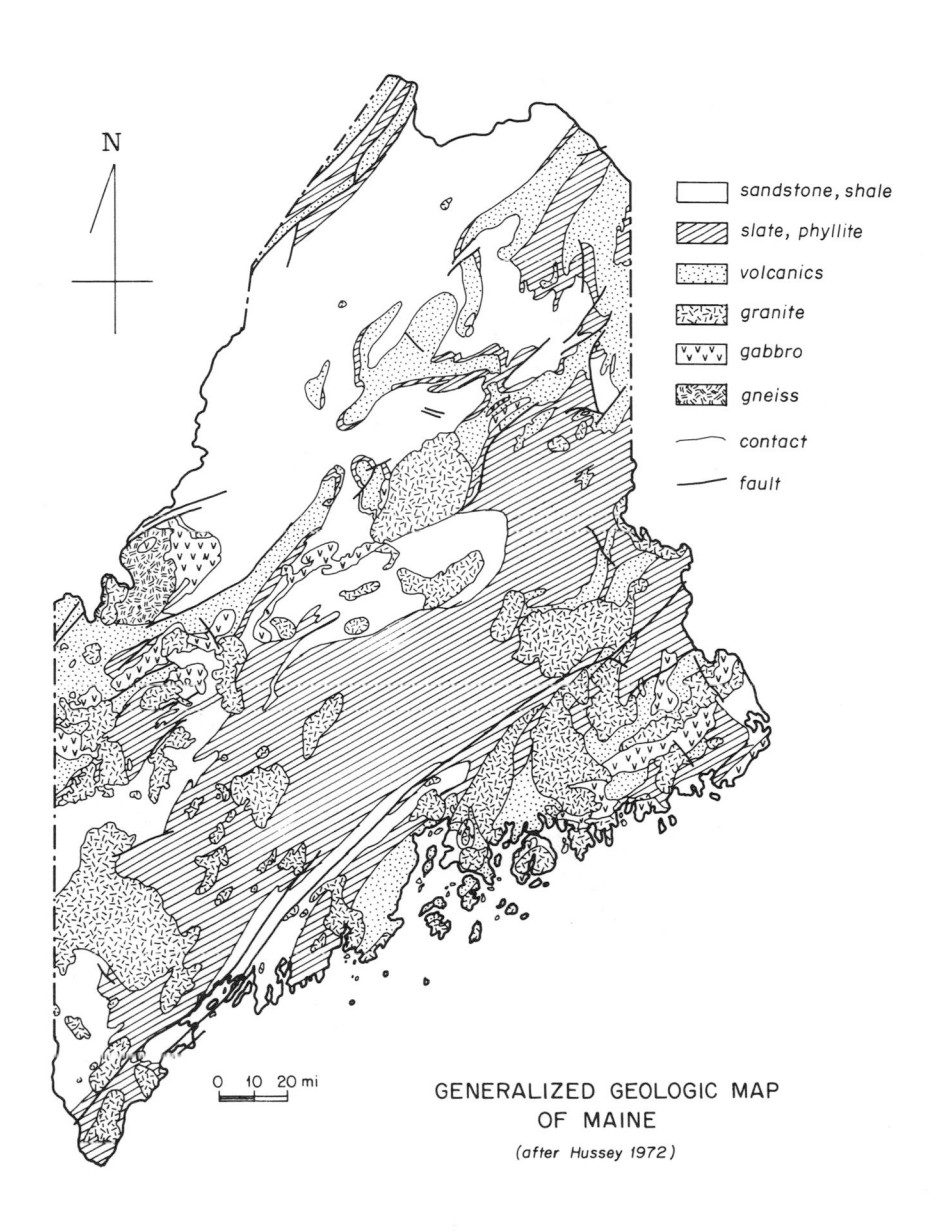

N

sandstone, shale
slate, phyllite
volcanics
granite
gabbro
gneiss
contact
fault

0   10   20 mi

GENERALIZED GEOLOGIC MAP
OF MAINE
(after Hussey 1972)

Granite, you will notice, has particles of contrasting color grown together; these are mineral crystals. As they grow, the minerals interfere with each other, preventing development of the sharp points and flat faces we ordinarily expect in crystals, but the arrangement of atoms inside is always the same for each kind of mineral, and that is the technical definition of crystal. It is only when there is a space, such as where a bubble existed in the magma, that well-formed crystals can grow.

Igneous rocks can be divided on the basis of mineral (that is, chemical) content into two major families, and, fortunately, for general purposes these can be distinguished by color. Members of the granite family are lighter, not only in weight but in color because the major components of granite are light-colored minerals with a high proportion of aluminum and potassium. The darker crystalline rocks belong to the **basalt** family, whose minerals are rich in iron and magnesium and are mostly dark green and black. Remember, though, that rocks are mixtures of minerals, and there are many gradational types in between.

The form of igneous rock easiest to visualize is **lava,** molten igneous rock of either family poured out on the surface. Everyone has seen pictures of red hot molten rivers of lava streaming down the flanks of a volcano to cool on the lower slopes or perhaps to plunge into the sea. Volcanoes are long gone from Maine, removed by erosion over the many millions of years since their activity, but evidence for them exists in the form of thick, widespread beds of lava and ash, especially in northern Piscataquis and Aroostook counties.

Near **Eustis** in northwestern Maine, along Route 11 south of **Winterville,** and on the **Barred Islands** in Penobscot Bay, there are interesting examples of basaltic lava that apparently poured into an adjacent sea where it formed large more or less spherical masses called *pillows*. The formation of pillow lavas has actually been observed and filmed in Hawaii by scuba divers who watched lava emerge from cracks in older flows beneath the sea. The lava quickly chilled into soft, plastic blobs with glassy coatings, tucking into the spaces between other pillows before they finally hardened.

Some magma forces its way into cracks in the encasing crustal rocks and hardens there before reaching the surface, forming *dikes*.

Pillow lava on Barred Islands, Penobscot Bay.

These are common along the coast in roadcuts and sea cliffs. Some are especially well displayed on **Schoodic Point,** where black dikes of basalt cut straight through red granite. The sea has excavated blocks of the more readily weathered basalt, leaving straight-walled, narrow chasms in which the sea surges back and forth. Dikes are useful to geologists unraveling the geologic history of an area. They are obviously younger than the rocks they cross, and sometimes they are cut by still younger dikes or fractures, outlining a sequence of events.

Grain Size of Minerals. The size of the mineral grains (crystals) in an igneous rock is significant; a simple analogy explains what crystal size reveals. Imagine a box partly full of ping-pong balls. When you shake the box all the balls move, bumping against each other at random, but when the shaking stops the balls will settle. If the stop is abrupt, the balls will be left in a random pattern. If you decrease the shaking energy slowly, however, the balls will have time to nestle together in a closely packed structure, neatly taking up all the space.

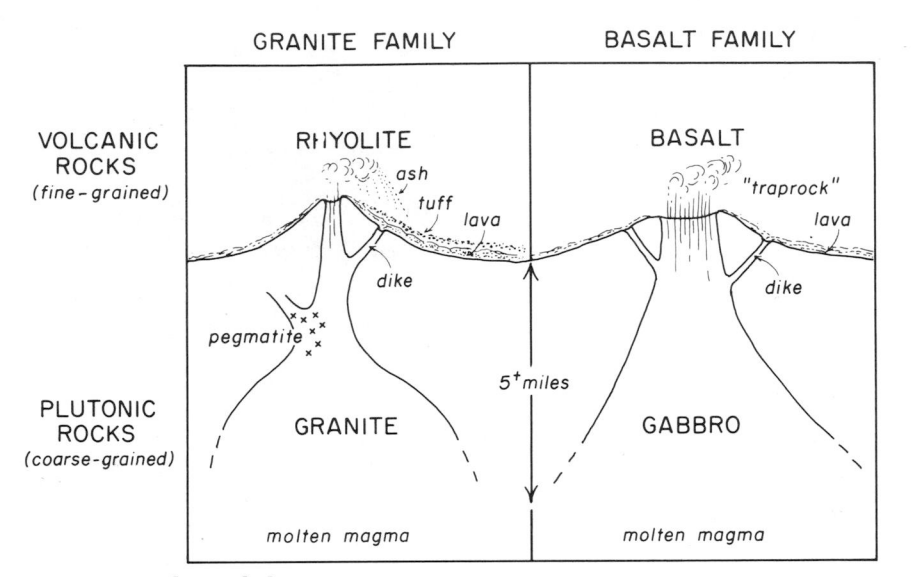

Igneous rocks and their origin.

Similarly, a mass of molten rock is a collection of atoms free to move as long as the temperature remains above the melting point for that rock. As the mass cools, the atoms will slow down and begin to form minerals, grouping themselves according to their chemical affinities, melting points, and so forth. The slower the cooling, the more time for large minerals to grow. If the rock melt cools quickly, the atoms will hardly have time to arrange themselves and the crystals will be very small, perhaps microscopic. The grain size of igneous rocks is therefore an important clue to their history.

Volcanoes can be studied directly, and their products are found to be fine-grained, just as you would expect for quickly cooled rock. Other igneous rocks are much coarser textured. The crystals of granite, for example, are readily seen without the aid of a lens. In fact, in some varieties of granite, crystals of several inches—and occasionally of several feet—in length have been found. Since it requires slow cooling—on the order of tens of millions of years—for crystals of this size to grow, it is clear that they solidified miles below the surface of the earth, where the insulating blanket of crustal rock would not only slow the loss of heat but also confine the water vapor and other gases needed for crystal growth. The heat and pressure

involved were immense—high enough to leave a halo of baked and hardened rock in the enclosing crust. Rocks that have cooled at great depth are called *plutonic*, after Pluto, god of the underworld. Large bodies of granite are frequently referred to as *plutons*.

Igneous rocks thus may be grouped according to mineral (chemical) composition, as belonging to either the granite family or the basalt family. They may further be separated by grain size, as volcanic (fine-grained) or plutonic (coarse-grained). The many gradational possibilities have separate names but they will not be used here.

Two of the igneous rocks in the diagram have not yet been mentioned. **Rhyolite,** the fine-grained member of the granite family, is found on **Traveler Mountain** in the Katahdin range and **Mount Kineo** on Moosehead Lake. It is very dense rock, dark gray with tiny flecks of lighter crystals. Near **Eastport** you can find dark red to maroon rhyolite, while **Haystack and Quaggy Joe mountains** near Presque Isle are the same rock but buff to yellow in color.

Gabbro, the coarse-grained basalt family rock, is widely found in Maine, notably at **Cape Neddick** on the Southwest Coast and in the cliffs of **West Quoddy Head** on the Downeast Coast. The Cape Neddick gabbro body is circular on the exposed surface but in cross-section it is cone-shaped. During the upward intrusion of the molten mass, pressure built until the enclosing rock cracked in a pattern of inward dipping, concentric fractures. These fractures were filled by gabbro in two episodes, each of slightly different chemical composition. The outer portions of the body are the older, first-stage emplacement of igneous rock. The cape and its tiny island, **The Nubble,** site of a picturesque lighthouse, stand out from the shoreline as a more or less circular promontory.

Basalt is far more abundant, globally, than is granite. It is the rock of the ocean basins, and most volcanic rock is basalt. It also occurs in large flows as *traprock* in many places of the eastern United States, and similarly in many other parts of the world. Granite, on the other hand, is found mostly in the cores of mountain ranges and in interior continental areas that are believed to have been the site of former mountain ranges. Maine, of course, is part of a continent, and for this reason granite is more abundant here than basalt and gabbro.

Basalt magma probably originates at depths of thirty-five to fifty miles, even below the crust. Granite is generally associated with metamorphic rocks, suggesting a much shallower origin. Some granite, in fact, appears never to have been quite molten at all, but formed essentially in place by intense heat and pressure during the mountain-building process.

If granites and gabbros crystallized from magma many miles below the surface, how did they get to the surface where we see them today? The answer is that as whole segments of the crust were slowly uplifted, their surface layers were simultaneously eroded. Layer by layer the cover was planed away until finally the deep core was exposed. When we look at crystalline igneous masses such as Mount Katahdin or Cape Neddick and realize that literally miles of rock have been removed to reveal them, we begin to get a glimmer of the immensity of geologic time.

Sedimentary Rocks

Rocks of the second great group, sedimentary, are characteristically found in layers because the sediments from which they formed were carried by water or wind and settled out by gravity. Close examination will show that they are made of individual particles that are simply stacked, not grown together like the crystals of igneous rocks, although they have been compressed and cemented together to form true rock.

Sediments are derived from disintegrating older rocks. Water transporting and depositing the particles also tends to sort and classify them. Some operating gravel pits have cut into three different sediment types: the finest-grained silt and clay, coarser sand and gravel, and finally cobbles and boulders. In many places the beds alternate and repeat, indicating a varied history of stream and lake patterns during the time of deposition. How this happened in the past is easily visualized because mud, sand, and gravel banks are familiar sights today.

Where slopes are steep, streams move fast and have plenty of energy. Erosion is active and the gravel fragments are large and rounded, often recognizable pieces of the original rock. These deposits are close to the bedrock source of the gravel; they do not travel far because the fragments are heavy and settle out quickly

Fine silt and clay layers deposited over layers of sand and gravel, exposed in a gravel pit near Winterport Station.

when the current subsides. Gravel beds, compacted and cemented, eventually form a sedimentary rock known as **conglomerate.** A beautiful example is found on the top of **Mount Battie** in Camden Hills State Park.

If the grinding and winnowing process continues, the fragments are separated into individual minerals. Harder minerals, especially quartz, endure as individual grains and form sand. Beds of sand may eventually become buried and subjected to great pressure, and minerals dissolved in the water buried with them cement the particles. The resulting rock is called **sandstone,** ranging in hardness from crumbly to quite solid. Grindstones and whetstones were made from it by early settlers.

Silt is the result of even finer grinding. In Maine, most of what is commonly known as clay is in reality silt, the difference being the degree of fineness. Silt feels faintly gritty between the fingers and when wet will not roll into a cohesive string or ribbon as does wet clay. It settles fairly quickly from muddy water. Clay, the finest fraction of all, is as smooth as toothpaste and is a long time in settling from muddy water. Mud layers, a mix of both silt and clay, when compressed and hardened, form **shale.** A thin-bedded and rather

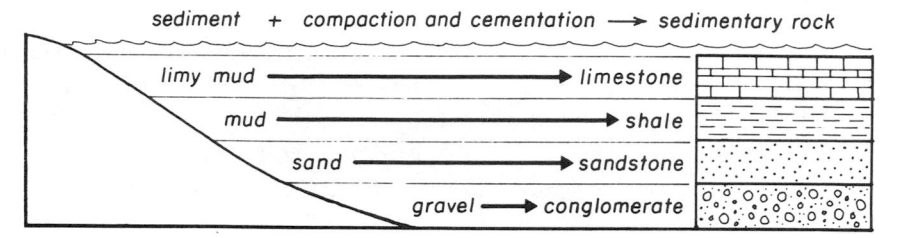

Each type of sediment forms a characteristic sedimentary rock.

flaky sedimentary rock, shale is readily broken with a hammer and tends to split in small, flat fragments, often revealing shiny mica grains lined up parallel with the split face. Most shale in Maine has been further modified by heat and pressure to form slate, a much harder rock.

During mountain-building episodes, volcanoes were active in Maine and produced a special kind of shale called **tuff** from their "ash." The word ash actually is not appropriate because it implies burning; instead, the particles are finely divided volcanic rock that cooled very quickly from molten rock sprayed high in the air by the enormous pressures of exploding volcanoes. Tuff is very hard and dense and is often gray-green and distinctly layered.

One more sedimentary rock found in Maine is **limestone.** This rock is also deposited from water but by a chemical reaction rather than as simply the physical settling of particles. Calcium carbonate precipitates from sea water, forming a limy mud, which in turn is compacted and hardened into rock. Limestone is important in Maine as the basis of the cement industry in the **Thomaston-Rockport area,** and is also mined for agricultural lime in a number of other localities. Limestone is readily distinguished from other rocks by the fact that it will fizz under a drop of dilute (1:5) hydrochloric ("muriatic") acid.

Marine shellfish have the ability to combine the calcium and carbon dioxide found in sea water into the mineral **calcite,** (chemically, calcium carbonate) and build their shells from it. Some limestone layers are built largely of shells.

Interpreting Sedimentary Rocks. Sedimentary rocks are useful in reconstructing earth history not only because their assortment of grain sizes, fossils, and mineral content reveals their ancestry, but

also because the layers readily reveal the amount of squeezing the crust has endured. All sedimentary layers were originally horizontal but in Maine most of the sedimentary beds have been folded and refolded, invaded by igneous intrusions, and buried under volcanic flows during mountain-building episodes. *Faults* (cracks marking where rocks have broken and slipped) cutting through homogeneous igneous rock leave no indication of how much the crust was displaced, but if the fault cuts through sedimentary layers, matching of beds on opposite sides of the break provides a measure of the amount and direction of motion along the fault.

Fossils are found in sedimentary rocks if plants and animals lived in the environments where the sediments accumulated. Most sedimentary rocks originated on the sea floor, and most of the biota found as fossils lived in the sea. Changes in the ocean environment occurred frequently during geologic time and are now recorded in fossil shells by their abundance and variety. Paleontologists are able to reconstruct the history and geography of the ancient earth with considerable confidence by analyzing the fossil content of sedimentary rocks.

Metamorphic Rocks

A metamorphic rock is literally a "changed" rock. If sedimentary beds are drawn deep into the earth where high temperatures and pressures prevail, the first change is the recrystallization of the minerals. Mineral grains grow, filling the spaces between particles to form a harder, denser rock. At higher temperatures, and especially under the influence of increased pressure, the atoms rearrange themselves. Minerals tend to line up parallel to each other. Under these conditions shale, which ordinarily has little strength, metamorphoses into much harder and more durable **slate.** Slate cleaves in broad sheets,which makes it useful for a variety of familiar products—roofing, flooring, blackboards, and so forth. **Monson** has had a long history of slate quarrying. Roadcuts near Monson display good examples of slate.

With increasing temperature and pressure, further growth of platy minerals takes place. **Phyllite,** a common rock in Maine, is the product of the next level of metamorphism. Here the minerals, although too small to be seen without a lens, give the split rock a

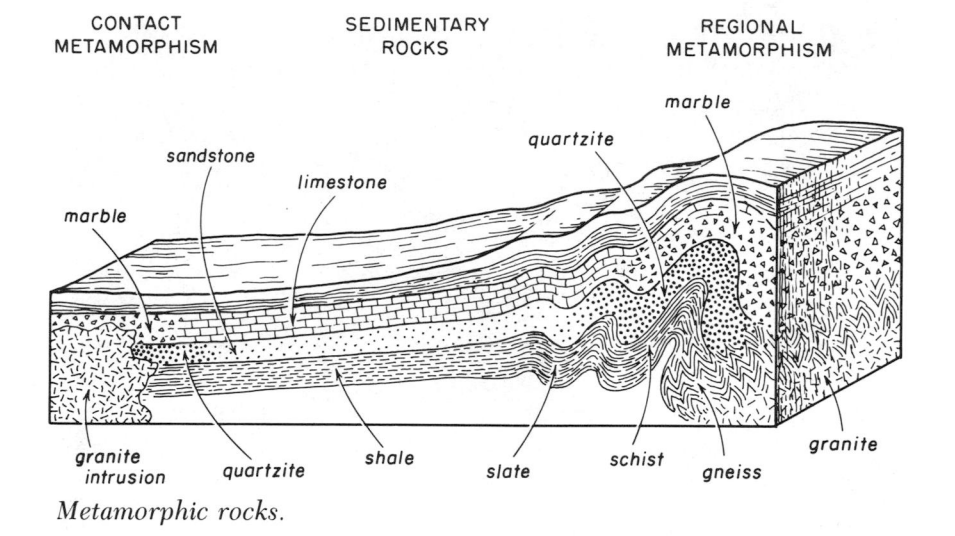

CONTACT METAMORPHISM   SEDIMENTARY ROCKS   REGIONAL METAMORPHISM

marble

quartzite

sandstone

limestone

marble

granite intrusion   quartzite   shale   slate   schist   gneiss   granite

Metamorphic rocks.

silky sheen. Along Interstate 95 in **Bangor,** crinkly sheets of vertically standing phyllite are well exposed.

If the minerals are large enough to be seen on a broken surface, and they are lined up parallel, the rock is called **schist.** Because of the leaflike appearance of these rocks they are said to be *foliated.* Usually a number of minerals have developed, depending upon the temperature reached in the metamorphic process; mica, garnet, and quartz are familiar examples. Roadcuts on I-95 between **Topsham** and **Richmond** display brown-weathering schist.

Coarse bands up to several inches across of alternating light and dark minerals form at the highest levels of temperature and pressure, producing a rock called **gneiss.** Some gneisses are so coarse-grained that they can hardly be distinguished from granite, and this has led to controversy among geologists. In some places it is not clear whether a mass of rock is plutonic, that is, crystallized from magma, or a highly metamorphosed rock brought very close to the melting point. The distinction has implications in earth history, and can lead to significant differences in interpretation. The fact that granite can itself be metamorphosed does not simplify the problem! In any case, it is interesting that material that started out as bits of disintegrating granite goes through the sedimentary process, and after enduring

Gneiss exposed in I-295 roadcut near Falmouth.

the highest grades of metamorphism may finally emerge again indistinguishable from granite.

All sedimentary rocks are changed by metamorphism, even sandstone. Sandstone consists of essentially one mineral, **quartz.** Because only two elements, silcon and oxygen, are available, no new minerals are formed during metamorphism; sandstone simply becomes much more tightly cemented, forming **quartzite.** You can tell quartzite because on a broken surface the fracture will have gone straight across the sand grains rather than around them, leaving a glassy face. Quartzite, because it lacks any platy minerals, is said to be *nonfoliated.* **Marble,** another nonfoliated rock, is the product of metamorphosing limestone. The process tends to increase the grain size and to purify the limestone. Marble is found in a variety of colors—black, grey, pink, red—due to impurities in the original limestone. In the extreme it becomes the familiar white crystalline rock used in buildings and statuary. (It must be mentioned that much polished rock used in the building trades, though called "marble," is of different composition and origin from that just described.)

Metamorphic rock, folded and refolded, faulted and crushed and recrystallized, is found wherever crustal plates have collided.

Folded and fractured metamorphosed sedimentary rocks at Boarstone Mountain.

Surface rocks are drawn to depths of six to ten miles, and molten rock—magma—is commonly intruded into the squeezed and kneaded layers at the same time. High temperatures are maintained for one to ten million years, producing radical changes to vast amounts of rock—most of New England, for example.

It is possible to duplicate in the laboratory (on a small scale, of course) the high temperatures and pressures of the outer few miles of the crust and to study the effects of these conditions on minerals. In this way geologists have discovered the sequence in which minerals change from one form to another as conditions change. By mapping the occurrence of certain key minerals in the field, it is apparent that higher-temperature forms are found in the southwestern part of Maine. The "hot spot," the center of highest temperature and pressure, was evidently beyond the borders of Maine to the southwest. Wrapped around this area like stripes around a bulls-eye are narrow belts of progressively lower-grade minerals (that is, ones formed at lower temperatures and pressures). The northeastern half of Maine experienced relatively low-grade metamorphism. This explains why the only abundant fossils in Maine are

igneous plutons

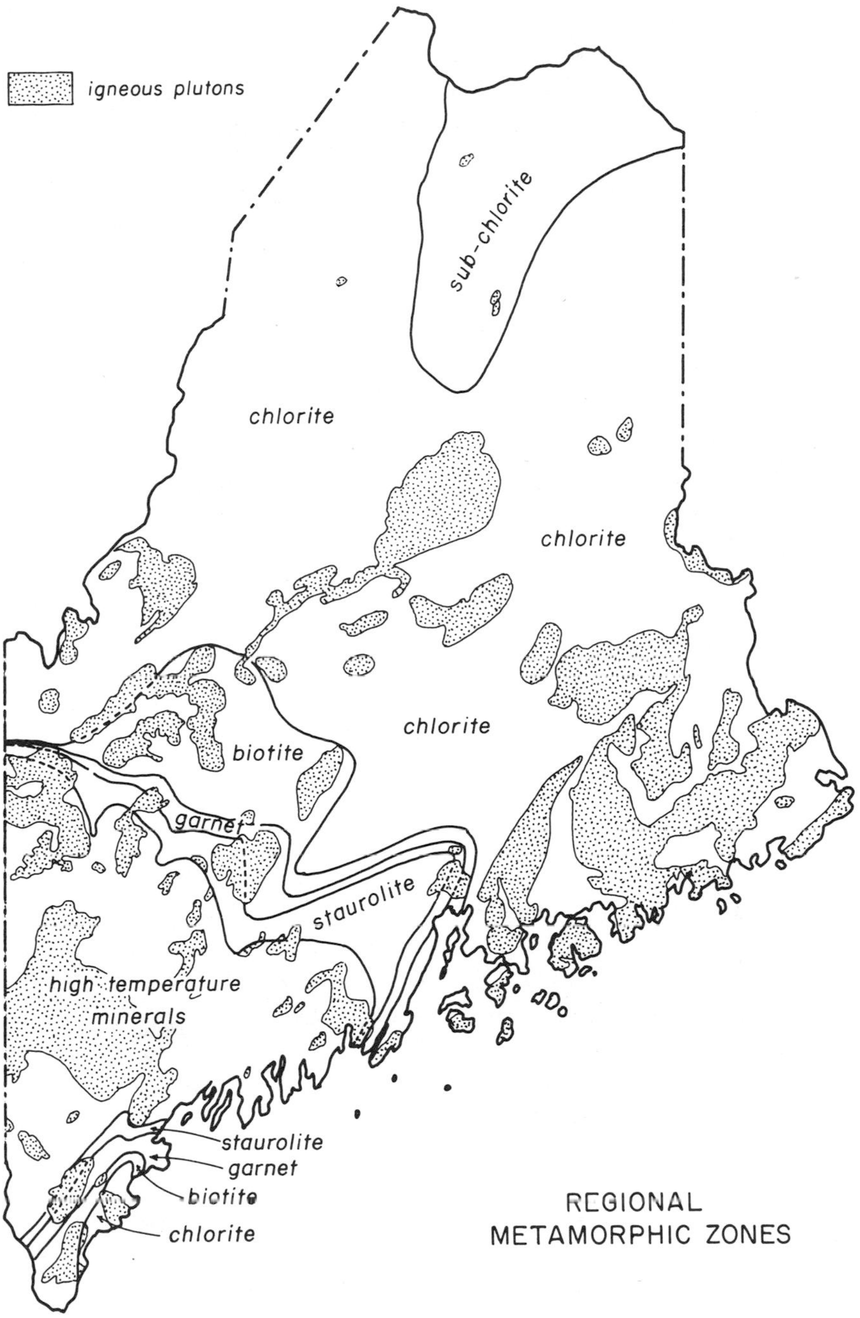

sub-chlorite

chlorite

chlorite

chlorite

biotite

garnet

staurolite

high temperature minerals

staurolite
garnet
biotite
chlorite

REGIONAL
METAMORPHIC ZONES

found here; farther southwest the fossils were obliterated by metamorphism.

Nearer the earth's surface—say, within three miles—where molten rock invades cooler crustal rock, *contact metamorphism* produces intense local changes. New minerals are formed by combining chemical components from the invading magma with those in the adjacent crustal rock. Cooling is accomplished comparatively quickly—in 10,000 to 100,000 years—and the effects generally are observable only a few hundred yards from the contact zone. Geologically this is small-scale, though locally a significant effect.

Contact metamorphic zones are found near the margins of many of Maine's large igneous bodies. Many of the state's mountains are formed from harder, more resistant contact zones surrounding eroded granite bodies. For example, **Mount Bigelow** is part of the contact zone surrounding the granite body that underlies Flagstaff Lake. **Big Squaw Mountain,** near Greenville, is hardened contact rock surrounding a mass of gabbro extending under Moosehead Lake. A readily accessible outcrop of a contact zone is found along U.S. Route 1 south of **Fort Knox State Park,** at the west end of the suspension bridge over the Penobscot River. Here vertical beds of fine sandstone were metamorphosed into very hard quartzite by the Mount Waldo granite pluton, the center of which is 4½ miles west, near the village of Prospect.

A more violent effect on host, or "country," rock is revealed on Mount Desert Island, where the granite of Cadillac Mountain invaded older igneous rocks and schists, shattering the walls of the magma chamber and intruding into the broken rock. A zone of this rock surrounds Cadillac Mountain and can be seen in many places along the eastern and southern sides of the island. Look for dark fragments of all sizes up to a foot or two, suspended in light-colored, crystalline granite matrix.

Minerals

Several thousand natural minerals exist, but fortunately for landscape appreciators only a few are involved in the rocks we are likely to encounter. Much has been said already about granite and basalt, sandstone, schist, and gneiss, and in all those rocks only a handful of minerals are important. A few more minerals have an

economic value because of the metals or other commodities that can be extracted from them, and a very few are valuable as gemstones.

Minerals and Atoms. Minerals are natural chemical combinations of a few kinds of atoms in a definite proportion. Which minerals

Silicate structures. (From Stokes, Judson, and Picard, Introduction to Geology: Physical and Historical, *2nd edition, ©1978, pp. 67, 69. Reprinted by permission of Prentice-Hall, Inc., Englewood Cliffs, N.J.)*

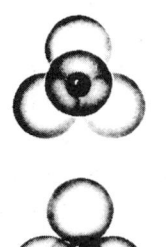

The silicon-oxygen tetrahedron is the most important complex ion in geology, since it is the central building unit of nearly 90 percent of the earth's crust. Upper view is from above and lower is from the side.

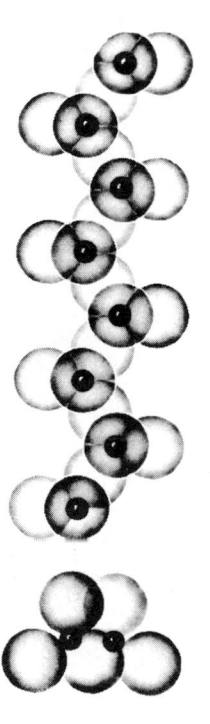

Top: *Single chain of tetrahedra viewed from above.* Bottom: *Viewed from an end. Each silicon ion (small black sphere) has two of its four oxygen ions bonded exclusively to itself and shares the other two with neighboring tetrahedra fore and aft. The resulting individual chains are in turn bonded to one another by positive metallic ions. Since these bonds are weaker than the silicon-oxygen bonds that form each chain, cleavage develops parallel to the chains.*

The glacier-carved U-shaped valley of Witherle Ravine, Mount Katahdin.

A pocket beach between rocky headlands, Acadia National Park.

Coast Guard Beach, Popham.

The tombolo at Barred Islands, Penobscot Bay.

Mount Katahdin from Route 11, South Twin Lake in foreground.

Looking north to Doubletop Mountain, Baxter State Park.

Horse Mountain, Baxter State Park.

Lower South Branch Pond, Baxter State Park.

Weathered granite point at Mount Katahdin, Chimney Pond in the distance.

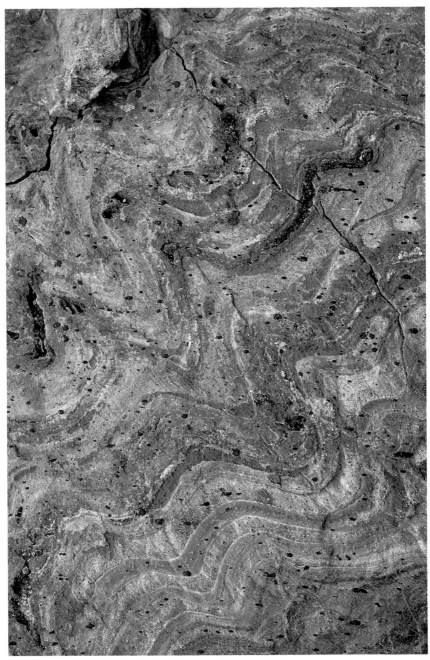

Tight folding of sedimentary rock, off Route 156, near Wilton Intervale.

View from Indian Hill rest area on Route 15, Greenville.

will form depends upon not only the kind of atoms available but, more important, the temperatures and pressures in effect during crystallization.

Atoms are arranged in a unique and unchanging pattern for each mineral, and most of the characteristics of the mineral are due to this atomic arrangement. For example, **quartz** is a very simple mineral made of only two kinds of atoms, silicon and oxygen, in a proportion of two oxygen atoms for each silicon atom, or SiO$_2$. The atom of silicon in chemical combinations actually requires four oxy-

Top: *Double chain of tetrahedra viewed from above.* Bottom: *Viewed from an end. The doubling of the chain is accomplished by the sharing of oxygen atoms by adjacent chains. Hornblende molecules show this arrangement.*

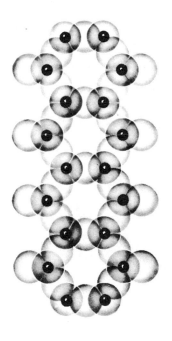

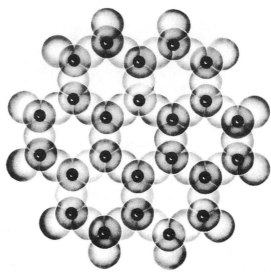

In tetrahedral sheets, as in mica, each tetrahedron is surrounded by three others, and each silicon ion has one of the four oxygen ions to itself, while sharing the other three with its neighbors.

gens, but in quartz it satisfies this need by sharing two oxygens with other silicons, thereby bonding itself to the other atoms and building a strong framework. Quartz is a hard mineral as a result. The shape of a crystal is also a direct result of the atomic structure. Quartz is sometimes found as glassy, clear, pointed needles, but only if the crystals faces have been allowed to grow unimpeded. Normally, as crystals grow from many separate centers they run into each other and none of them develop the outward appearance of crystals as we think of them. At the atomic level, however, the structure is the same whether faces are developed or not.

Quartz is usually recognized by its glassy luster and its clear or milky color, rarely tinted with rose or black. Quartz is a component of granite, usually accounting for 10 to 40 percent of the total minerals. In addition, as igneous and metamorphic processes cool down and minerals crystallize, quartz tends to remain in solution longer than most other minerals. That is why it is common in veins of all sizes cutting across other rocks, representing the last phase of igneous or metamorphic action.

The other major mineral component of granite is **feldspar,** which occurs in two varieties, **orthoclase** and **plagioclase.** Both are silicates, combinations of silicon and oxygen plus a few metal atoms. Like quartz, the silicon-oxygen unit is bonded together, but in the case of feldspar an atom of aluminum substitutes for every fourth silicon, creating an electrical imbalance. This is corrected by the inclusion of atoms of potassium, sodium, or calcium in the feldspar structure. Orthoclase has potassium, and plagioclase takes up sodium and calcium. The atoms are strung out in chains that are cross-linked to form a three-dimensional framework with a distinct linearity. This structure is responsible for one of the identifying characteristics of this mineral: the fact that feldspars cleave along flat, uniform faces. Orthoclase is frequently found in granite as pinkish or white coarse, rectangular crystals, sometimes inches on a side. Plagioclase occurs in shades of gray to almost black, and is found in gabbro as well as granite. Both feldspars attain sizable dimensions in pegmatite, a very coarse variety of granite.

Mica, a minor mineral component of granite, is familiar to many people. It too is a silicate, and in this case the silicon-oxygen group is bonded to other atoms to form sheets. Within the sheets atoms are bonded tightly, making the flakes strong and flexible, but the sheets are bonded together weakly with atoms of potassium, allowing the mineral to be split into very thin flakes, the distinctive characteristic of mica. White or clear mica is called **muscovite.** It contains aluminum in addition to the silicon and oxygen. Some muscovite is pink or green, and in thick crystals it can be brown. **Biotite** is black; it contains iron and magnesium instead of aluminum. In both varieties, atoms of potassium loosely tie the sheets together.

If you see black, needlelike crystals in granite, they are probably the mineral **hornblende,** one more silicate. Once again the crystal form reflects the atomic arrangement: chains of silicon and oxygen atoms linked by iron and magnesium as well as calcium, sodium, and aluminum.

These four—quartz, feldspar, mica, and hornblende—are the main components of granite. Gabbro and basalt, which is too fine-grained for its minerals to be identified without a microscope, are also silicate rocks but they do not contain quartz. The silcon and oxygen are combined with iron and magnesium to form two principal minerals: **olivine,** named for its olive color, and dark green to black **pyroxene.** These two, plus plagioclase feldspar, are the major components of the basalt family and are responsible for its dark color.

Calcite, the mineral of limestone and marble, is calcium carbonate. It is soluble, accounting for the hardness of water in some areas and for the rapid deterioration of statuary and gravestones exposed to the weather. Calcite is sometimes found as clear, milky crystals that are soft enough to be scratched by a knife, distinguishing it from quartz.

Tourmaline, coal-black and shiny in its commonest form, is the State Mineral of Maine and is common in coarse granite and pegmatite.

Most metal ores occur as sulfides, metal atoms plus sulfur atoms. The commonest is **pyrite,** iron sulfide, which is very often the source of the rusty color on weathering rocks. Sulfides of zinc, copper, nickel, and lead have also been found in Maine, locally in commercial quantities, but they are not sufficiently abundant to be significant as rock-forming minerals.

Minerals as Indicators. **Chlorite** is a dark green mica mineral that contains atoms of iron and magnesium. It is a significant mineral because it is an indicator of low-grade metamorphism. About half of Maine is underlain by rocks that were metamorphosed to chlorite-grade temperatures and pressures. Biotite, already described, is an indicator of the second level of metamorphism.

Garnet, a silicate of calcium and magnesium, is often found as tiny red or purple crystals in schists and gneisses. It is an indicator

Gold

Gold, a mineral that is composed of a single element, is almost totally nonreactive, so natural compounds are not found. It occurs widely but very sparsely in rocks, generally in trace amounts. Because of the high value people have always placed on it, even very low grade deposits can sometimes be mined profitably.

Gold usually occurs in association with quartz veins, often called *lodes.* If the lodes should be crossed by a stream, the heavy gold particles are carried away by the water to collect in the deeper pockets of sand and silt. These sediments can be "panned," or washed, in a wide shallow bowl; a frying pan will do. The sediment, plus of the third metamorphic grade. Higher grades are characterized by rarer minerals, which are only infrequently visible to the unaided eye.

Recycling Rocks and Minerals

All rocks on the surface of the earth are subject to weathering and erosion and thereby contribute to sediments and sedimentary rock. Any rock—sedimentary, volcanic or plutonic—dragged deep enough can be subjected to sufficient heat and pressure to be metamorphosed, and if the process should continue long enough, melted. There is much evidence that earth materials have been cycled and recycled, again and again. Many rocks along the coast show the effect of multiple periods of folding and refolding. Under the microscope, some mineral grains can be seen to have been metamorphosed and deformed not just once but two and three times. Minerals form under certain prescribed conditions of heat and pressure, and if those conditions change, as they are likely to in metamorphism, the mineral reacts. In many cases the reaction is stopped in its tracks before it is complete, and the resulting mineral records the change in its partially altered composition or structure. It is a delightful paradox that the history of global events is often revealed by microscopic examination of mineral grains.

Recycling tends to refine rock materials. When the young molten earth first crusted over, all rocks were probably basaltic. As

plenty of water, is sloshed around and carefully spilled, leaving the tiny "colors" (flakes) of gold behind. Panning seldom pays by itself; it is generally used to locate the "mother lode." The prospector patiently works his way upstream, checking each tributary until he finds the one contributing the gold.

Today gold is panned from streams in western Maine, notably the **Swift River** near Byron, and **Kibby Stream** north of Eustis, by mineral hobbyists and a few die-hard, eternally optimistic prospectors.

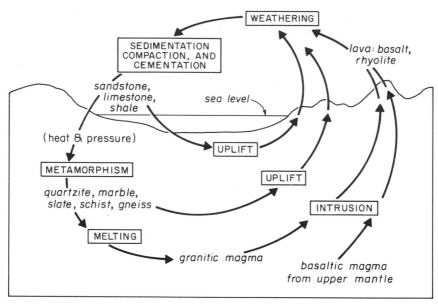

The rock cycle.

weathering broke down the rocks and dissolved the more soluble minerals, the iron and magnesium from the dark, heavy basalt was carried away in sea water. The relatively lighter cleaned-up sediments, richer in aluminum and potassium, were metamorphosed and even melted during mountain-building episodes. Over time, part of the crust began to take on the chemical composition of granite. These bits coalesced around a few nuclei, forming coherent masses, and ultimately great continent-size bodies of granite "floated" on the heavier basalt.

Though the number of cycles and amount of time involved varied considerably in different parts of the earth, it is safe to say that most of the crust has been recycled several times during the several billion years of geologic history.

7
Plate Tectonics

Nearly 400 million years ago two immense slabs of earth's crust, dragged by unimaginable forces, slowly slid toward each other like gigantic ice floes in a polar sea while the ocean separating them steadily shrank. The continents finally collided, not with a sudden crash but in a slow, inexorable crush over many millions of years, grinding and buckling the edges of the slabs and thrusting the great slivers into mountain ranges as high as any on earth today. They crumpled the sea floor between them, forcing much of it down to great depths, to be melted and returned to the surface in violently erupting volcanoes. North America was firmly joined to Euro-Africa.

Two hundred million years ago great tensional forces pulling on this huge landmass tore it apart along north-south fractures. Water rushing into one of these spreading rifts formed a new ocean, the present Atlantic, and the continents we now know as Europe and North America began to move their separate ways.

Maine is right on the scene of the action, and its crumpled rocks record many titanic events, but geologists have had to piece together data from around the world and from many different scientific specialties to outline the full scope of this almost incredible history. How they did it is the subject of this chapter.

This Earth Is a Peach

The behavior of earthquake waves in their travels through the earth reveals that in cross-section the earth shows three layers: *crust*, *mantle*, and *core*. The boundaries between them are not sharp, and the transition zones between layers amount to many miles.

143

To visualize better the relative thicknesses of these layers, take a string one meter (thirty-nine inches) long and strike an arc with chalk or pencil. This represents a sector of the earth's sphere, about four thousand miles in radius. Using the same center and about half the string, strike another arc inside the first. This inner arc is roughly the boundary between core and mantle, about eighteen hundred miles below the surface. You could also draw a still smaller arc with about one-fourth the string to show an *inner core*.

Since one meter on this drawing represents four thousand miles, one millimeter represents four miles. The crust beneath the ocean is three to five miles thick, or just about one millimeter on this scale drawing. This is probably less than the thickness of your chalk line. It is easy to see that, proportionately, the crust of the earth is as thin as the skin on a peach.

The eruption of lava at 1200 degrees Celsius from volcanoes is

Waves in Matter

Waves pass through matter in two principal forms: compression and shear. Compression waves can pass through gasses, liquids, and solids; sound waves are an example. Compressions and expansions of air are deciphered by your ear and brain into sounds. Sounds can be transmitted underwater and also through solids. Shear waves, the other form, get their name because the particles of the material being disturbed can be thought of as sliding past each other, or shearing, as the wave goes by. A taut rope pulled sideways and snapped also produces a shear wave, an S-shaped wave that moves the length of the rope. Shear waves cannot be transmitted by liquids because there is no elasticity to make the particles snap back after they have been pulled out of their original positions. In both cases it is apparent that the wave form, or energy, is carried along, not the particles; they are dislocated very little.

Besides producing ripples in the earth's surface, which may damage structures and landscape features nearby, earthquake vibrations travel through the earth in both shear and compression waves, but at different speeds. Compression waves, traveling almost twice as fast, reach remote seismographs before shear waves. They leave a small wavy mark on the seismogram, followed in due course evidence of high temperatures beneath the surface, and in fact might be taken as evidence of the molten interior of the earth. Lava originates in the uppermost part of the mantle, however, only about sixty to one hundred miles below the surface. Below that, in spite of temperatures increasing to well over 2,000 degrees Celsius, to judge from the behavior of earthquake waves the mantle is solid rock, not liquid. This is due to the pressure of many hundreds of miles of rock above. At the mantle-core boundary, about eighteen hundred miles below the surface, the temperature has increased to 3700 degrees Celsius. The pressure here is not sufficient to maintain a solid state against that kind of temperature, and the solid mantle gives way to the liquid core.

Seismograms indicate that the core, about 2200 miles thick, is liquid, while the earth's density and electromagnetic characteristics

Continued on page 148.

by the larger mark of the arriving shear wave. The greater the time separating the arrival of the two waves, the farther the waves have traveled and thus the farther the earthquake from the seismograph. By using simple triangulation, data from only three seismographs are required in order to pinpoint the location of a particular earthquake.

Certain areas on the surface of the earth, at prescribed distances from each earthquake, fail to receive shear waves, although compression waves do show up. It has been deduced that the vibrations detected in these areas have gone through a zone that permits compression waves to pass but not shear waves; in other words, a zone that acts like a liquid. This is the evidence that the earth has a liquid core about 1800 miles beneath its solid shell of mantle and crust.

Finally, within the liquid core is a region, 3,000 miles below the surface and 1,000 miles in radius, in which earthquake waves are affected as they are when they pass through a solid. Thus, the inner core of the earth, at least in respect to its influence on waves, is believed to be solid.

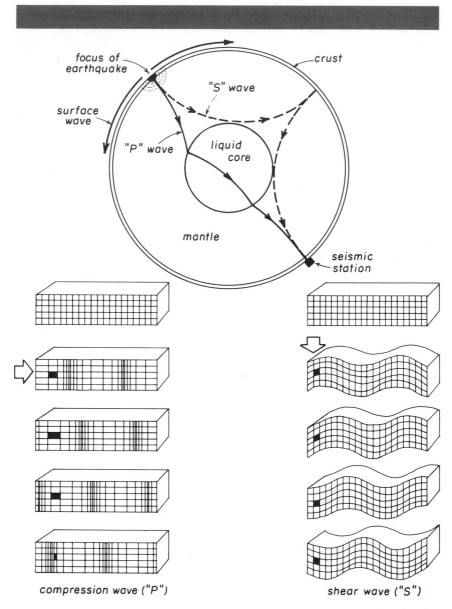

Compression waves and shear waves travel at different rates through earth's core. (After illustration in Earth, *fourth ed., by Frank Press and Raymond Siever. Copyright 1974, 1978, 1982, 1986, W. H. Freeman and Co.)*

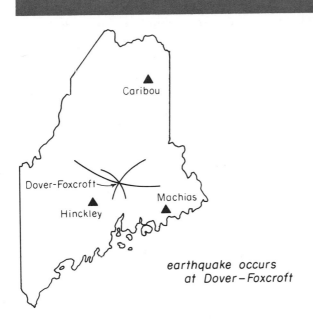

earthquake occurs
at Dover–Foxcroft

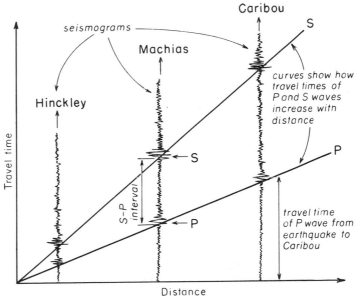

Typical seismograms.

suggest that it is made of nickel and iron. Finally, there is an inner core, which deflects waves passing through it in such a way as to indicate that it is solid. These temperatures and pressures, let alone the depths, cannot be observed (measured) directly, of course. All the evidence for them is in jagged lines scratched on seismograms by earthquake waves.

The crust is much thicker under the continents, twenty to sixty miles as compared to only four to six miles under the oceans. The continents rest on the mantle like icebergs in the ocean, with much more of their mass submerged than showing, and for the same reason: the granitic continental rocks are a bit lighter than the mantle basaltic rock.

The Global Jigsaw Puzzle

It is intriguing the way South America fits into the west coast of Africa. You can also close up the Red Sea and the Persian Gulf, and fit Madagascar neatly into the nearby coast of Africa, making a solid mass of Africa and Asia. With a little rotation, North America snuggles against Western Europe, and so forth. Probably as soon as accurate maps were available, certainly by the eighteenth century, people noticed this; anyone can play the jigsaw puzzle game, fitting the continents together.

By the early 1900s some geographers had begun to inquire seriously into the possibility of continents splitting apart and drifting about on the surface of the earth, but no mechanism then known could produce such prodigious migrations.

Until mid-twentieth century, most geologic features had been studied individually and in isolation, and often problems arose when people tried to devise explanations for what they had observed. For example, identical fossil animals were found on opposite sides of oceans. How could ancient land animals have migrated across wide oceans? Fossils of tropical plants and animals are found in present-day Arctic and Antarctic regions. How could the ancient climate of the polar regions have been so radically different from today's? What accounts for global belts of volcanoes and earthquakes? A few imaginative geologists proposed that if the continents had split up and moved across the face of the earth, many of these difficulties would be reconciled, but the idea languished because there was too little evidence that these motions had actually taken place.

World War II, and the navigational needs of the world's navies, especially for submarines, resulted in the accumulation of an immense amount of new information about ocean basins. The sea floor, mostly unknown until the war, was found to be fully as complex as the terrain of the continents. The topography of the ocean bed was mapped with great accuracy, delineating vast plains, deep valleys, and long mountain ranges—the mid-ocean ridges. Moreover, these ridges were found to be split lengthwise by a continuous valley, or cleft. New instruments measured the flow of heat from these mid-ocean ridges and revealed a surprising fact: more heat was escaping here than the average for sea floor, and it was leaking through the floor of the cleft. The cleft turned out to be the active seam through which new sea floor is extruding.

Sea Floor Spreading

Picture a pot of tomato soup on the stove, preferably a glass pot through which you can see swirling currents of soup. As the pot warms, convection currents of soup rise from the bottom and move

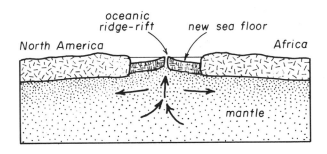

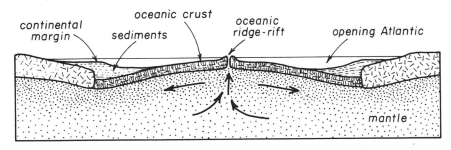

Sea floor spreading. (After illustration by Bunji Tagawa, Scientific American, *March 1972.)*

outward toward the edges. Here the soup cools and descends to the bottom, where it will be heated and rise once again in a cycle driven by the heat of the flame. At the surface, meanwhile, a froth begins to form, which is pushed and dragged to the edge by the circulating soup. The heaver, cooler soup near the edge descends in a sloping path beneath the crinkling, folding margin of the floating froth.

Here is a mechanism, a convection cell of molten rock, that could drive continental drifting. The warming soup example, suggested about twenty-five years ago, is a crude analog of what takes place during *sea floor spreading*. All of the oceans are scarred by open wounds, cracks in the mid-ocean floor. Rising molten basalt from the topmost layers of the mantle moves through these cracks and forces apart slabs of sea floor, creating parallel ridges of basalt with new sea floor between them. The molten rock moves laterally in a gigantic convection cell, dragging the covering crustal slab with it, opening the ocean and spreading the sea floor. The process actually can be seen taking place in Iceland, famous for its volcanoes and hot springs, where the Mid-Atlantic Ridge is above sea level.

As it approaches the outer limit of the cell, the heavier sea floor cools and sinks back into the mantle. Lighter granite islands and microcontinents with their sediment blanket, analogous to the froth on the tomato soup, are scraped off and added, crumpled, to the accumulating continent. The sea floor slab is *subducted*, or pulled down under the edge of the continent and melted down, becoming lava, which eventually erupts from the volcanoes along the active edge of the continent. .

A new concept in geology known as *plate tectonics* began to emerge in the 1960s. According to plate tectonics theory, the outer crust of the earth has broken into a few large pieces called plates. These plates have slipped over the surface of the Earth in the past, permitting new sea floor to form along the mid-ocean ridges where they spread apart. They grind and shake where they slide past each other and produce mountain ranges where they collide. Plate tectonics had the effect of suddenly bringing entire fields of geology, oceanography, geophysics, and geochemistry, each with myriad observations and facts, into a unified and understandable framework, much as the theory of evolution had done for biology nearly a hundred years before. Supporting evidence continues to flood in.

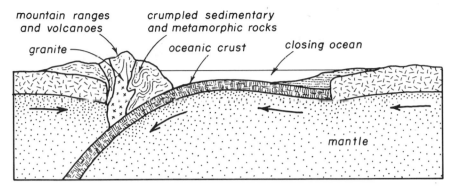

mountain ranges
and volcanoes

crumpled sedimentary
and metamorphic rocks

granite

oceanic crust

closing ocean

mantle

COLLIDING CONTINENTS

(After Bunji Tagawa, Scientific American, *March 1972.)*

Frozen Compasses

In recent decades geologists using extremely sensitive instruments have learned that some rocks possess *remanent magnetism,* a record of the magnetic field as it was when the rocks were formed. Igneous rocks—particularly basaltic lavas, which contain iron-bearing minerals—erupted onto the surface of the earth and cooled quickly, but not before the minerals, like tiny compasses, had aligned themselves with the earth's magnetic field. When the rocks solidified, these tiny compasses were frozen into position. As field data accumulated it became evident that remanent magnetism in rocks within the same area but of different ages sometimes recorded different locations for the magnetic pole. Plots in some cases suggested the north magnetic pole had once been much further south, nearly on the present equator.

This could explain the presence of tropical features like coral reefs and coal beds in Alaskan rocks, but astronomers and geophysicists objected. This "polar wandering" is far more than could reasonably be attributed to changing declination—the small changes in the relative position of the magnetic and true north poles. Moreover, they argued, it is not likely that the axis of rotation has changed since the primordial dust cloud became a planet. It is far more likely that something else moved, namely, the continents. Here, from an independent line of research was support for plate tectonics.

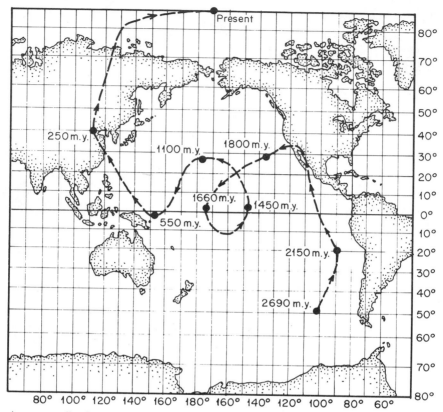

Apparent "polar wandering." (After T. M. Gates, in Earth, *fourth ed., by Frank Press and Raymond Siever. Copyright 1974, 1978, 1982, 1986, W. H. Freeman and Co.)*

A Magnetic Clock

The oldest rocks on the Atlantic sea floor are only about 200 million years old, a small fraction of the 3.5 billion–year age of the oldest rocks. Geologists suddenly realized that the sea floor everywhere, far from being the most stable and ancient part of the earth, is young and mobile. Geophysicists studying remanent magnetism in sea floor basalts discovered that not only did the minerals record the position of the magnetic pole at the time of deposition, but also showed that the polarity of the field had reversed from time to time. Basalt flows at increasing distances on opposite sides of the mid-ocean cleft, where new sea floor is extruding, reveal a remarkable symmetry of normal and reverse polarity. The pole that we call north was, in fact, a magnetic south pole 700,000 years ago. This north-south flip-flop, for which no cause is yet known, has occurred more than 170 times in the last 76 million years.

Comparing the magnetic data with records of known changes in polarity over time, it is possible to date individual basalt flows. The map shows parallel stripes, progressively older with increasing distance from the crack. This not only confirms sea floor spreading and moving continents, but actually measures the rate at which continents are moving. For the North Atlantic the rate is about two to five centimeters a year, about the same as the growth of your fingernail. Not fast, but over the 200 million years since the Atlantic Ocean began to open, this has separated Europe and North America by three thousand miles.

Subduction and Earthquakes

Earthquakes in Japan, the Aleutians, South America, and else-where on the rim of the Pacific Ocean, when plotted on a cross-section of the crust, are found to lie along a well-defined zone plunging thirty-five to fifty degrees under the land. Shallower earthquakes are found seaward, while earthquakes nearer to land are deeper. The deepest are found right under the land. No earthquakes plot deeper than 450 miles because at this depth the rock is plastic and responds to pressure by flowing, not fracturing.

This discovery became an important link in the chain of reasoning behind plate tectonic theory. The line of earthquakes evidently marks the pathway, the subduction zone, where the moving plate of heavy ocean floor plunges into the upper mantle as it approaches the lighter continental margins. The descending slab eventually reaches melting temperature, and the lighter gasses and lava make their way back up through zones of weakness in the stressed crust to spew forth as volcanoes. Here is the explanation of the intimate association of earthquakes and volcanoes, the "ring of fire" around the Pacific Ocean.

Matching mountain chains, like the Applachians in North America and the Caledonides in Scotland, are found on opposite sides of intervening oceans because continents breaking up do not necessarily separate along the older collision line marked by a scar of mountains. Instead, the break can cut right across mountain ranges and sedimentary basins, with their fossil plants and animal remains,

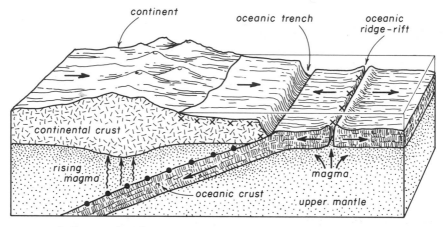

x *shallow earthquakes*
● *deep earthquakes*

Earthquakes in the subduction zone, where spreading sea floor meets edge of continent.

leaving fragments of each behind, like unlucky passengers on opposite ends of a broken ship.

Earth's Magnetic Field

One of the consequences of a moving, molten iron-nickel core in the center of the earth is the development of an electrical field around the planet. This field encloses a vast area beyond the surface of the earth, far out into space. It has a north-south polarity that is easily detected by the magnetized needle of a compass. The field, and thus the position of the poles, is relatively fixed and has provided a point of reference for navigators and explorers ever since the compass was invented, over eight hundred years ago. The fact that the pole of rotation, true north, and the electrical pole, magnetic north, closely coincide is more than fortuitous. Most geophysicists agree that the rotation of the earth, with its solid mantle and liquid metallic core, creates the field.

Two qualifiers in the preceding paragraph need to be examined in more detail: "relatively fixed" and "closely coincide." Because the earth's magnetic field is dynamically generated, it changes over time.

Geologists now have a new comprehension of earth history. In addition, natural hazards like volcanic eruptions and earthquakes are now better understood and there is a theoretical basis for their prediction. Plate tectonics still has rough edges to be smoothed and some gaps to be filled. Some enthusiasts may have extended their ideas too far, but practically all geologists around the world today accept the general premises of plate theory.

In our time on earth, Maine is part of the trailing edge of the continent, more or the less in the center of the North American Plate, which includes the western Atlantic sea floor. The whole plate is sliding westward, but things are quiet, geologically, in Maine. Earthquakes are rare and mild, and of course volcanoes are unknown. The tectonic "action" is far to the east on the Mid-Atlantic Ridge, and to the west along the Pacific coast. Where the North American Plate meets the Pacific Plate the crust splinters and quakes along great faults—like the San Andreas Fault running the length of California—and spews volcanoes, like the recent eruption of Mount St. Helens in Washington. In past geologic eras, most recently 300 million years ago, the situation was quite different, with volcanoes

The magnetic north pole is located in northern Canada 1100 miles south of true north. A compass pointing to magnetic north does not point to true north, except when it is on the line that passes through both poles. This line passes through Cincinnati, Ohio.

Maine is well east of this line, so here a compass needle swings to the west of true north. The angle between the north line of a compass and true north is called *declination.* It ranges from about sixteen degrees in western Maine to twenty-two degrees in eastern Maine. The declination changes over time, usually a small fraction of a degree per year. Most topographic maps show the declination and the year it was measured. Woodsmen and hikers crossing large stretches of roadless land by compass must take careful account of the magnetic declination. A day's hike on a compass bearing that is wrong by only a few degrees can make you very late for supper.

and earthquakes in Maine marking the closing of an ancient Atlantic
Ocean and the collision of continents along the line of the present
Appalachian mountains.

As we think about the relative motions of continents floating
about and colliding, we are apt to assume, unconsciously, that Maine
has always occupied the same place on the globe. If anything has
"stood still," it is probably the axis of rotation of the earth. We have
already mentioned that the earth's magnetic poles coincide closely,
though not exactly, with the rotational poles. Assuming that this has
always been the case, and using the remanent magnetism in rocks,
geologists are able to reconstruct the positions of the land masses
in remote times. It turns out that Maine has been anything but fixed
in its present place on the globe. The history of Maine's wanderings
is the subject of the next chapter.

8
Maine Through Geologic Time

Maine's geologic history brings to mind an old Mainer's joke: "If I was going there, I wouldn't start from here." Our previous descriptions of opening and closing oceans, of migrating and colliding continents, of mountain ranges and intrusions of molten rock, imply a long and complicated history. It will be easier to understand how Maine's geologic history is unraveled if we first look at rocks that have been almost undisturbed since they formed. The Colorado Plateau, a layer cake of sedimentary beds dissected by the Grand Canyon in Arizona, is a good place to start.

Reconstructing Geologic History

It is obvious in the walls of the Grand Canyon that sedimentary beds are laid down one on top of the other, and that the lowest beds are the oldest. No area on earth contains the complete record of earth history, but the Grand Canyon displays over 300 million years' worth. Working from one area to another it is possible to *correlate*, or match, beds and expand the time scale. A bluff or mesa many miles away from the Grand Canyon, for instance, might contain some of the same beds that form the canyon rimrock beds, plus several more layers on top of them, thus extending the record upward (younger). Another canyon might similarly extend the record downward (older). Locating and measuring sedimentary sequences and correlating their matching portions is a large part of what geologists do.

Placing events in the proper order—say, whether a period of volcanism came before or after the deposition of a particular bed—is simply a matter of noting the position of the volcanic rocks in the sequence of layers. This is easy enough in an undisturbed pile, but in Maine, where the rocks have been folded or even overturned and broken, it becomes more complicated. Nevertheless, determining the top and bottom of sequences of sedimentary rocks is routine for field geologists.

Many sedimentary rock layers were made from muddy water carrying an assortment of particle sizes. The coarsest material, gravel and sand, settled out first, and finer silts and clays came to rest later. In Maine beds like these are common. Such a sediment bed, grading upward from coarser to finer particles, reveals its bottom and top even when it is vertical or overturned. Beds of conglomerate, coarse sand and gravel, are also useful in working out relative ages. For example, in the valley of **Trout Brook** north of Mount Katahdin a bed contains pebbles of **Traveler Mountain** volcanic rock evidently eroded off the mountain. Obviously, the gravel was deposited after the volcanism. Further information can be gleaned from what are called *cross-cutting* relationships. An igneous dike cutting through other rocks must be younger than those rocks. In fact, in some places a dike has cut across part of a series of sedimentary beds but not the rest—evidence that the dike is younger than some beds but older than the others.

Most rock layers in Maine have been compressed and warped and broken. These breaks, called faults, are also cross-cutting features and can usually be dated by which rocks they offset. Many faults, in turn, are cut by younger plutons, a fact that further increases the precision of ordering geologic events.

Using Fossils. Fossils are an important part of the record of geologic history, but good fossil exposures are rare in Maine. Across much of the state the rocks have been deformed and metamorphosed to an extent that has destroyed the fossils, but in a band stretching across northern Maine from **Moosehead Lake** to **Shin Pond,** and in the northeastern part around **Presque Isle,** lightly metamorphosed sedimentary rocks still contain the imprints of ancient sea life and the remains of some of the earliest land plants found anywhere. These plants, forming coal-like beds only millimeters thick in **Trout Brook** valley, were probably alive 350 million years ago.

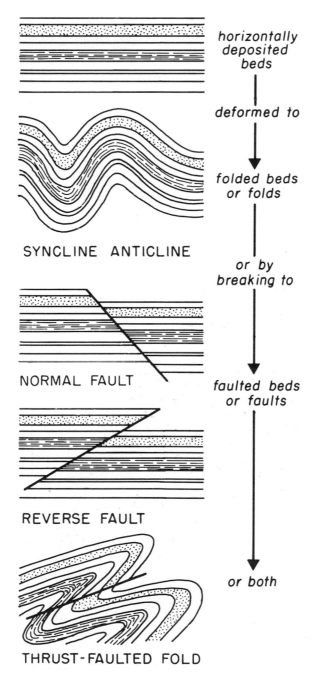

horizontally
deposited
beds

deformed to

folded beds
or folds

SYNCLINE   ANTICLINE

or by
breaking to

NORMAL FAULT

faulted beds
or faults

REVERSE FAULT

THRUST-FAULTED FOLD

or both

*Rocks may be deformed by both faulting and folding. (After illustration
in* Earth, *fourth ed., by Frank Press and Raymond Siever. Copyright 1974,
1978, 1982, 1986, W. H. Freeman and Co.)*

Fossils are important in their own right, of course, because they reveal the evolution of life over geologic time. They also provide data on the environment in which the organism grew: the water depth, temperature, and clarity; the nature of the sea bed; whether it was hospitable to many forms or only those specially adapted, and so on. Probably the most important detail learned from fossils is the age of the rock in which they are found. A few key fossils, those which are widespread but known to be restricted to a narrow range of time, can tie a bed, wherever it is found, to a certain portion of the geologic time scale.

There is a complication: most rocks in Maine are altered from their original condition by metamorphism. The great heat and pres-

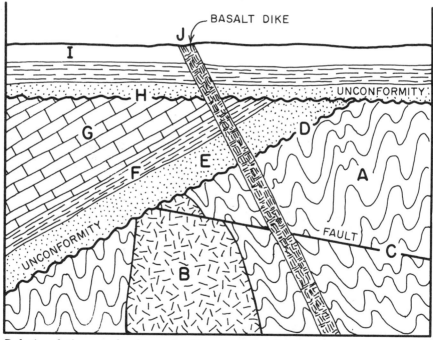

Relative dating can be determined by observing field relations.
(A) Sediments deposited and later deformed; (B) granite intruded into
sedimentary rock; (D) unconformity caused by erosion; (E, F, G)
sediments deposited, then tilted and eroded to produce unconformity at
(H); more sediment deposited; (J) basalt dike intruded. (After illustration
in Earth, *fourth ed., by Frank Press and Raymond Siever. Copyright 1974,*
1978, 1982, 1986, W. H. Freeman and Co.)

sure that accompany mountain-building have made new minerals
from old and in some cases radically altered the appearance of the
rocks. Geologists are aware of these changes and can recognize that
what might now appear to be an igneous rock originally may have
been a bed of shale or dirty sandstone.

Using facts and deduction, geologists slowly and patiently put
together a story of events in a portion of the earth's crust. For
example, a geologist might reason from his observations as follows:
1) accumulating sediments indicate the presence of a sea; 2) the beds
are folded and faulted, indicating a period of mountain-building; 3)
there are igneous rocks, and their temperature and rate of cooling
will be suggested by the minerals formed and the metamorphic
effects on the surrounding rocks; 4) part of the sequence is missing,
so uplift above sea level and subsequent erosion can be inferred; 5)
followed by more sediments, indicating a time of subsidence beneath
the sea once again, and so on. This kind of work has gone on all
over the world for over two hundred years.

A Geologic Time Scale

Placing geologic events in the proper sequence is known as
relative dating. By the end of the nineteenth century geologists had
worked out a relative calendar for large portions of the earth, but
assigning dates and time spans to these events was uncertain. The
geologic column, the basic device for organizing geologic knowledge,
has been divided into short pieces for easier reference. *Eras* are the
largest units, like volumes in a library. *Periods* are chapters, and
Epochs are paragraphs.

As geologic history unfolded it became apparent that the time
required for all the events and processes to take place was beyond
the wildest imaginings of most historians. The earth had to be millions, maybe hundreds of millions, even billions of years old. At the
turn of the century the discovery of radioactivity suddenly provided
the clock that was needed. *Absolute*, or numerical, dating became
possible.

Dating by Radioactivity. Many elements exist in two or more
forms, called *isotopes*, and many of these isotopes are unstable and
radioactive; that is, they disintegrate into another element sponta-
neously, radiating energy in the process. The rate of change for each

THE GEOLOGIC CALENDAR

ERA	PERIOD	MILLION YRS. AGO	EVENTS IN MAINE
CENOZOIC (Mammals)	QUATERNARY	1 — 2 —	10,000 years ago last ice melts. Continental glaciation. Man appears on earth.
	TERTIARY	25 — 65 —	Uplift, rejuvenation of rivers. South Atlantic Ocean opens. North America drifts west. Erosion to plain.
MESOZOIC (Reptiles)	CRETACEOUS	136 —	Cape Neddick gabbro intruded. North America drifts northwest.
	JURASSIC	190 —	North Atlantic Ocean opens. Rifting of Fundy Basin. Intrusion of basalt dikes.
	TRIASSIC	200 — 225 —	Pangaea splits. Mount Agamenticus granite. Erosion to plain.
PALEOZOIC (Marine life)	PERMIAN	280 —	Alleghenian orogeny. Granite in southwest Maine.

Period	Age (millions of years)	Events
CARBONIFEROUS	325	Sebago Pluton.
	345	Land plants, shellfish.
DEVONIAN	380	Major granite masses intruded (Mt. Katahdin, Downeast mtns.). Major faulting. Regional metamorphism. Acadian orogeny. Avalonia collides with North America. Iapetus closed.
SILURIAN	390 / 395	Iapetus shrinking. Volcanism, subduction of island arcs and shelves with sediments.
	430	Taconic orogeny (Mass., N.Y.).
ORDOVICIAN	470	Attean Pond granite intruded. Cape Elizabeth rocks folded.
	500	Cape Elizabeth rocks deposited.
CAMBRIAN	570	
PROTEROZOIC (Primitive life)	1600	Iapetus open. Chain of Ponds gneiss, oldest rocks in Maine; no record of their history.
	2600	
ARCHEOZOIC (Molecular organic structures)	3800	Oldest rocks on earth.

element is constant, and the time required for one-half of the atoms of an isotope to change is called its *half-life*.

One of the many elements useful for radioactive dating, because it is found in common minerals like feldspar and mica, is potassium-40, one half of which in 1.3 billion years will have converted to calcium-40 and argon-40. By determining the amount of potassium-40 as compared to the products calcium-40 and argon-40 remaining in the rock, and applying the known rate of change, the absolute age of the rock can be calculated. This is especially useful in igneous rocks, which contain no fossils to reveal their ages.

It is not surprising that geologists, like historians, know the dates of more recent important events with greater precision. The rise of the dinosaurs and the formation of coal beds can be dated with a small percentage of error. Dates for events older than 600 million years, however, are sparse and more widely spaced, both chronologically and geographically. Unfortunately, about 85 percent of geologic history took place before 600 million years ago (see table).

It is a tribute to the brilliance of the geologists of the late nineteenth century that many of their estimates of age, based on sequences of evolving fossils and inferences as to the rate of geologic processes, were remarkably close to the radiometrically determined ages of the same intervals. As laboratory instruments and field data improve, the accuracy of radiometric dating will continue to increase. Assigning numerical values to the geologic calendar through the study of radioactive elements is one of the finest scientific achievements of the twentieth century.

A Geologic Time Meter

The electric meter, that face of four or five dials which records the amount of power consumed, is familiar to nearly everyone. Let us imagine a geologic time meter of the same design. Four dials arranged horizontally will record the passage of time. From left to right the meters will record billions, hundred millions, tens of millions, and millions of years. Each dial must go around ten times for

The Oldest Rocks

The oldest rocks found on earth so far, in Greenland, have been dated as 3.8 billion years old. It is really impossible to comprehend this amount of time, but some grasp of it might be gained by imagining a scale model of time. If 3.8 billion years were to be compressed into one year, and earth history began on New Year's Day, the oldest rocks in Maine, the **Chain Lakes** rocks, were formed about the middle of May. The oldest rocks with hardshell fossils found in Maine appeared in late November. The plate collision forming the Appalachian Mountains began about December first and continued for a week or so. The continent split apart again about December 15. Dinosaurs appeared about December 20 and disappeared ten days later. Man arrived about 7 p.m. on the last day of the year. The great ice sheet flowed over Maine during the last two hours and has been gone only fifteen minutes. Recorded human history occupies the last one and a half minutes.

The oldest rocks in Maine, at a venerable 1.6 billion years, are in a small circular body northwest of Eustis known as the **Chain Lakes massif.** This ancient mass is largely gneiss, part of the foundation core of North America. Little is known of the past of these rocks beyond the fact of their antiquity. No doubt this is all that remains of some ancient *terrane*, or minicontinent, long ago welded onto North America. It was eroded flat and became the platform on which younger rocks were deposited, deformed, and built into mountain ranges, which in turn were eroded away. A lot can happen in 1.1 billion years.

the dial on its left to go around once.

For the first dial (farthest left) to go around once, the fourth dial (farthest right) must go around a thousand times. It will take ten million years for the fourth dial to go around once. If, as astronomers and geologists agree, the earth is a bit less than five billion years old, the left dial has yet to complete one-half of one rotation!

A Piece of the Really Old World. If you were to stand on the cliffs of **Cape Elizabeth,** near Portland, and sing, "My bonnie lies over the ocean," you would be closer to the truth than you might imagine. You are standing on a slice of Europe that about 400 million years ago became welded onto North America. Far to the east, somewhere across the ocean, lies the rest of the land that used to be attached to the rocks under your feet. How Cape Elizabeth, and most of the New England coast, came to be left behind in North America when Europe broke away 190 million years ago is an interesting story whose details are still being unfolded by geologists.

Most of coastal New England and much of the Canadian Maritime Provinces are part of a block of crust known as *Avalonia*, which 500 million years ago was not part of North America at all but was on the other side of the ocean. Someone with a sense of humor named this predecessor of the Atlantic after Iapetus, who was the father of Atlas ("Atlantic").

North America and Avalonia began to converge, probably in response to convection currents deep in the mantle, buckling the floor of the Iapetus Ocean. Slabs of crust, with their thick layers of sand and mud, plunged down along steep fault zones dipping toward the land, where they melted. Molten rock found its way back to the surface to form chains of volcanic islands near the coasts of both continents, similar to Japan and the Aleutians today.

On relatively shallow shelf areas, sand and mud surrounding the islands, like today's clam flats, were hospitable to shellfish and other organisms. Occasionally beds of ash and lava from the volcanoes were added to the accumulating pile of sediments eroded from the land. As drifting of the plates continued, the westward-moving Avalonia overtook and collided with the island chain off its west coast, folding and deforming the layers of ash and sediment.

Similarly, the islands off North America were dragged westward, and about 445 million years ago collided with the continent. Whole sheets of crumpled sediment beds and volcanic debris were bodily shoved over the rigid edges of the continent, obliterating most fossils. Although this collision was responsible for the Taconic Mountains in western Massachusetts and Vermont, there is little evidence of it in Maine. Part of the collision zone, from **Coburn Gore** to **Attean Pond,** is marked by dark green pods of **serpentine,** a soft basaltic rock quarried there at one time as soapstone. Granite produced by melting of downwarped portions of the crust was intruded into what is now the Attean Pond area near Jackman.

Iapetus was much reduced. For many millions of years sediments eroded from the land, and thick layers of mud interbedded

Continued on page 171.

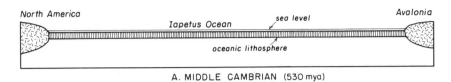

North America   Iapetus Ocean   sea level   Avalonia

oceanic lithosphere

A. MIDDLE CAMBRIAN (530 mya)

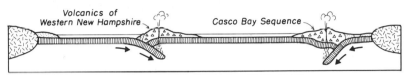

Volcanics of
Western New Hampshire   Casco Bay Sequence

B. LATE CAMBRIAN TO EARLY ORDOVICIAN

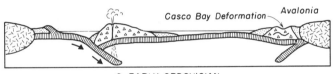

Casco Bay Deformation   Avalonia

C. EARLY ORDOVICIAN

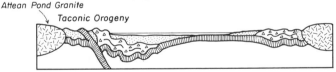

Attean Pond Granite
Taconic Orogeny

D. LATE ORDOVICIAN TO MIDDLE SILURIAN

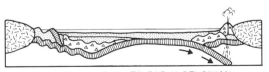

E. LATE SILURIAN TO EARLY DEVONIAN

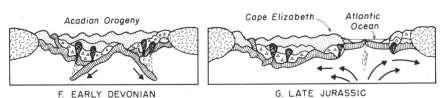

Acadian Orogeny   Cape Elizabeth   Atlantic
Ocean

F. EARLY DEVONIAN   G. LATE JURASSIC

(After Hussey, Two Lights and Crescent Beach State Parks, *M.G.S. Bulletin 26, 1982.)*

Folding and Faulting

If you push your hand on a tablecloth you can force the sliding cloth to form folds at a right angle to your hand. If you tried the same movement with a sheet of rolled-out pie crust dough, some of the folds would break and the broken upper portion would continue to slide, overriding the lower portion. A similar process produces folds and faults in thin layers of crustal rocks when pushed by great lateral pressures.

Compression during the collision of Avalonia with North America forced the rocks into folds called *anticlines* (tent-shaped) and *synclines* (down-sags). These folds, which may be from a few feet to many miles across, are usually independent of the hills and valleys in today's landscape; the present surface is the result of erosion that, in a mature landscape like Maine's, often has cut across the internal structure of the rocks. Many roadcuts expose folded and faulted rock on a small scale, but rock layers dipping one direction in one cut and quite a different direction in the next, also indicate folding or faulting that may involve thousands of feet of crustal rocks. Only careful measurement and mapping, followed by drafting of interpretive third-dimension views, reveal the true structure of the bedrock.

Very large folds, called *anticlinoria* and *synclinoria*, are like swells on the ocean, superimposing their structure on the smaller crests and troughs of the waves. On the flanks of these large structures are innumerable smaller anticlines and synclines.

The bedrock of Maine has been warped into three major northeast-trending synclinoria. The broad Central Maine synclinorium stretches from New Hampshire to New Brunswick and measures nearly fifty miles across. Much narrower are the Moose River synclinorium and the Connecticut Valley–Gaspé synclinorium of the St. John River region. Between the synclinoria are the Lobster Mountain–Weeksboro anticlinorium and the Boundary Mountain–Munsungum–Winterville anticlinorium.

A wedge-shaped block of coastal rocks, extending from Cape Elizabeth into New Brunswick and bounded on the north by a line from Portland through Bangor to Vanceboro, is a remnant of Avalonia welded onto North America. It has been deformed by large-scale, low-angle faulting. The northern boundary, a zone of crushed rock about two miles wide called the Norumbega Fault Zone, is the surface trace of at least three parallel faults. These together define the lower side of a block of older rocks that slid northwest at least six miles over younger rocks. The fact that this line is straight and undeformed indicates that this *thrust faulting* occurred during the latter stages of plate collision; there was little disturbance of the

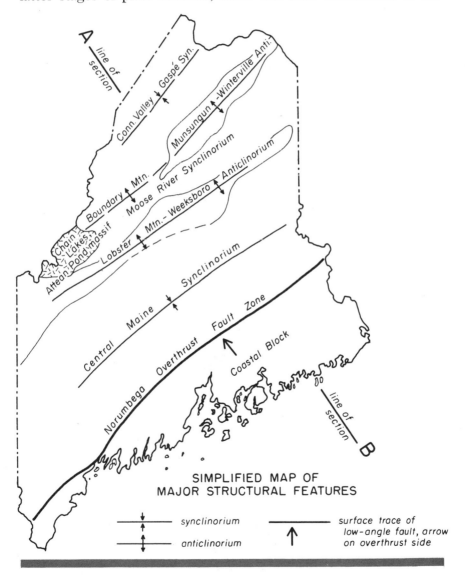

SIMPLIFIED MAP OF
MAJOR STRUCTURAL FEATURES

crust after the thrust faulting. Unfortunately, erosion and glacial debris obscure the traces of these great breaks in the rock, and they are revealed to geologists only by careful mapping and interpretation of crushed rock in scattered outcrops.

There is apparently no correlation between earthquakes experienced in historic times with known geologic faults, suggesting that these faults are well healed and no longer active.

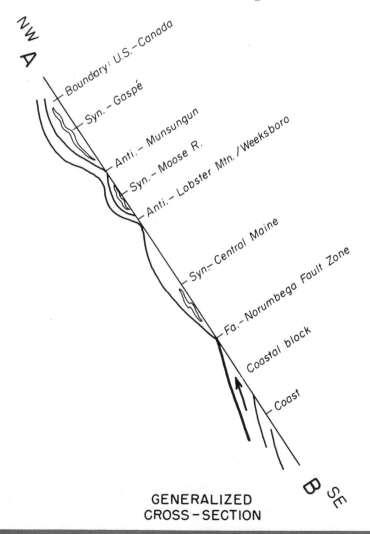

GENERALIZED
CROSS-SECTION

with thin beds of clayey sand accumulated in its shallow waters. Overall, the sedimentary pile totaled about five thousand feet, and here is an anomaly: shallow-water deposits five thousand feet thick! The explanation is that while the sediments were being laid down the sea floor was sagging beneath the load, maintaining a shallow basin.

The sediments became compacted and cemented into shale, micaceous sandstone, and sandy limestone. These rocks are now found widespread over central and northern Maine.

Iapetus continued to shrink, and Avalonia, bearing down on North America, finally collided with the continent about 390 million years ago, pinching and folding the rocks caught in between. This episode of collision and crumpling, the major mountain-building event in Maine, is known as the *Acadian orogeny*. Vast amounts of crust and covering sedimentary rock were subducted, forced down into the mantle where high temperatures and pressures metamorphosed the shales and limestones into slates and marble, the sandstones into quartzites and schists. Much of the crustal material was dragged deep enough to produce black-and-white-banded gneiss injected by light-colored veins. These folded rocks are well displayed in roadcuts along Interstate 95 from **Portland** to **Gardiner.**

Much rock was actually melted, and great masses of molten magma intruded into the surrounding crustal rock, cooled and crystallized, and became the granite plutons now found in the mountains and the coast of Maine. Uplift of this mass of igneous and metamorphic rock over the next few million years probably created a mountain range as lofty as today's Rocky Mountains.

Avalonia was only the first part of the encroaching Eurasian continent to collide with North America. About 70 million years after the Acadian orogeny the full mass of Africa and Eurasia pushed into North America. Most of the effects of that collision are recorded in the Appalachian Mountains south of the Hudson River. Maine and New England, perhaps shielded by Avalonia firmly welded onto the continent, show little disturbance related to this **Appalachian orogeny.**

The closing of Iapetus by the collision of the continents with their bordering island chains, the metamorphosis of the down-folded crust, the intrusion of huge amounts of granite into the collision zone—all were parts of a long process occupying 200 million years. Had you been there it would have been unnoticeable: an occasional earthquake, volcanic eruptions now and then, slow but steady erosion of the land. In short, a time about like our own on earth. In fact, that is just what is taking place today in Japan and the southwest Pacific islands, Mexico, Chile and Peru, the Mediterranean, and many other regions of geologic activity.

The huge landmass formed by this consolidation of all the continents was called Pangaea, and Maine, 250 million years ago, lay near the center of it, the latitude about 5 degrees north, and longitude about 0 degrees. This point today is in Ghana, in the bight of Africa. Who knows what the climate was like, but an area so near the equator and in the center of a landmass probably was hot and dry. No rocks of that time exist in Maine, but those remaining in other parts of the country confirm this interpretation.

The modern pattern of continents and oceans began to develop nearly 180 million years ago. Pangaea split parallel to the equator,

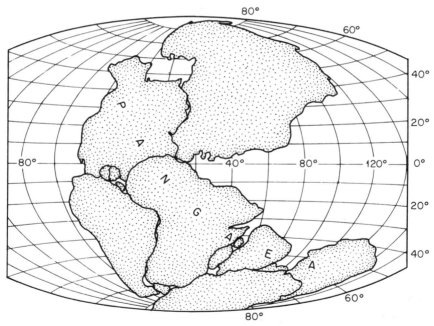

Pangaea, 200 million years ago. (After illustrations by Tom Prentiss in "The Breakup of Pangaea," by R.C. Dietz and J.C. Holden, Scientific American, *October 1970. Copyright 1970 by Scientific American, Inc. All rights reserved.)*

forming two parts corresponding roughly to the present northern and southern hemispheres. The northern hemisphere slowly moved north and eventually split to form long, narrow rift valleys, as Africa and the Arabian peninsula are doing today. The ocean found its way into one of these valleys, and North America and Europe went their separate ways. The break in the supercontinent occurred near, but not along, the old collision seam marked by the Appalachian Mountains. Part of former Avalonia was left behind as Europe moved away to the east. Fossils animals are found now in the limestone quarries of **Thomaston** (as well as other parts of New England) that were living in Avalonia before the welding of Pangaea; they belong to Europe, not North America.

By the time dinosaurs had become extinct, about 65 million years ago, North America had rotated thirty degrees counterclockwise, and had moved Maine to about 35 degrees north, 40 degrees

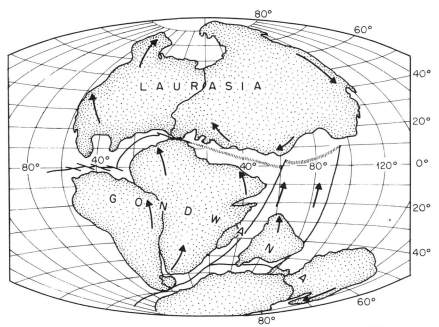

180 million years ago. (After illustrations by Tom Prentiss in "The Breakup of Pangaea," by R.C. Dietz and J.C. Holden, Scientific American, *October 1970. Copyright 1970 by Scientific American, Inc. All rights reserved.)*

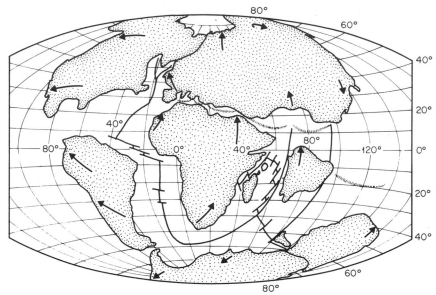

65 million years ago. (After illustrations by Tom Prentiss in "The Breakup of Pangaea," by R.C. Dietz and J.C. Holden, Scientific American, *October 1970. Copyright 1970 by Scientific American, Inc. All rights reserved.)*

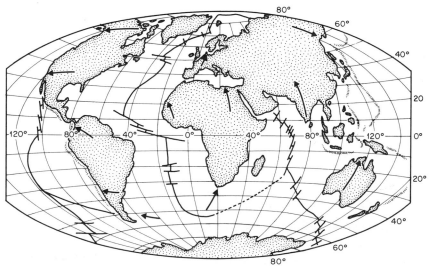

Present position and motion of continents.

west. The major North Atlantic rift shifted from the west side to the east side of Greenland and penetrated to the Arctic Ocean, thus completely separating Eurasia from North America.

Central Maine is now at 45 degreees north and 69 degrees west. Motion of the North American Plate is now essentially westward; Maine may not shift any farther north. Fifty million years from now perhaps Maine will have moved to 90 degrees west, the present longitude of Minneapolis. North America and Europe to this day continue to drift apart. (If you are planning to go to Europe, perhaps you had better go soon; the Atlantic Ocean gets wider by two inches every year.)

The Latest Episode: The Ice Age

Eastern North America, though sliding steadily westward like a huge raft, has had no great changes in the past 80 million years. Streams and rivers have carried away vast tonnages of rock, smoothing the landscape to a gentle plain. There is geologic evidence that 20 million years ago uplift of the plain rejuvenated the rivers, causing them to run faster and erode new valleys until finally there was little of the old plain remaining. This was the landscape found a million years ago by encroaching ice, oozing down from the north like pancake batter spreading over a griddle.

"Ice age" usually refers to the last million years, the Pleistocene Epoch. There were many advances of continental glaciers during this time, separated by "retreats," or periods of melting, longer than the glacial advance periods.

North America was covered by glaciers, uncovered by melting, and re-covered again at least four times, and possibly as many as ten times according to evidence in the Midwest. We can presume that this was the case in Maine also, but the last major advance completely wiped out the traces of earlier major episodes. In some localities in Maine, including **Roque Bluffs,** southeast of Jonesboro, two distinct tills deposited at different times indicate small-scale advances and retreats of ice within the last major ice stage.

What caused the great build-up of ice over the land? Obviously the climate was colder then. Studies of pollen and fossils in marine clays indicate that the mean annual global temperature was about five degrees colder than at present. (For comparison, annual fluctuations now average a few tenths of a degree.) But pollen and fossils do not explain *why* the temperature was colder. If the energy received from the sun has varied over geologic time, this should result in warmer and cooler periods, but there is no way to determine whether this happened. On the other hand, (assuming constant output of radiation by the sun) if there were changes in the earth's orbit, the heat received by the earth, and thus the temperature, would vary. Small changes in the orientation of the earth's axis, its distance from the sun, and a "wobble" in the earth's orbital plane, do repeat in regular patterns. When they all combine in just the right way, the energy received from the sun by the earth is reduced to the point where large amounts of snow at high latitudes can survive the summer, and an icepack can accumulate. Some geologists favor this explanation.

This does not explain why ice ages only come along every few hundred million years, as the geologic record indicates. Perhaps the pattern of moving continents is a factor. For example, in the last 30 million years the Arctic Ocean has been cut off from warm equatorial currents by the migrating Northern Hemisphere continents, while at the same time Antarctica slipped away from South America and Australia to take up its position astraddle the South Pole, protected from tropic waters. The colder climate at both poles, of course, favors ice accumulation.

Will the ice come again? The time since the last ice advance is shorter than the average for interglacial periods, so we probably cannot expect another ice age for several million years yet. On the other hand, burning of fossil fuels by humans may be affecting the balance of gases in the atmosphere in such a way as to warm the earth far more than can be offset by cooling from astronomical variations. We may have had the last ice age.

The Final(?) Chapter

In a few hundred million years the Pacific Ocean may have been closed and another Pangaea formed by colliding North America and Asia. We cannot know for sure, but there is every reason to think that crustal plates will continue to split and drift, volcanoes will spew, and earthquakes will groan and snap. Geologic processes will go on, regardless of mankind's small affairs. In the words of James Hutton, one of the founders of modern geology, "No sign of a beginning—no prospect of an end."

9
Geology in Human Affairs

Mention geology and most people think of rocks and minerals. Only when some unusual event happens—an earthquake, a landslide, disastrous erosion of beach frontage, or the announcement of a valuable mineral find—does the average person ordinarily become conscious of geologic processes. The geologic foundation and the operation of natural geologic processes, both in the past and continuing, play a part in human affairs whether we recognize it or not.

The location of mountains, lakes, and bogs, and the north-south orientation of the rivers and their flat, fertile floodplains—the shape of the land—dictated where the people would spread from the early coastal settlements. Maine's rock and mineral resources attracted the attention of surveyors and engineers in the early decades of the nineteenth century. Perhaps the earliest formal report, in 1829, was by Moses Greenleaf, who was interested in applying geological knowledge to the development of the state. In the following century and a half, fundamental geological knowledge and application of that knowledge have increased in parallel.

Mineral Resources

Granite. The most profitable mineral commodity in Maine over the years has been granite. The heyday is over, but at its peak during the late nineteenth century there were more than 100 quarries operating, most along the coast, on islands, or along rivers—wherever water transportation was available to ship the product to markets and railheads on the eastern seaboard. Maine granite was shipped from New York by rail as far inland as Chicago and St. Louis.

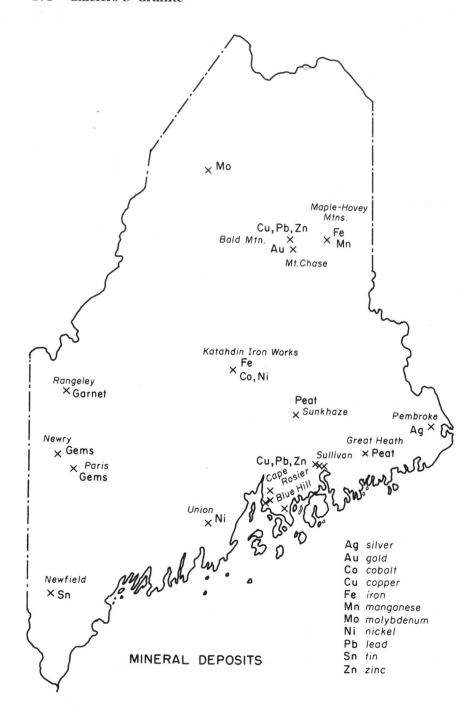

× Mo

Maple-Hovey Mtns.

Cu, Pb, Zn
Bald Mtn. ×   Fe
                 × Mn
Au ×

Mt. Chase

Katahdin Iron Works
× Fe
  Co, Ni

Rangeley
× Garnet

Peat
× *Sunkhaze*

Pembroke
Ag ×

Newry
× Gems
    × *Paris*
    Gems

Great Heath
× Peat

Sullivan
Cu, Pb, Zn ××
Cape Rosier
× *Blue Hill*
×
×

Union
× Ni

Newfield
× Sn

MINERAL DEPOSITS

Ag *silver*
Au *gold*
Co *cobalt*
Cu *copper*
Fe *iron*
Mn *manganese*
Mo *molybdenum*
Ni *nickel*
Pb *lead*
Sn *tin*
Zn *zinc*

Granite is not rare in the Appalachians and by no means did Maine have a monopoly, but the quality was high and certain characteristics of color and grain of Maine granite were in great demand. During the expansionist years of the late nineteenth century the nation experienced a boom in construction of imposing banks and office buildings, public buildings and monuments. **Vinalhaven** was the site of one of the larger operations, and it was there that huge columns were turned for the Cathedral of St. John the Divine in New York City. In Augusta at that time, the state Capitol, the Post Office, the Courthouse, and many other buildings were built of **Hallowell** granite. Paving blocks were turned out by the millions.

Quarrying had declined by early in the twentieth century as simpler building materials were found for construction and paving. Most of the quarries are closed today, except for special orders for decorative architectural stone and monuments. The State Museum in Augusta has an excellent display, including a full-scale diorama of a granite quarry, samples of granite from various quarries, and tools used in the industry. It is well worth a visit.

Limestone. Lime is another mineral commodity that has been important in Maine's economy, but rocks suitable for "burning" into lime are nowhere near as widespread in Maine as granite. The coast near **Thomaston** was the original site of the lime industry and remains active today. The town of **Rockland,** split off from East Thomaston, became the major locale for the industry during its greatest years, 1850 to 1900. Unlike granite cutting, the quarrying of limestone continues to flourish today.

Limestone is heated to drive off carbon dioxide, leaving "quicklime," a basis for plaster, mortar, and cement production. Originally this was accomplished in crude kilns fired by wood, at first in abundant supply in Maine. In later years wood was imported from Nova Scotia in schooners, which hauled out lime on the return trip. Today the roasting is an automatic, continual process carried out in huge oil-fired kilns. At present the Dragon Cement Company operates a modern plant at Thomaston and supplies its product to Maine and other eastern markets.

In Aroostook County, in the vicinity of **Caribou, Fort Fairfield** and **Limestone,** are many small limestone quarries once operated to make lime for cement, mortar, and agricultural purposes. Some was probably used in the late 1800s to make iron. The limestone is of good quality but of low commercial value because it occurs as very narrow, steeply dipping beds, on the order of one to two inches thick separated by shale beds several inches thick. The real value of this limestone is in the soil (called the Caribou silt loam) that developed from it, which is the basis of the important agricultural economy in this area. Lime is quickly leached from the soil, however, resulting in lower crop yields and significant soil erosion if it is not replaced.

Slate. The slate industry began at **Monson** in the 1870s and is still active. Large blocks of the dense, easily split rock were lifted out of deep quarries and were made into roofing, flooring tile, blackboards, slabs for sinks and countertops, and many other products. The Portland Monson Slate Company ships finished slate to New York for wider distribution, including back to Maine for retail sale. An abandoned quarry is easily seen from Bray Road at the west edge of the village, along the shore of Lake Hebron.

Acquiring Geological Information

Geologists make observations in the field, identifying rocks and noting how they lie in the ground. This information they add to the basic document of the science, the geologic map. The map is a summation of thousands of bits of information and measurement made by field geologists, plus a generous amount of interpretation.

The geologic map of Maine in some respects resembles an artist's palette. It's an old and well-used palette: streaks of contrasting color run diagonally across the map and splotches of bright color are dabbed here and there, seemingly at random. Each color represents a particular type of rock. Wherever an individual bed or igneous body is encountered it is given an identifying symbol and color code on the map. Folded beds and cross-cutting igneous intrusions create the stripes and blotches that make geologic maps so visually interesting.

Except on the coast and in the higher mountains, extensive exposure of bedrock in outcrops is scarce. When found, the rocks

Sand and Gravel. Although it is not a very glamorous industry, the production of sand and gravel, together with lime and crushed rock, is by far the largest part of Maine's mineral economy today. Most of the expense in the sand and gravel business is associated with transport of these low cost, high bulk materials. A few decades ago it would have been hard to conceive that Maine would experience local shortages of sand and gravel, given that practically all of the state is buried under glacial debris, but today that is indeed the problem in some areas. A gravel pit located in an area of expanding construction is a valuable asset.

Peat. Peat is another mineral in abundant supply, but currently of low value in Maine. The U.S. Bureau of Mines has officially designated peat as a mineral, probably because it is excavated and is essentially nonrenewable on a meaningful human time scale. The state has more than 100,000 acres of commercially valuable peatland, most of it in Washington and southeast Aroostook counties. The **Great Heath,** six miles north of Cherryfield, is a typical peatland. Most of the reddish brown "peat moss" that is taken is relatively

exposed are likely to be distorted and altered, and two geologists examining the same outcrop can sometimes reach quite different conclusions as to the rock's history. A geologic map really represents the combined judgments of a group of geologists, with their contemporary wisdom built in.

As understanding increases, maps are revised. Several state geologic maps of Maine have been published in the past century and a half, most recently in 1985. Undoubtedly more will be published in the future, each representing the best knowledge at the time.

Students often find the great variety of rock and mineral names bewildering, and all too often the actual rock picked up in the field does not seem to fit any of them. This problem is handled in a number of ways. On one student's map, a classmate of mine, the symbol FRDK appeared with considerable frequency. He said it stood for "Funny rock. Don't know."

compact and partly decomposed. It is used for agricultural and horticultural purposes. The famous peat of Ireland and Scotland, by contrast, is dark brown to black humus peat with few remaining identifiable plants. Humus peat is not mined in Maine. A few years ago, when the price of oil had skyrocketed, there was a flurry of activity centering around the use of peat pellets for fuel, but this potential new mineral industry passed into limbo when oil prices declined and both private companies and government lost interest in energy alternatives.

Metal Mining

As early as 1830 there was interest in iron mining north of Brownville Junction, off Route 11, where eventually **Katahdin Iron Works** was established. Here, iron ore was extracted from deeply

Types of Geologic Maps

Geologic maps generally involve either the bedrock of an area or its surficial material (sand, gravel, and landscape features). Mineral prospectors, quarry men, builders, highway designers, and others concerned with hard rock, as well as academic and research scientists studying basic processes and principles of geology, use bedrock geologic maps. The pattern of colors on the map is used by geologists to draw cross-sections and to infer the three-dimensional structure of the crust beneath their feet. Cross-sections are diagrams similar to roadcuts, but the beds are projected much deeper, usually many hundreds or thousands of feet. They reveal the pattern of folding and faulting of bedded rocks and the intrusion of igneous rocks as interpreted from surface data. Bedrock geologic maps and cross-sections are made from thousands of observations and inferences, and they will be as accurate as the information and skill that go into them.

The surficial geologic map is made the same way: a combination of observation and inference. Gravel pits, road banks, excavations, stream banks, and many other openings reveal the kind of material underlying the soil. Distinctive landscape characterisitics left by the glacier are also shown on surficial geologic maps. Many people use this information for town planning, locating and protecting water weathered gabbro. Today a State Historic Site there preserves one blast furnace and a "beehive" oven used for making charcoal, one of the ingredients used in reducing iron ore to metal.

After the Civil War, when the exploration of the West began to reveal the riches in that part of the country, a few people realized that Maine had rocks similar to the ore-bearing rocks of the newly opened territories. The fever of the 1870s fueled a boom in mining speculation that rivalled the goings-on in the West. Most of the activity was concentrated in Hancock County from Blue Hill to Sullivan, where volcanic rocks proved to be host for ores of silver, copper, lead, and zinc. The hysteria of the time also inspired the organization of a few companies that, in the words of John Rand, onetime State Geologist, "found the possibilities of taking a profit from the sale of common stock considerably more appetizing than

supplies, finding construction materials, siting landfill and disposal areas, and so on. Research geologists studying the history and the effects of glaciation on the land also make use of these maps.

Geology, like all sciences, is constantly growing and changing. As geologists collect new information and revise their interpretations, old maps become outmoded and new ones are issued. It is a never-ending process.

A Rock "Library"

A systematic collection of rocks and minerals is an essential part of geologic research; a specimen is usually far more informative than a written description of the rock. In addition to hand specimens, samples are taken by drills with hollow bits that remove a core as they drill down in the rock. Cores are taken routinely by engineers designing foundations for heavy buildings and bridges, and by exploration geologists searching for mineral deposits.

Rock samples and cores form a "library" of information. The Maine Geological Survey is a repository for samples and cores from many locations around the state, donated by individuals and companies for the use of anyone interested.

digging a hole in the ground." Most of these "ores" proved to be deposits too small to mine profitably, but a few mines in this area have produced ore in times of favorable metal prices. The last mine shut down at Blue Hill in 1977.

During World War II an extensive effort was made to locate minable deposits in Maine, and considerable tonnages of valuable ores were found, particularly iron and manganese in Aroostook County. So far, metal prices have not been high enough to justify opening these deposits.

Hope springs eternal in the prospector's breast, however, and the search continues even today. In 1977 the discovery of a huge deposit of copper, gold, and silver ore in Aroostook County near Portage (the **Bald Mountain** deposit) was announced, and in 1983 a similar find near **Mount Chase** in northern Penobscot County was revealed. These deposits—and others of iron-manganese, cobalt, nickel, and, molybdenum—while significant, must wait for higher metal prices before being attractive to mine developers.

Oxford County is well known to mineral collectors. Large veins of pegmatite have been opened up in a number of places, and it is said that 200 varieties of minerals are found here. Gem-quality beryl (aquamarine), apatite, garnet, and pink, green, and black tourmaline, have been taken from this area to be shipped to jewelry manufacturers in America and in Europe. Amateur collectors also are the basis of a small amount of business for old mines around **Paris.**

Groundwater Resources

The proper siting of water wells may bring the average person into contact with geologists, particularly if the amount of water required is large. The abundant rainfall in Maine, averaging about forty inches per year, makes it likely that water will be encountered at a reasonable depth almost anywhere you dig. About three-fourths of the precipitation runs off to lakes and streams or is evaporated. The rest makes its way downward as groundwater, infiltrating between the grains and particles of unconsolidated sedimentary deposits and finally into the cracks of bedrock. The most abundant water supplies, flows up to 100 gallons per minute, are found in stratified sand and gravel beds. Wells drilled into bedrock almost anywhere are likely to find water flowing in the range of three to ten gallons per minute, sufficient for most domestic purposes.

Most bedrock wells in Maine are between 100 and 200 feet deep, although 600-foot wells are not unusual. If the well site is on the top of a hill, the well probably must go deeper to find adequate water. Most well drillers will simply drill the well where it will be most convenient. Normally geologists are not called in to help locate wells in these situations, but a client requiring hundreds of gallons of water per minute (say an industrial or recreational developer) is likely to call in geohydrologists.

Modern water prospecting often begins with detailed analysis of aerial photos to find traces of aquifers, which might be either sand and gravel deposits saturated with groundwater or near-surface fracture zones in the bedrock. Electronic sensing devices and computer modeling can be applied in the effort to set a drill in the most promising sites. Professional geohydrologists have shown that a geologic understanding of the occurence of groundwater vastly improves the chances of success in difficult situations.

Waste Disposal Sites

Groundwater is susceptible to pollution from improperly handled sewage; fluids leaching from solid waste landfills; dumped household, farm, and industrial materials; and many other sources. Poisonous substances dissolved in the water can seep into the aquifer, and once there they are very hard to remove. The siting of disposal facilities for wastes, particularly hazardous wastes, is an extremely important and difficult problem, and the expertise of geologists can be valuable in these cases.

Maine has attracted attention because of its large amounts of granite, the preferred rock for underground disposal of radioactive wastes. Many other criteria beside the presence of granite must be taken into account, however, before selection of a disposal site can be made. For one, the repository must be dry and isolated from groundwater, so the high rainfall, together with the abundance of fractures in the granite, should rule out Maine as a disposal site for high-level radioactive wastes.

Earthquakes

Maine is not prone to large earthquakes, but small ones do occur. Most regions except for the Mountain Upland experience mild shocks from time to time. For an earthquake to be felt it must

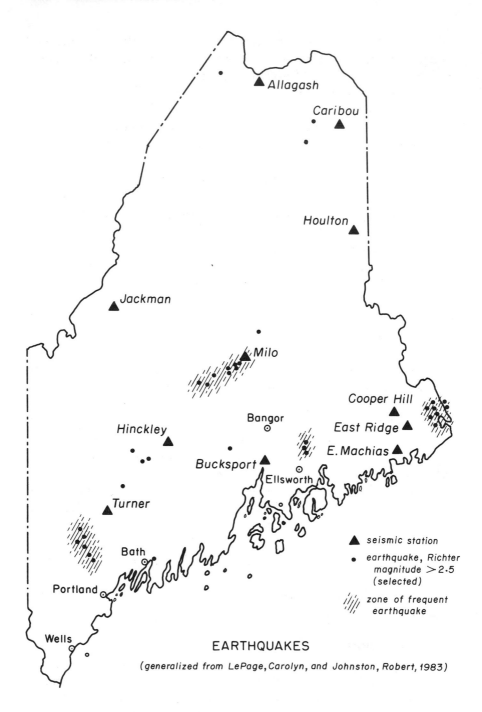

Allagash

Caribou

Houlton

Jackman

Milo

Cooper Hill

Bangor

East Ridge

Hinckley

E. Machias

Bucksport

Ellsworth

Turner

▲ seismic station

• earthquake, Richter
   magnitude > 2·5
   (selected)

/// zone of frequent
   earthquake

Bath

Portland

Wells

EARTHQUAKES

(generalized from LePage, Carolyn, and Johnston, Robert, 1983) register over 2.5 on the Richter Scale, a logarithmic scale of magnitude on which each whole number is ten times the value of the preceding number. Damaging earthquakes measure over 5.0 in magnitude. The strongest in recent history in Maine occurred in 1979 between **Bath** and **Wiscassett,** measuring 4.0 in magnitude.

Earthquakes are produced by breaking rock as it slips and adjusts to crustal forces. Maine has been inactive tectonically for many millions of years, so strong earthquakes, though not impossible, are not likely. Since 1975 a network of modern seismographs has been monitoring Maine earthquakes continuously, and the record shows that earthquake sites are widely scattered, though there are several zones where mild earthquakes are clustered. One of these is between **Gray** and **Auburn** and a few miles west of the Maine Turnpike. Somewhat more active is a zone between **Milo** and **Dover-Foxcroft** on routes 6 and15. A third zone is north of **Ellsworth** along the east side of Graham Lake. An area along the **St. Croix River** in Washington County has received a number of very mild shocks. None of the earthquakes recorded to date has done any damage.

Geological knowledge benefits the public in many ways. Areas prone to flooding or landslides, soils that are shallow or excessively wet, potential ore bodies, valuable deposits of sand and gravel, and vital aquifers can be identified and their presence made known to municipal leaders so that the activities of developers can be guided wisely. Marine geologists help seacoast communities cope with coastal erosion. Highway geologists use geologic maps to locate roadcuts and supplies of fill, as well as suitable sites for storage of road salt. Geotechnical engineers use basic geological knowledge when designing foundations for buildings and bridges, and soil scientists apply an understanding of surficial geology to farm problems. Not the least, an aquaintance with geologic principles can increase any person's understanding of many natural events like volcanic eruptions, landslides, and earthquakes when they occur, and at all times can be a source of intellectual pleasure. The science of geology has contributed, and will continue to contribute, in many ways to the well-being of Mainers.

10
Road Logs

Many people are hikers and canoeists, some are sailors, and a few are aircraft pilots, but most of us view scenery only from the road. Consciously noticing and recognizing the landscape along the way can make an otherwise monotonous trip more interesting.

The roads selected for description in this chapter are frequently traveled and also present good cross-sections of different parts of the state. Reading ahead before your trip—or better, having a passenger read while you drive—can make a car trip an interesting experience. Technical terms already introduced earlier in this book are used freely, and, similarly, a number of geological sites mentioned here have already been discussed. Further explanations should be sought in appropriate chapters.

Southwest Coast

Interstate 95, Kittery to Portland. From the entry into Maine at Kittery on the Piscataqua River, the highway crosses rolling, sandy land covered with pine trees, where glacial meltwater streams loaded with sand and gravel, met the sea. There are very few landmarks and no outcrops of bedrock to be seen for a number of miles, but from Mile 10 to Mile 12, and at the Cat Mountain Road overpass, about three miles north of Exit 1, light-colored granite of the Agamenticus Pluton shows in low roadcuts.

Near Exit 4, in **Biddeford,** are more granite outcrops, this time of the Biddeford pluton, which is older by 100 million years than the Agamenticus rocks. Some horizontal slabbing, or "sheeting," can be seen.

From here to Portland the rocks are low-grade metamorphic quartzites and schists. Outcrops and roadcuts are few, although there are several large outcrops of these rocks near Exit 5 at **Saco**.

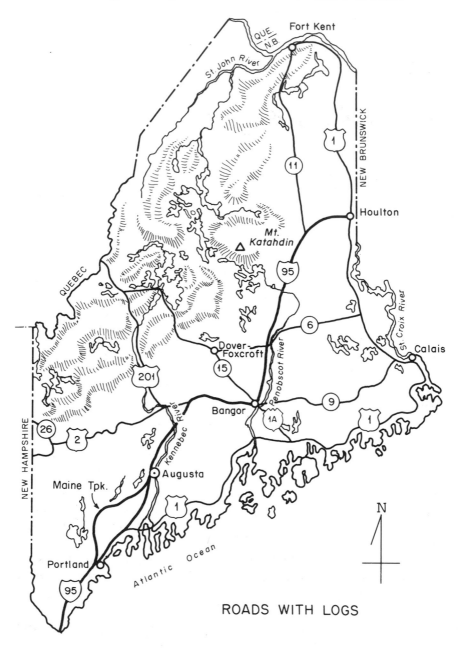

ROADS WITH LOGS

I-295 through Portland offers good views of the estuaries of the Fore and Presumpscot rivers, exposing wide flats of the glacio-marine silt and clay at low tide.

Near the town line of **Falmouth** are excellent exposures in high roadcuts of banded schist and gneiss dipping sharply to the east. These rocks, part of Avalonia, the coastal block, have been shoved up along the Norumbega Fault Zone. I-295 rejoins I-95 in a mile or so.

Central Upland

Interstate-95, Portland to Gardiner. Interstate 95 follows the strike, or trend, of two of the oldest rock beds in Maine, and it exposes them in some excellent cuts. These rocks are quartzites, gneisses, and schists—coarse-grained metamorphic rock distin-guished by the banding in light and dark colors. Originally these rocks were layers of sediment and volcanic rock deposited in the basin between the colliding continents that formed, and deformed, Maine. In some places you can see intruding veins of pegmatite cutting between and through the layers. Many of the roadcuts reveal contorted and faulted beds that indicate the forces and stresses the rocks endured.

At Exit 10, in **Falmouth,** is a cut many feet high and several hundred feet long. Although stopping is prohibited here, it is pos-sible to get a good impression of the rocks at a slow speed. The alternating light and dark layers of schist and gneiss dip to the east. From here to Exit16, in **Yarmouth,** bedding is more or less parallel to the road and there are a number of similar large, clifflike cuts.

From **Freeport** eastward toward **Brunswick,** the beds of schist, more drab and uniform in color, continue to dip east at a low angle. Gentle warping can be observed in some places.

The highway bridges the Androscoggin River near the U.S. Route 1 exit, and although there is little sign of it, the road also crosses a major fault. Mapping of the rock types has shown that at this locality older rock layers, perhaps 500 million years old, have been thrust up northwest along a low-angle fault that dips southeast. Under the fault are similar appearing beds that are about 480 million years old. The great force that pushed this slab was part of the Acadian orogeny, or mountain-building time, when Avalonia col-lided with North America 390 million years ago. From here north-

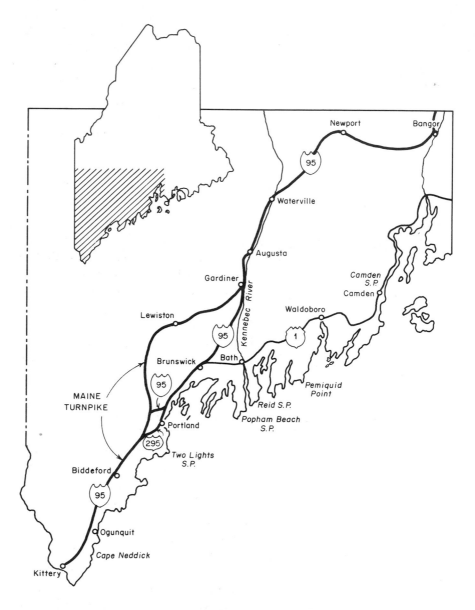

ward, although there is little change in general appearance, the
schists and gneisses belong to the older group of rocks. Their similar
appearance is due to a similar origin and to the fact that these beds
were all subjected to the same high temperature and great pressure
associated with the orogeny.

Roadcuts and outcrops of schists and gneiss are common along the highway, with little change from one mile to the next because the highway follows the strike; that is, the road is more or less parallel to the bedding of the rock. In numerous places pegmatite has intruded into the beds. Much of this rock weathers to a rusty color, owing to iron-bearing minerals. Mica flakes, particularly in the pegmatite, glisten in the sunlight.

At **Mile 78,** northbound, there is a large exposure on the right (east) of sheared pegmatite. A fault, revealed by the intensely broken and crushed rock, cuts through the center of the cliff. There was an old quarry here from which road material has been excavated in the past.

At **Exit 26** there is a fine exposure of gray gneiss and schist, unweathered and displaying some interesting folding and warping. Veins of pegmatite cut through the outcrop. Thin banding of contrasting dark gray and white brings out the structure of the rock very well, making this a good outcrop for study. The best cut is along the on-ramp for the southbound lane, and since the road is wide here it is probably safe to examine the rocks on foot.

Interstate 95 joins the Maine Turnpike at Gardiner, and further descriptions will be found in the turnpike log.

Maine Turnpike: Portland to Augusta. The Maine Turnpike leaves the coast at Portland and from there travels up the axis of the Central Upland. Although the upland is underlain by metamorphic rocks such as schists and gneisses, in this southern portion there are few outcrops or roadcuts in solid rock. Most of the land is buried under a thick cover of till and glacial debris reworked by meltwater from the wasting glacier. At the **Sabbattus River** (Mile 82) a large sand bank, mined for commercial use, exposes the nature of this material.

At the Route 9 overpass, about **Mile 83,** and locally from Mile 94 to Auburn, low roadcuts show contorted metamorphic bedrock. From **Auburn** (Exit 12) to Lewiston (Exit13), outcrops and roadcuts in dark schist become more common and increasingly are cut by coarse-grained pegmatite veins whose flat feldspar crystals and large flakes of mica reflect the sun.

From Lewiston to Gardiner there are few roadcuts in the low and swampy landscape but occasionally you can glimpse vertical thin-bedded slates and phyllites. These are the principal rocks of the Central Upland and are encountered in roadcuts and outcrops from here to Houlton.

About two miles north of Exit 14, near the town line of **West Gardiner,** outcrops show intense folding and the intrusion of granite. At the **Litchfield Road** overpass, a quarry on the west side exposes intensely folded metamorphic rocks with granite in the core of the folds. These exposures border the large mass of granite that underlies Hallowell and Augusta. At **Mile 103** the eastern abutment of the Maple Street bridge displays a good example of reaction rims, light-colored borders on fragments of schist that were engulfed and chemically altered by intruding molten granite.

The Maine Turnpike merges with Interstate 95 at Exit 14 in Gardiner and ends at Exit 15 in Augusta. Interstate 95 continues north.

Interstate 95, Augusta to Houlton. Hallowell granite, which was used to build the Maine State House, is exposed in cuts from the turnpike tollgate to about one-half mile north of Exit 31. The massive gray granite is broken by horizontal cracks, sometimes confused with bedding at first glance. This "sheeting," well displayed at the **Old Belgrade Road** overpass, is due to the release of pent-up strain developed in the rock during cooling.

At the city line north of **Augusta,** high roadcuts expose vertical slaty rocks, mostly metamorphosed shales and siltstones. The bedrock of the Central Upland has been deformed into tight vertical folds, and because the road closely parallels the strike of these folds, the same rock type appears in numerous roadcuts all the way to Newport. There is a quarry and rock crushing operation at Exit 32, Lyons Road, **Sidney,** where limy slate is made into a variety of construction materials. The machinery is visible on the west side of the highway.

At Exit 34 in **Waterville** the roadcut is deeply stained with rust. This is the the result of oxidation of small veins of pyrite (iron sulfide), common in these rocks.

The land is flat from Waterville to Pittsfield, for this was once the bottom of a lake of glacial meltwater. East of the highway only a mile or two, a vast region of spruce bogs streaked with glacial eskers stretches from Winslow to Newport. I-95, like the railroad before it, makes a wide swing to the north to avoid this inhospitable land.

East of **Newport** (Exit 39) the highway crosses a number of ridges, each revealing in cuts at the top somewhat finer-grained metamorphic rocks than those in the Augusta-Waterville area. In many places these are folded and shattered. The normally gray rock weathers brown and yellow, even green in some places. Where soil and vegetation are missing we can see that the tops of these outcrops were smoothed and rounded by glacial action.

At **Mile 161** (Exit 42) there is a view of the Bangor Basin, a flat confluence of rivers and bogs where the Penobscot River starts its cut through the Downeast Mountains to the sea. There are few outcrops from here to Bangor but at the city line one gets a view of the bare slopes of Peaked Mountain beyond Bangor on the other side of the basin. There are no views of the Penobscot River from the interstate highway.

In **Bangor,** between exits 47 and 48, the highway crosses the narrow valley of the Kenduskeag River and passes through deep cuts in shimmering silver-gray phyllite.

North from Bangor the highway cuts through a few low outcrops of slaty rocks and at Exit 53 emerges in a wide space occupied by **Alton Bog.** No open water is visible, but the bog—a vast, flat expanse of low, shrubby "heath" plants dotted by small clumps of larch and spruce trees—stretches away on both sides of the road. A deep layer of sphagnum moss, destined to form peat, carpets the area. This is a "raised bog," which means the peat layer separates the vegetation from the goundwater and its dissolved minerals. The only nourishment the plants receive is from rain water.

After crossing the town line for **T1 R6** (in this sparsely settled region many towns are known only by surveyed land coordinates), a roadside scenic overlook provides a fine view of Mount Katahdin, a large mass of granite with several summit peaks and glacial cirques, and Traveler Mountain, the eroded remnant of a very hard volcanic rhyolite flow. To the southwest are White Cap, Saddleback, and other mountains.

About three miles north of **Sherman** (Exit 58) the highway rises on the side of a hill presenting a fine view across Thousand Acre, or Crystal, Bog. In the background is the Katahdin-Traveler skyline, and to the north, the sharp peak of Mount Chase, carved from hard volcanic rock.

The highway continues to cut through metamorphic rocks, slates, schists, and quartzites. Rounded mountains to the east are made of granite and hard contact-zone rocks. From Exit 60 to **Houlton** and the Canadian border, the view opens to fields and farmland, the southern part of the famed Aroostook County potato land.

U. S. Route 1: Houlton to Fort Kent. When you drive north from Houlton you enter a part of Maine that is like no other. The forests and mountains southwest of Houlton are left behind as U.S. Route 1 heads north, straight as an arrow, through Littleton, Monticello, and Bridgewater. It goes past farms with large, square farmhouses, and big white barns, partly submerged underground. Broad fields stretch across the landscape to low ridges, most of them capped by remnant stands of spruce and pine. On some of the ridges are the spires of churches and the silhouettes of small communities. It is a landscape typical of Wisconsin more than Maine. This is southern Aroostook County, the land of the Maine potato.

Once again the scenery reflects the geology, for the underlying rock is unmetamorphosed limestone and limy shale, here spread wider than in any other part of the state. The glacier pulverized the rocks and left the debris to be formed into the rich, loamy, Caribou soil that makes for good farmland. In roadcuts the weathered limestone is buff to yellow, but a fresh piece is dark blue-gray. Some beds are as crystalline as fine sugar, and they fizz merrily under a drop of acid, the sure test for limestone.

Dominating the view to the north is **Mars Hill,** over sixteen hundred feet high and an anomaly in this flat country. The sharp crest, carved from resistant conglomerate and sandstone, is visible from Houlton, thirty miles away; indeed, the highway runs straight at it. From the town of Mars Hill, west of the hill, you can see that the peak you have been watching as you approached from the south is only the end of a long narrow ridge, covered with forest but streaked with ski trails.

Aroostook State Park, four miles south of Presque Isle, features Quaggy Joe Mountain, a double peak of hard, volcanic rhyolite (lava

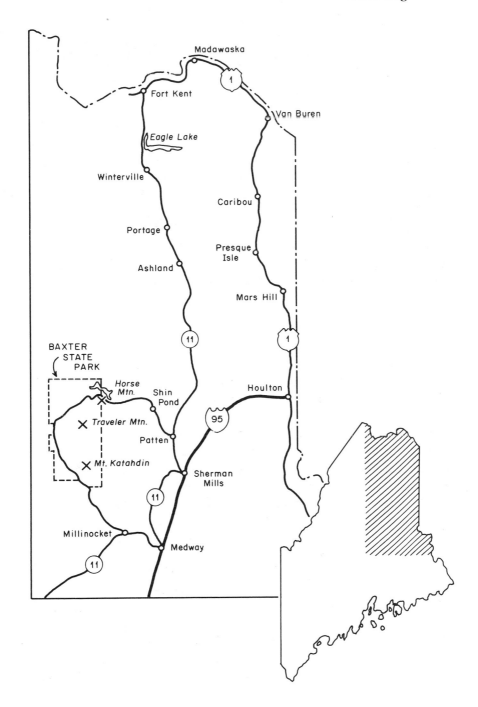

Mars Hill is visible for miles across Aroostook County farmland.

with the composition of granite but without its crystallinity). The mountain rises 600 feet above Echo Lake, reaching a total of twelve hundred feet above sea level. It offers good views to the north and northwest. A similar peak, **Haystack Mountain,** is reached by a ten-mile side trip west on Route 163 from Presque Isle, through Mapleton, across open farmland more rolling than that farther east. This sharp, prominent peak is also carved from dense rhyolite, weathered yellow to buff. A short, steep climb to the top provides a 360-degree view, and from here it is clear that Haystack Mountain, part of the Castle Hill ridge, marks the boundary between the farmland of the Aroostook Valley and the spruce-fir forest to the west.

U.S. Route 1 crosses the Aroostook River at **Presque Isle** and follows the high ground, with views in every direction. Farming has determined the scenery here. The river meanders in wide, ten-mile swings across this portion of "the County," marked by the towns of Washburn, Presque Isle, Caribou, and Fort Fairfield. Near the outskirts of **Caribou** a picnic area provides a view of the river. There is also a good roadcut in steeply dipping, thin bedded, limestone cut by white calcite veinlets. Apparently solutions with dissolved calcium carbonate penetrated along fractures and deposited the mineral.

As you drive north along U.S. 1 a line of hills to the west seems to close in, narrowing the belt of farmland. There are smaller farms along the ridge and even west of it. Here the bedrock, though limy, is more silty and shaly, and thus more resistant to erosion, accounting for the hills. East of the highway, farms give way to a vast cedar bog as you approach **Van Buren.** From a height of land about two miles south of the city there is a wide view of the St. John valley, although the deeply incised river is not visible.

The St. John River flows in a floodplain that is a mile wide in some places, and the shoulders of the valley rise on each side another half-mile away. Tremendous volumes of sand and gravel alluvium are distributed along the course of the river, and many islands appear in the streambed at low water levels. U.S. 1 follows the south bank closely and provides numerous views of the swift-flowing water. A small bluff at the **Madawaska** town line reveals the slightly limy fine sandstone and shale, thin bedded and vertical, that account for the hilly farmland to the south. At Madawaska the river narrows considerably, and large mills on both sides of the river indicate the development of hydropower. The highway follows the river's winding course, past a fine view upstream from **Frenchville,** to Fort Kent, where U.S. Route 1 ends.

Route 11: Fort Kent to Sherman. The thirty-seven miles of this route south from **Fort Kent** to **Portage Lake** has been designated a Scenic Highway, and it is well named. The road rises from the confluence of the Fish and St. John rivers at Fort Kent. Within a mile and a half the road has gained enough elevation to present fine views to the east of ridges with fields and farms. Numerous shale outcrops along the road explain the hilly landscape. The presence of cleared land, and thus good soil, also suggests that the rock must contain some limy layers. Route 11 more or less marks a boundary between the forested Northern Region on the west, underlain by shale and sandstone, and the more fertile Aroostook Valley, with its limestones and limy shales, to the east. This becomes evident as you drive along, generally with forest on your right and farmland to the left.

At **Soldier Pond** the road climbs steeply, and at the summit is a roadside picnic area with a fine view over the village and the surrounding landscape. At Plaisted the road descends to Eagle Lake and follows the shore for five miles. Two narrow arms make up the lake, joining at the village of **Eagle Lake.** A picnic ground just north of the village commands fine views north and east of each arm.

South of **Winterville** the road climbs steeply. A roadcut at the crest explains the ridge: it is held up by hard volcanic rock. Dark green-grey basalt lava, exposed for 300 feet along the road, is especially interesting because of "pillow" structures in the rock. Numerous high-angle faults and fractures filled with white calcite cut the rock, and a few bits of pyrite can be found. Deep weathering at the top of the exposure has dissolved the calcite and emphasized the pillows.

For five miles the highway picks its way over volcanic rock, between Hedgehog and Pennington mountains, emerging finally to a view south over the upper portion of Portage Lake. For the next several miles there are beautiful vistas to the west across the marshy flats of Fish River, with a range of mountains on the skyline. In the volcanic rocks of these mountains one of the great mineral finds of the century was made in the 1970s: the Bald Mountain deposit. Many millions of tons of copper-gold-silver ore were discovered, but development of a mine awaits more favorable metal prices. Between Portage Lake village and Ashland there are frequent glimpses of a sharp peak on the eastern skyline: Haystack Mountain, also carved from a lava flow.

The road crosses the Aroostook River at Ashland and then for thirty miles heads south through a green canyon of forest almost unrelieved by breaks except for logging roads and one or two crossroads communities. The land is covered with glacial debris, but shale and sandstone bedrock is exposed in rare roadcuts. A mile or two south of **Knowles Corner,** a dark green, fine- to medium-grained crystalline igneous rock is exposed in a rounded, weathered outcrop. This rock, called diorite, is intermediate in composition between basalt and granite.

The road emerges from forest a few miles short of **Patten,** where there are good views of Mount Katahdin to the west and Mount Chase to the north. An especially fine viewpoint is a scenic turnout on **Ash Hill,** three miles south of Patten, from which (with binoculars) you can easily see North and South basins, cirques on the east flank of Mount Katahdin. To the east is Crystal Bog, a Nature Conservancy preserve of 4,000 acres of bog and peatland. Granite knobs of the Oakfield Hills make the skyline to the northeast.

Where Route 11 meets Interstate 95 at **Sherman** there is a fine exposure of silvery phyllite in the abutment supporting the overpass at the interchange.

Midcoast and Downeast Coast

U.S. Route 1: Brunswick to Bucksport. For a mile or two east of Brunswick the highway parallels the Androscoggin River on its way to Merrymeeting Bay, where it will join the Kennebec River. Near the **West Bath** exit is a large mass of pink granite.

At **Bath** a high bridge gives a fine view of the estuary of the Kennebec. Near here was the largest earthquake to strike Maine in recent years, but at Richter Magnitude 4, it was scarcely felt except by instruments. From Bath to Wiscasset there are numerous exposures of metamorphic rocks intruded by veins and masses of pink and white pegmatite. Wide mud flats are exposed at low tide at Wiscasset.

Good roadcut exposures at **Edgecomb** reveal vertical bands of gneiss and pegmatite. An especially fine, deep cut in the same rocks has been made just west of **Newcastle.**

East of **Thomaston** you will get glimpses of the Dragon Cement plant and its enormous quarry. This large deposit of limestone has been lightly metamorphosed to marble. Some fossils related only to European animals have been found in this rock, evidence that this coastal land was once joined to Europe.

From Rockland you can see the Camden Hills to the north. Beautiful views of Penobscot Bay open up as you drive toward Bucksport. Large clifflike exposures in roadcuts as you approach the suspension bridge to Verona Island are largely slates and similar slabby rocks.

U.S. Route 1: Bucksport to Calais. At Bucksport the bedrock is schist, poorly exposed, although there is an outcrop at the junction with Route 46. In **Orland** there are outcrops of sheeted, coarse-grained granite, part of a large pluton stretching to the north and

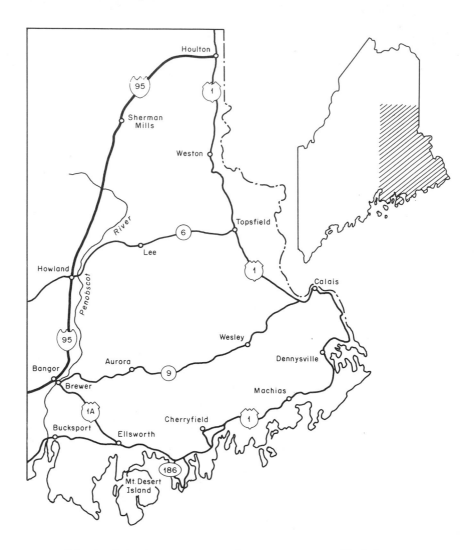

crossed by both U.S. Route1A and Route 9. It is called the Lucerne granite because of the beautiful exposures of it near that place.

At the town line of **Ellsworth** the highway leaves granite and crosses into dark mica schist but outcrops are not common; most of the land is covered with glacial debris and forest. From Ellsworth to Hancock there are a few roadcuts in dark greenish schist.

The usual route from Ellsworth to Machias is to leave U.S. Route 1 at Franklin and take **Route 182** to Cherryfield, where you rejoin Route 1. This cut-off is a scenic highway, with glimpses through the trees of Tunk Lake and Spring River Lake. You can also see to the north the bare, slabbing slopes of Tunk Mountain, an isolated monadnock of granite.

At **West Sullivan,** where the road crosses an upper arm of Frenchman Bay, granite is once again encountered. From Sullivan there is a fine view southwest across Frenchman Bay to the rounded summits of Cadillac and Champlain mountains on Mount Desert Island. A short distance south of Sullivan, red granite, part of the pluton that makes up Cadillac Mountain across the bay, appears in outcrops and roadcuts.

A *side trip to Schoodic Point:* Route 186 leaves from West Gouldsboro and heads south for Winter Harbor. From here a loop road, clearly marked by a sign, provides a very scenic side trip around **Schoodic Point,** part of Acadia National Park. An unusual display of dark greenish-gray basalt dikes cutting through the red granite is a principal feature of the point. There is fine rocky coastal scenery along the rest of the loop road, which rejoins Route 186 at Birch Harbor. Route 186 meets U.S. Route 1 again at Gouldsboro.

From the junction of Route 195, between West Gouldsboro and **Gouldsboro,** U.S. Route 1 travels across dark-green rock that resembles basalt. Actually, it is gabbro, the coarser-grained member of the family, exposed in road cuts from here to the Washington County line. At the county line there is a deep cut in pink granite, and the rest of the way to Milbridge the road is in and out of gabbro and pink granite.

Milbridge is a pretty coastal town with fine views of Narraguagus Bay. Most travelers take advantage of U.S. Route 1A, a shortcut from Milbridge to Harrington; the main route goes to Cherryfield.

From Cherryfield to Eastport, the easternmost corner of Maine, the road is in volcanic rocks. For the most part these are lava flows, red rhyolite being common, but they also include ash beds consolidated into the dense, very fine-grained rock called tuff. Some of these beds accumulated as sediments in an environment where shellfish could flourish, and a few fossil localities have been discovered here. Some twelve miles east of **Machias** the rock changes from dark gray and greenish-black to maroon and purple, reflecting a change in composition of the lavas from basaltic to a more granitic type.

At Whiting Route 189 leaves to the east for Lubec and West Quoddy Head State Park, a site of considerable interest described in Chapter 3. At **West Pembroke** a sign points right to the town-owned park at **Reversing Falls,** a side trip of six miles along Leighton Neck Road, which becomes rough and narrow but is worth the time. Here the changing tide from Cobscook Bay, rushing to fill (or empty) Dennys and Whiting bays, is forced through a narrow passage between two peninsulas. The huge, roaring saltwater river creates great whirlpools and standing waves, and six hours later the show will be repeated, with the tide flowing the other way. There are other reversing falls on the Maine coast, but this one is the most impressive.

From **Pembroke** eastward, the rocks exposed are volcanic flows and ash beds until you reach the town of **Perry,** where you find conglomerate, a rock made from identifiable pebbles of older rocks. Embedded in the conglomerate along with volcanic rocks are pieces of red granite (which will be encountered in the bedrock a few miles up the road). The Perry conglomerate, at about 345 million years, is one of the youngest sedimentary rock formations in Maine.

At the village of **Red Beach** there is a turnout for St. Croix National Monument. In addition to the historical interest, this is a good place to see the red granite in detail, weathering away along crystal boundaries. The sand at the water's edge is largely pink or red feldspar grains.

From here on, there are numerous outcrops of red granite along the road, with grey granite more common closer to **Calais.** Just short of the town there is a roadside rest with a fine view upriver. North from Calais to Topsfield, where U.S. 1 crosses Route 6, the land is low, forested, and swampy. There are few high prominences and little to be seen from the road, but about two miles north of **Topsfield** the highway rises over a granite knob on top of which is a large communication tower. Just beyond the tower is a large roadcut through strongly weathered, coarse-grained pink granite, the northern tip of a large pluton that extends more than eighty miles to the southwest, probably all the way to Mount Desert Island. This is an old roadcut, and weathering has emphasized the sheet structure by eroding along the close-spaced fractures until the granite almost looks layered.

A scenic turnout north of **Danforth** presents a view of Mount Katahdin on the skyline to the northwest, while just a little further on, near **Weston,** is a local landmark: the Million Dollar View of the Chiputneticook Lakes. These lakes, of which East Grand Lake is the largest, occupy the eroded crest of a large granite dome off to the east. Much of the landscape you see from here is in Canada. The view is wide and handsome, and fortunately you do not have to be a millionaire to enjoy it.

From here north to Houlton the landscape is hilly and open. There are numerous vistas to the west over forest and farmland, with a few rounded granite crests in the distance.

Downeast Mountains

U.S. Route 1A, Ellsworth to Brewer. North of Ellsworth the highway crosses glacial till left by the melting ice sheet. A few road banks show marine silt and clay beneath the thin vegetative cover. There is little to be seen except spruce forest for ten miles, but then rather suddenly the road gains elevation and roadcuts reveal coarse-grained gray granite separated into horizontal slabs by "sheeting." The weathered tops of the hills are rounded, and soil is thin or absent. The glacier polished the shoulders of some of these hills. For a few years after highway construction, these polished surfaces can resist the pitting and deterioration caused by the weather, and they glisten when the light is right.

From **Lucerne** there is a splendid view to the southwest. Although there is no scenic turnout, it is possible to pause safely for a few moments in the fire station lot. Phillips Lake lies below, and directly across is Dedham Bald Mountain, so-called to distinguish this one from many other "Bald Mountains" in the state. A fire tower and numerous communication antennas are on top. This and other peaks in the neighborhood are carved from the Lucerne granite. Weathering is slabbing off concentric sheets, and rockslides are evident.

A couple of miles farther north, across from the **Dedham School,** a large cut exposes steeply dipping thin-bedded quartzites and other metamorphic rocks that have been broken by faults. This is one of the better roadcuts to observe slickensides, smoothed and polished surfaces along which the bedrock slipped during some long ago earthquake. Elsewhere on the rock face it is possible to see drag folds and crushed rock, also attesting to faulting at this location. Less than half a mile to the south are outcrops of granite, so this is very near the edge of the Lucerne granite pluton.

From the Hancock County line to **Brewer** the bedrock is metamorphic schists and quartzites, exposed in roadcuts and forming the high knobs to the south of the highway.

Route 9: Brewer to Calais. After following the Penobscot River upstream from Brewer for a few miles, Route 9 heads east at Eddington. From here the road crosses many miles of low, boggy land, the monotony of which is occasionally interrupted by protruding masses of granite and related rocks. The first of these is in the vicinity of **Clifton,** where a prominent cliff rises above the eastern shore of Parks Pond. Roadcuts nearby are in dark, fine-grained igneous rock called diorite, a rock between granite and gabbro in composition.

Within a mile or so, roadcuts expose very coarse, light-colored granite, part of the granite pluton also crossed by U.S. Route 1A at Lucerne. The road becomes more hilly, and to the north the rounded summits of **Peaked and Little Peaked mountains** are visible. Great concentric sheets of granite have spalled off these mountains, leaving very steep, slightly rounded south faces.

About one mile west of **Amherst** a roadcut reveals vertical beds that have been contact metamorphosed by the granite pluton into hornfels, a very hard and tough rock. This cut also shows minor faults along which movement of a few inches can be discerned. The valley at Amherst is carved from more easily eroded metamorphic rocks, but at **Aurora** the road is back in granite. Silsby Hill, to the north, and numerous rounded knobs showing through the thin soil to the south, are granite.

East of Aurora the road turns southeast and runs along the top of a remarkable high, straight gravel ridge. This is the **Whalesback,** a portion of a large esker left when the ice sheet melted. The ridge is higher than most of the trees, and you have the feeling of traveling on an elevated highway. There are several turnouts from which to admire the view. On both sides the land is flat "muskeg" (bog). On the north, the Middle Branch of Union River makes its meandering way through the swampy ground. Looming in the east, eight miles away, is Lead Mountain, a monadnock carved from resistant granite and left standing above the relatively flat plain after the passing of the glacier.

East of the Whalesback the road crosses an area of glaciated flat land dotted by piles of erratic granite boulders, some as large as twenty feet in diameter. The boulders are somewhat rounded but quite solid and unweathered, indicating that they have not been here very long, geologically speaking.

Well before the invention of the airplane Route 9 was called the Airline, no doubt because compared to the coastal route it cut straight from Bangor to Calais. Its name is further justified today because it is used for visual navigation by small aircraft flying across this otherwise trackless land.

A roadcut at the junction with **Route 193** reveals the sandy, well-washed and sorted glacial outwash over which the road is built. Ice blocks left buried in sand by the retreating glacier finally melted, creating the kettle hole lakes that dot the area.

Near **Wesley** the road climbs, reaching a height of land at the junction with Route 192. This higher land occurs over heat-hardened rock in contact with the granite pluton. There are good views from here, a welcome contrast to the forest-walled road of the past few miles. Blueberry barrens stretch across these sandy uplands, and many granite boulders are scattered over the fields. Settlements are more numerous from here eastward.

At **Crawford** another zone of hard contact rocks has preserved a rise in the topography, while at **Farrar Hill** there is a roadcut through rusty, weathering quartzite with pyrite-filled fractures running parallel to the road.

Just before meeting U.S. Route 1 west of **Baring,** the road once again enters granitic terrain. One mile east of the junction, on U.S. Route 1, good exposures on both sides of the road show how granite intruded quartzite. The interesting mosaiclike patterns were made by the molten granite penetrating into the surrounding fractured quartzite.

Route 6, Howland to Topsfield. The highway crosses the Penobscot River at West Enfield and follows the east side of the river to Lincoln, winding over flat, forested land with little to see. Glacial drift lies thick over the land and most of the boulders, brought from the north, are fine-grained metamorphic rocks, schists and quartzites.

East of **Lincoln** the landscape becomes more hilly and more interesting as the road enters granitic terrain, the northern edge of the Downeast Mountain region. There are views to the south of rounded knobs of granite, and boulders of granite are common in the glacial debris. About ¾ mile west of the **Lee** town line, an interesting roadcut exposes medium- to coarse-grained light gray granite in contact with thin-bedded slate and quartzite. For the next mile or so the blue-gray, and very hard, metamorphic rock shows the effects of intense heat and chemical alteration accompanying the intrusion of the granite body hundreds of millions of years ago.

About one mile east of **Springfield,** and from there to **Carroll,** are good views west over the flat, forested, and swampy landscape to rounded hills of granite in the distance. Almost three miles east of the Carroll town line is a fine view northwest to Mount Katahdin. The road continues to follow the northern edge of the Downeast Mountain granite terrain. A few farms and orchards and some open fields are found on this gently rolling upland, but generally the land is only lightly settled.

A picnic area on the shore of **East Musquash Lake** is a good stop. Across the lake is a prominent rounded knob of granite. The same coarse-grained pink granite is exposed in outcrops on the south side of the highway, where it is easy to get a close look. A mile or so farther east the highway joins U.S. Route 1 at Topsfield.

Mountain Uplands

Route 15: Bangor to Dover-Foxcroft. From Bangor to Kenduskeag, Route 15 more or less follows the course of Kenduskeag Stream. At Bangor the stream flows in a steep-walled narrow valley, but upstream from the city the valley is gently rolling to flat, and in places there is a fairly wide floodplain. From the road there are glimpses of wide meandering curves and rapids in some places. North of **Kenduskeag** the road is built on segments of "horsebacks"—narrow, winding eskers scarcely wider than the road in some places, and as much as twenty feet higher than the surrounding low land.

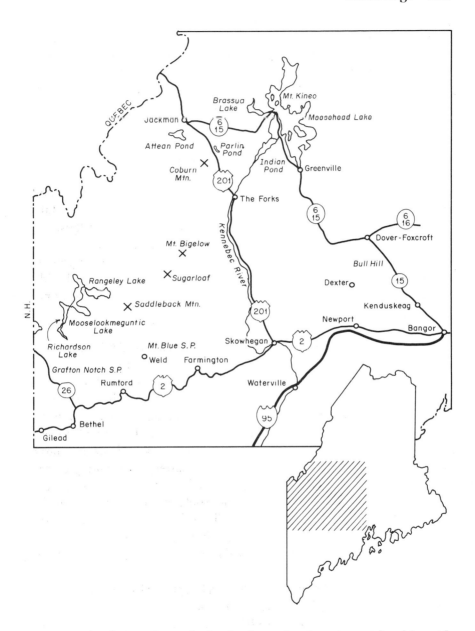

North of East Corinth the highway has been considerably widened and improved. Near the height of land in **Charleston,** the northern edge of the Bangor Basin, roadcuts have exposed steeply dipping beds of metamorphosed sandstones and shales, locally distorted and warped by folding and faulting. Some of these beds are also iron-stained, indicating the presence of pyrite in the slaty rock.

From the top of **Bull Hill,** at the entrance to the Charleston Correctional Facility, there is a fine view northward of the Piscataquis Valley and the Mountain Upland beyond, including a glimpse of Mount Katahdin. Well into May, the snowcapped mountains are a beautiful backdrop to the soft greens of the valley. There is no roadcut on Bull Hill but the next ridge, **Norton Hill,** has a deep cut in nearly vertical phyllite. The microscopic mica particles shimmer with a silky sheen. The northern part of the cut exposes thin-bedded quartzite in a pinstripe of brown and blue-gray layers. The resistant quartzite layer is responsible for the northeast-trending ridges.

Dover-Foxcroft, like most old inland Maine communities, was located at a falls in the river where power could be developed. It developed as a twin city, with separate governments on each side of the river, but today only the name still indicates the original arrangement.

Routes 15 and 6: Dover-Foxcroft to Jackman. At Dover-Foxcroft, Route 15 is joined by Route 6. The combined highway follows the Piscataquis River upstream, heading west to Guilford, and then turns north shortly before entering Abbott Village. The view from the bridge over **Kingsbury Stream** in the village is worth a stop. There is a waterfall here and, not surprisingly, the site of an old mill. Layers of quartzite, up to twelve inches thick and cut by quartz veins, appear flexed like a thick pad of paper. The fold plunges toward the bridge at a steep angle. Hard, polished rock surfaces, called slickensides, reveal where the rocks slipped during earthquakes many millions of years ago. (While these particular faults are long inactive, it is interesting to note that the Dover-Foxcroft area is the locale of infrequent present-day earthquakes, none of them destructive.)

A pronounced change in grade at **Abbott** marks where the road leaves the Central Upland and enters the mountains.

At the south edge of the village of **Monson** the highway cuts through a small rounded outcrop of slate, the cleavage vertical and diagonal to the road. The top of this outcrop has been smoothed by the grinding action of the glacier. Slate has been the basis of an industry at Monson for one hundred years, and it is still quarried east of the village. Most of it is shipped to New York for wider distribution. An abandoned quarry is easily seen from **Bray Road,** a short side-trip from the center of town to the west. The great, square hole is filled with groundwater now, but it is easy to picture how the slate was split off in huge blocks and lifted from the quarry to finishing sheds on the rim. Pieces of waste rock are piled in windrows, which reach into Lake Hebron.

About 3½ miles north of Monson the road makes a pronounced left swing around a large outcrop of slate, providing a good close-up view of the rock. An igneous dike, intermediate in composition between granite and basalt, cuts through the outcrop. From here to **Greenville** the road crosses low, swampy areas separated by fairly large hills with views across the forest. Thin, bouldery till covers most of this area.

Shortly before **Greenville** a roadside rest area offers a stunning view of large mountains to the north and east: Big Squaw, Baker, White Cap, and numerous smaller summits. In another mile or so, from the crest of **Indian Hill** there is a fine view of the southern part of Moosehead Lake with its broad reaches deep blue in the morning sun. Several large islands seem to float just offshore.

Several places in the village of Greenville offer glimpses of Moosehead Lake, and beyond **Greenville Junction** numerous views open up. The level of Moosehead Lake was raised when East and West outlets, a few miles up the road, were dammed to control water flow in the Kennebec River, but Moosehead was already the largest lake in Maine when the dams were built.

The mountains surrounding the southern end of Moosehead Lake are carved from rock in the contact zone of diorite, an intruded igneous rock intermediate between granite and basalt. The hardened contact rock was more resistant to erosion when it was exposed by being uplifted many hundreds of millions of years later. Big Squaw Mountain, west of the lake, and other mountains to the southwest owe their origin to this process.

Where the highway crosses the town line separating **Big Squaw Mountain** and **Little Squaw Mountain** townships there is a cut through the diorite, which here is crumbling in a peculiar nubbly pattern. Where weathering has softened it sufficiently the coarse-grained rock appears at first glance to be made of pebbles and boulders, like a sedimentary conglomerate. On fresh rock faces there is no sign of this weathering pattern, but near the upper part, where the diorite has partially weathered, a fine network of cracks indicates where it will eventually crumble. Beyond this cut are other exposures of the diorite and its peculiar weathering pattern. One is at the entrance to Squaw Mountain Lakefront development.

A side road on the left to **Squaw Mountain Lodge** is marked, and a side trip to view Moosehead Lake from this vantage point is worth the time. Across the lake two prominent rounded peaks, Big and Little Spencer mountains, remarkably similar in shape, dominate the skyline.

The highway follows the west shore of the lake for a number of miles to **Rockwood,** crossing branches of the Kennebec River at East and West outlets on the way. Looming to the northeast of Rockwood is **Mount Kineo,** less than a mile away but on the opposite, or eastern, side of the lake, which at this place pinches down to a narrow passage separating the northern and southern parts. From the village and for another mile or so along the road there are fine views. The mountain, made of resistant rhyolite lava, has a profile common to many Maine mountains: the northern end slopes up gradually to a cliffy south-facing side. The glacier, in its southward flow, rode up over the mountain, smoothing the upstream side but plucked rock away the opposite side, leaving steep cliffs.

Highways 6 and 15 leave Moosehead Lake and follow the Moose River upstream for a couple of miles. To the south (left) is Blue Ridge, named for the color of the rock, the same hard rhyolite rock of Mount Kineo.

About three miles from Moosehead Lake the highway makes a sharp left turn and then a right, dropping down through a cut in the rock. The Kineo rhyolite is so dense that weathering has little softening effect on it, and it shatters to a flinty broken surface showing tiny sparkling flecks against a bluish-gray background. These are minerals stopped in the process of crystallization by sudden cooling.

The highway skirts the edge of an arm of Brassua Lake before crossing the railroad. About five miles west of the railroad crossing, the highway cuts through one more exposure of the Kineo rhyolite. Beyond this the road follows the Moose River upstream, with little to be seen other than forest and occasional glimpses of Long Pond. The area is covered with a layer of glacial till. Routes 6 and 15 join U.S. 201 on the southern edge of Jackman.

U.S. Route 2: Skowhegan to New Hampshire. U.S. Route 2 approaches **Skowhegan** from the east along the edge of the Kennebec River. Just east of the city is the Great Eddy, a formidable whirlpool during high water, where the river pours out of a narrow gorge and makes a sharp right turn. The gorge is cut through thin-bedded slates and quartzites and can be seen from the parking lot of the Municipal Building. Upstream the river splits around an island, and here the city of Skowhegan was developed. Before the present dams were built there were two waterfalls at this location. Indians must have speared salmon here; the name Skowhegan means "fish-watching place." The highway now crosses the river via the island, and both dams are visible.

West of the town of **Norridgewock** pastures and fields accentuate the hummocky nature of the land, due to the glacial debris deposited in irregular mounds as the ice melted away.

A little east of the town of **New Sharon** the highway enters the floodplain of the well-named Sandy River. The river meanders widely in its floodplain of sand and minor amounts of gravel. Across the flat land there are glimpses of the mountains to the north and west.

At **East Wilton** the landscape becomes abruptly more hilly, the streams smaller, more rocky, and narrow; obviously this is the edge of the Mountain Upland. Roadcuts expose schist and gneiss, the principal rock type of the Mountain Upland.

The highway crosses into the valley of the Androscoggin River at **Dixfield.** This river lies in a narrow but flat-bottomed valley, which confines its meanders. Ahead lies the huge Boise Cascade paper mill at Rumford, located at the site of former falls now dammed for power.

At **Rumford** the highway climbs the side of the narrow gorge of the Androscoggin, gaining 175 feet of elevation. Upstream to the west, the river once again is found meandering in a flat-bottomed (though wider) valley. At Rumford Point a wide swing in both the river and the highway affords a fine view of the floodplain. The sandy soil through which the river is flowing is exposed in stream banks in a few places. From here to Newry there are a few roadcuts exposing gray mica schist. Pegmatite and quartz veins increase in abundance as you go west.

At **Newry,** Route 26 leaves to the right (north) to Grafton Notch State Park. (This is a side trip well worth taking for its interesting alpine geologic features. See the separate road log below for this stretch of Route 26.)

From Newry to **Bethel** the valley becomes narrower. The Androscoggin valley upstream from Bethel is scarcely wider than the river, and the highway steadily climbs westward. There are good views, especially to the north, of rugged, steep mountains with many bare cliffs but rounded tops. The highway leaves Maine in scenic mountain country.

Route 26: Newry to Grafton Notch. Route 26 leaves U.S. Highway 2 at Newry and follows the Bear River upstream. The river has developed small, flat bottomlands separated from each other by short sections of steep and rocky streambed. In New England these flat lands are called intervales and are the only farmable land in the mountains. There are numerous roadcuts through mica schist along the highway, and beyond **North Newry** pegmatite veins are common, the coarse-grained minerals visible even from the car.

At the lower end of one of the intervales a sign marks the south boundary of **Grafton Notch State Park.** The upper end of the intervale is closed off by one of the more interesting of Maine's natural features: **Screw Auger Falls.** Here the Bear River has followed joints and fractures in solid granite bedrock, cutting a very narrow, twisting gorge. The stream tumbles down granite steps in short waterfalls, and the swirling water with its load of sand has sculpted and smoothed the sides of the gorge in half-round cusps and vaults. The medium-grained black-and-white granite is washed clean in the stream bed and displays some interesting patterns of crystallization.

Mother Walker Falls and **Moose Cave,** farther up the valley, have a similar origin. The latter is a very narrow defile partly cut through and around large talus boulders that have slid from the steep cliffs above. Frost action has broken out a huge slab that has slipped down a few feet to completely cover part of the gorge where it is only three or four feet wide, forming the "cave."

From Moose Cave the valley turns north and narrows. It is evident that a valley glacier squeezed through this constriction, carving a deep canyon between the buttresslike shoulders on each side. The solid rock sides are steep, rounded, and bare—good evidence of glacial action.

Hiking trails leave from a parking lot in **Grafton Notch.** To the west, trails ascend to Old Speck and to the Eyebrow, a glowering cliff made by the spalling of arcuate slabs of granite, leaving behind an eye-shaped scar on the mountainside. From below this is a formidable cliff, and the trails up this side of the notch are among the steepest in Maine. The reason is that the glacier, cutting deep into the valley, carved the main channel much deeper than the side, or tributary, valleys.

From the **Spruce Meadow Picnic Area,** at the upper end of the park, there are good views down the notch, the U-shaped profile carved by the glacier being quite evident.

U.S. Route 201: Skowhegan to Jackman. Running north from Skowhegan U.S. Route 201 cuts across a wide swing of the Kennebec River. It rejoins the Kennebec at **Solon.** The land is rolling and hummocky due to underlying glacial deposits. Mountains appear on the skyline to the north. Near Solon are roadcut exposures of sand, deposited on the floor of some vanished lake formed by the wasting glacier. After the lake had dried up, wind heaped the sand into dunes, eventually fixed in place by encroaching vegetation. At Solon the highway joins the Kennebec River, which it follows upstream closely for thirty miles. At **Bingham** the valley narrows conspicuously. Swift-running Austin Stream, entering the Kennebec from the east, is capable at high water of spreading sizable boulders, and it has been channeled to protect the town of Bingham.

Wyman Dam was built at **Moscow** to generate electric power, and Wyman Lake stretches ten miles to the north. The highway follows the edge of the lake and provides some fine scenic and historic roadside stops, which are worth taking the time to visit. The public landing for the town of Moscow offers a good view of the lake. A level line visible across the lake marks the elevation of an older, higher floodplain on which a road and houses have been built.

Construction of the highway required some large cuts in the cliffs, which now expose rusty, weathering, thin-bedded quartzites and phyllites, slaty rocks in vertical layers. About eight miles north of Moscow the valley becomes very narrow as the river squeezes past Henhawk Ledge on the west side of the river, almost at the head of Wyman Lake.

A roadcut on Route 201 above Wyman Lake exposes vertical bedded rocks.

The Forks is the confluence of the Kennebec and Dead rivers. The town is built on a floodplain of boulders and cobbles well exposed in the banks and easily seen from the bridge over the Kennebec.

A side road, paved and well-traveled, leaves the highway on the right at the bridge and follows the Kennebec upstream. A trip up this road to visit Moxie Falls is rewarding. About two miles east on this road is a side road to the left marked **Moxie Falls Park.** A short walk brings you to one of the finest waterfalls in Maine. It is notable for its free fall of more than sixty feet, plus a long cascade upstream above the main falls. The bedrock in the stream shows some interesting small-scale folding.

From The Forks the highway climbs steadily, offering views of Johnson and Coburn mountains looming to the northwest. These mountains are formed from a very resistant volcanic rock called rhyolite, similar in composition to granite.

Parlin Pond, at an elevation of about 1600 feet, is at the height of land for this highway and is a landmark that will alert you to a spectacular view coming up in about five miles.

A roadside rest, cut from the hill on the right-hand side, provides a fine view of **Attean Pond** and its many islands. The pond is in a large basin weathered out of a pinkish, coarse-grained granite. The Attean granite is older than most granites in Maine, emplaced during the earliest rumblings of the construction of the Appalachian Mountains, more than 430 million years ago. There are outcrops of this granite at the roadside rest.

The highway descends to the village of Jackman, an important center for northwestern Maine. About 6½ miles north of Jackman there is a Roadside Rest at Little Falls. From here the road starts its climb over the Boundary Mountains to the Canadian line.

11
Sites to See

Here are listed, with short descriptions, some notable landscape and geological sites in each physical region of Maine. A large number of them are used as illustrative examples in the text. Most are accessible by car and many can be seen from the car window, but some require a short walk.

The list is by no means exhaustive; one could hardly hope to list all the mountains, all the splendid waterfalls and gorges, the spectacular coastal exposures, the wide vistas to be seen in the state. Many more can be found on maps in atlases and guidebooks. What follows is merely a sample, some of the writer's favorite sites.

Southwest Coast

Mount Agamenticus, the highest point in York County, can be reached by taking Cat Mountain Road from Cape Neddick village. At the end, a good hardtop road ascends the mountain, where a fire tower and numerous communications antennas, plus an abandoned ski lift, clutter the top. Nevertheless, the 360-degree view is well worth the trip. The deep blue of the ocean off Cape Neddick in striking contrast to the white beach of Ogunquit makes a stunning sight to the east and north, while on the western horizon you can see the White Mountains of New Hampshire. Mount Agamenticus is made of pinkish, coarse-grained granite weathered light gray to almost white. It was rounded by the glacier, and you can find long, parallel scratches on bedrock knobs. This granite mass, nearly circular and six miles in diameter, is related to the White Mountain

(New Hampshire) granites, which were emplaced later than most granites in Maine, probably about 200 million years ago. Mount Agamenticus was an offshore island when the rising sea invaded the depressed land during the retreat of the continental ice sheet 12,000 years ago.

Cape Neddick is a large promontory south of **York Beach,** and a public park on the tip of the cape makes it readily accessible. The cape and its tiny companion island, **The Nubble,** location of a picturesque lighthouse, are made of gabbro, a coarse-grained igneous rock of the basalt family. The Cape Neddick gabbro mass is circular on the exposed surface, and being more resistant to the battering of the sea than is the surrounding rock, the cape stands out from the shoreline as a more or less circular promontory.

Israels Head juts out south of Ogunquit and offers an unobstructed view of the ocean. From here, the **Marginal Way,** a footpath to Perkins Cove, provides an unusual chance to walk along a high sea cliff. The bedrock is steep, thin-bedded quartzites interlayered with phyllite and fine-grained schist more than 400 million years old. In many places basaltic dikes cut through, their weathered surfaces a rich chocolate brown. This is a good place, especially in stormy weather, to watch the power of waves surging into the cracks and crevices in the cliffs, gradually tearing the headland apart. To the north is the long white sweep of Ogunquit beach.

The long stretch of beach, a barrier spit, from **Ogunquit** to **Moody,** is partly reinforced with rock riprap and to some extent artificial, but the development of dunes is restoring a natural look. Public access is provided by a bridge at Ogunquit Beach, by the Footbridge (no cars) about one mile north of the town beach, and at the south end of the road in Moody Beach (opposite the water treatment plant). In **Wells** the beach is accessible via public walkways about every block. (The beaches are described in some detail in Chapter 3.) Between Moody and Wells most of the natural beach has been altered by construction of roads and densely packed seasonal homes.

At **Biddeford Pool** a ragged point of rocks juts out into the ocean. The name "pool" comes from a nearly enclosed tidal basin formed to the north by the sand spit of **Hills Beach** and the tombolo of sand connecting the rock with the mainland. The pool is very shallow, virtually drained at low tide. Located on the extreme end of the rocky point, the **East Point Sanctuary** is open to the public. This is an excellent place to study the geology of the area because the ocean has uncovered a wide expanse of the metamorphic bedrock. Here you can see folds and faults in the contorted layers, and invading basaltic and granitic dikes, all displayed in three dimensions.

Two Lights State Park, not far from Portland on **Cape Elizabeth,** is a fine place to examine the bedrock geology of the southwestern coast. Here, as at Biddeford Pool, rocky cliffs are being torn apart by storm waves, exposing folds and faults in three dimensions. These rocks, though older than those exposed at Biddeford Pool and Israels Head to the south, are similar metamorphic quartzites and schists cut through in some places with basaltic dikes. An excellent semitechnical publication (Maine Geologic Survey Bulletin 26, 1982) describes the geology here and at nearby Crescent Beach State Park.

Midcoast

Popham Beach State Park is the largest stretch of sand beach in the Midcoast. Dunes separating the road from the wide, gently sloping beach are protected in this vulnerable environment by boardwalks. **Fox Island,** a knob of granite just offshore, is connected to the beach by a tombolo of sand. Note that this sand is reddish in comparison to the sands of Old Orchard and Ogunquit farther southwest. The color of this sand, brought to the coast by the Kennebec River just to the east, is due to a larger percentage of weathered rock and mineral fragments. The ocean waves have only begun their work of grinding and winnowing away the softer minerals.

Damariscotta Reversing Falls is an interesting sight during the change of the tide. The waters of the Damariscotta River are forced to flow upstream into **Salt Bay** by the flooding tide, and the falls reverse when the tide ebbs. There are numerous reversing falls on the Maine coast, and this is an easy one to observe.

Pemaquid Point is typical of dozens of rocky tips in this region of long, narrow peninsulas and bays. At the very end of the point, large sausagelike stringers of coarse granite and pegmatite in folded black schists and quartzites are being dissected by the sea. On the west side the ocean has cut into soft layers, making narrow grooves in the tightly folded rocks. Boulders rolled back and forth in these grooves by waves are rounded into nearly perfect spheres.

Mount Battie, in **Camden Hills State Park,** is easily ascended by car on a park road and presents a stunning view of Camden Harbor and Penobscot Bay. Mount Battie is a knob of metamorphosed conglomerate, a former bed of sand, stones, and gravel up to six inches in diameter.

Mount Megunticook, the mountain of which Mount Battie is really a shoulder, can be climbed by the Tablelands Trail from the auto road. The south face of Megunticook is nearly vertical, with a talus slope of rocks pried loose by frost working in the joints and crevices of the hard quartzite rock.

The Blue Hill peninsula and Deer Isle separate the Midcoast from the Downeast coast. One of the finest views on the entire coast is from **Caterpillar Hill,** a mile or so north of Sargentville on Route 15. To the west, the Camden Hills form a backdrop for the upper part of Penobscot Bay. Spread before you straight south is Deer Isle; you can see the connecting suspension bridge, but it looks tiny from here. To the east is the open water of Blue Hill Bay and beyond loom Mount Cadillac and other rounded summits of Acadia National Park.

Downeast Coast

Mount Desert Island and **Acadia National Park** have been described in Chapter 3. **Mount Cadillac,** highest point on the East Coast, presents a stunning view of the ocean, the offshore islands, and the Downeast coast. A trip around the **Park Loop Road** offers an overall view of the park and some coastal vistas that are unmatched anywhere.

Grindstone Point, on the east side of Frenchman Bay near Winter Harbor, is open to the public. From here there is a fine view to the west, between forested islands, of Cadillac and other mountains across the bay. The bedrock here is coarse-grained red granite laced with basalt dikes.

Most of **Schoodic Point** is within Acadia National Park boundaries. An outstanding feature here, as at Grindstone Point, is the prevalence of dark green to black basalt dikes cutting through the coarse-grained red granite.

Great Wass Island, south of Jonesport, although accessible by road and open to the public, is largely kept as a natural preserve by the Nature Conservancy. It presents an unusual opportunity to explore an unspoiled granite island coast, with sandy pocket beaches separated by rounded knobs and prominences. The interior is a wild setting of jack pine and heath bogs.

West Quoddy Head State Park, the easternmost point in Maine, provides hiking trails along the top of high gabbro cliffs. **Gulliver's Hole** is a cleft in the rock that follows a fault zone. Several pebbly pocket beaches lie between rocky points.

Red Beach Cove, about eight miles south of Calais, is interesting for the coarse red sand made up largely of red feldspar particles. There is a National Historic Monument here marking St. Croix Island and its early history.

Central Upland

Thin soil covers most of the slaty ridges, long northeast-trending folds protruding above the general landscape, but a large dome of granite underlies **Sebago Lake,** notable for its sandy beaches.

"Fossil" sand dunes can be seen at **Desert of Maine,** a commercial attraction near Freeport. In the vicinity of **Wayne,** on Route 133, you can pick out dune shapes, especially where the wind has created "blowouts," or scars, in the sandy hills. Between and surrounding these towns a vast amount of sand is exposed in road banks.

The Kennebec River foams out of a steep gorge at **Skowhegan** and into a wide, swirling pool before making a right turn and resuming its southeastward path. The pool, known as **Great Eddy,** is an impressive whirlpool at high water and is easily seen from U.S. Route 2 just east of the city.

North Anson Gorge is another fine place to watch the interplay of rocks and water, although the sides of the gorge are not steep or especially high. Here the Carrabassett River cascades in a winding path over folded slates, forming several small falls and some rocky islands. The gorge is easily viewed from the bridge of highway U.S. Route 201A, and from Maine Route 16.

A prominent esker, **The Whalesback,** stretches southeast from Aurora on Route 9. This esker is high and the highway is provided with scenic turnouts so you can get an unhurried look eastward across the bog and its meandering stream to Lead Mountain. In places where gravel has been removed you can see the inner structure of the esker: well-washed sand and gravel with a wide variety of rounded rocks. This landscape has changed little from the swampy, gravel-strewn land left when the great ice sheet melted away.

On Route 15, **Bull Hill,** a prominent ridge within the Central Upland in Charleston is the rim of the Bangor Basin. From here you can see mountains on the skyline to the northwest, marking the northwest limit of the Central Upland. To the southeast, the low, rounded ridge of the Dixmont Hills bound the opposite side. Bull Hill is held up by resistant sandstone beds tilted to a steep angle, but you must drive north to the next ridge, **Norton Hill,** to find an exposure of these rocks. The **Piscataquis Valley** is to the north. Clay under the valley soil contains fossil sea shells, showing that when the glacial ice cover melted away, the sea flooded this far inland.

Grindstone Falls, about nine miles north of Medway on Route 11, is formed by the East Branch of the Penobscot River where it encounters vertical slates and other metamorphic rocks striking across its path and makes a sharp right turn. One or two small vertical drops are followed by several hundred yards of rapids downstream. There is a roadside rest area here.

A magnificent view of Mount Katahdin and other peaks in that range is presented looking west from **Ash Hill,** three miles south of Patten on Route 11. The skyline extends, smooth and rolling, from the sharp peak of Pamola to The Traveler at the northern end of the main mass. North of Patten is the pointed top of **Mount Chase.** To the east is the broad expanse of **Crystal,** or **Thousand Acre Bog,** a Nature Conservancy preserve.

From **Weston,** four miles north of Danforth on U.S. Route 1, the "Million-Dollar View" looks toward the rolling farm country of Canada across **East Grand Lake,** one of the Chiputneticook Lakes.

Aroostook County is almost a different land from the rest of Maine. Farms are large and the views are wide and long. The ride north from Houlton to Van Buren on a fine day is memorable for its general openness, a relief from the unending, enclosing forestland of the Downeast Mountain Region. It is punctuated with a steady view of steep and sharp **Mars Hill,** ahead to the north a number of miles. Eventually, as you approach Presque Isle, the view gives way on the west to glimpses of Quaggy Joe Mountain and Haystack Mountain, carved by erosion from rhyolitic lava flows some 375 million years old.

Mountain Uplands

Baxter State Park: Crisscrossed by numerous trails, **Mount Katahdin** is one of the premier mountain hiking sites of New England. There are other mountains within the park too, and all of them are rewarding climbs. In addition, a good gravel road runs from the southern gate at Togue Pond, around the west side between **Doubletop** and the main granite mountain massif, to Sourdnahunk Field campground. Views of the slide-scarred sides of Katahdin and Doubletop and the cascading waterfalls at **Ledge Falls** make this a rewarding drive. The road continues around the northern edge of the range to Trout Brook, then easterly to the northern gate at Grand Lake Mattagamon at the foot of beautiful cliffs of hard rhyolite on **Horse Mountain.** A short side trip to **Lower South Branch Pond** campground is rewarded with a fine view of the pond framed by birches, and beyond to **Pinnacle Ridge** jutting out from The Traveler.

Ripogenus Gorge: The name Ripogenus is surely unique to Maine. It is applied to a lake, a dam and a gorge, all of them near the southwest corner of Baxter State Park. The dam includes a chute once used for sluicing logs through the gorge. The two-mile-long gorge was cut by the West Branch of the Penobscot River between cliffs nearly two hundred feet high in some places. A road to the power plant, a mile or so down from the dam, is marked "Visitors Welcome," and it is a short walk to a view of the gorge from above, where the river passes through pink coarse-grained granite. The **Telos Road,** two miles below Ripogenus Dam, crosses the river and offers a fine point from which to see white water boiling between pink boulders and ledges and pouring into the Cribworks rapids just downstream. Two and a half miles below the bridge the river makes a 90-degree left turn and leaves the road. A short walk from here brings you to **Big Ambejackmockamus Falls,** one of the prettiest in Maine.

Mount Kineo is the vertical south-facing cliff and rounded peak of rhyolite lava that pinches Moosehead Lake into a narrow strait at **Rockwood.** There are good views of it from either direction on Routes 6-15.

Big Wilson Stream crosses the Elliotsville Road about seven miles northeast of Monson. The stream is wide and there are numerous minor falls and swimming holes. It is a good stop on the way to or from **Boarstone Mountain,** a sharp peak on the southeastern edge of the Mountain Upland, where an easy climb from the west offers a fine view of Lake Onawa and the surrounding mountains.

Moxie Falls is one of the highest in Maine and is easily visited because it is in a town park two and a half miles east of The Forks in Somerset County. Moxie Stream approaches the Kennebec River in a series of cascades over folded metamorphic rock. The final pitch is a thunderous spray-filled roar over a vertical drop of about sixty feet.

Smalls Falls, on Route 4 about ten miles northwest of Phillips, is really two sets of falls, one on Sandy River and the other on Chandler Mill Stream. Colorful sculptured cliffs, stained yellow and orange, guide the stream into numerous vertical falls and steep cascades. There is a picnic area here.

From the floor of **Carrabassett Valley** near Sugarloaf there are fine views to the north of Bigelow and Little Bigelow mountains. This is one of the few places in Maine where *glacial cirques* can be viewed from a road; two can be seen to the west on the slopes of **Crocker Mountain.** From **Eustis Ridge,** a mile or so south of the village of Eustis, there is a fine view of Mount Bigelow.

Mount Blue State Park: Stunning views of mountain scenery are easily available by car in this state park in the heart of the western mountains. From a scenic turnout on Center Hill Road, just over one mile northeast of the village of Weld, you look across Webb Lake, set in a basin ringed by mountains. To the north and northwest the **Tumbledown Range** makes a rugged skyline, ending at **Tumbledown Cliffs** silhouetted against more mountains beyond. A picnic area on the flank of Center Hill, further up the road, is higher and offers a scenic trail with more wide views. The two-hour hike to the top of **Mount Blue** is rewarded by a fine 360-degree view of mountain scenery from the tower.

The **Height of Land,** on Route 17 about twenty-four miles north of Mexico, offers a vista of mountain scenery that is unsurpassed in the state. To the southwest are the high summits traversed by the Appalachian Trail—Bemis, Elephant, and Old Blue—while before you to the north is the wide expanse of Mooselookmeguntic Lake. About four miles further north is a similar view over Rangeley Lake.

Rumford Falls is almost completely covered with two electric power dams and other development, but it is not hard to discern that at this point the Androscoggin River makes a pronounced change in elevation—175 feet to be exact. Parts of the original narrow chasm can be seen. There is no better place to visualize the relationship between geology and industrial power development than from the power house at the top of the falls, looking down to the huge Boise Cascade paper mill. West of the falls the river is relatively tranquil as it follows a meandering path through a broad, flat-bottomed valley.

Grafton Notch State Park, about sixteen miles north of Bethel, encompasses an alpine glacial valley and several fine waterfalls. Looking south from the picnic area in the upper part of the valley, you see the typical U-shaped profile and steep, scoured shoulders of a valley once occupied by a glacier. **The Eyebrow** is a prominent cliff on the west side where the main valley makes a pronounced turn. **Mother Walker Falls** and **Screw Auger Falls** are known for their deep potholes and curving, scalloped chasm walls carved by swirling, gravel-laden water.

Snow Falls Gorge, about two miles south of West Paris on Route 26, was the site of a mill built to take advantage of the drop of the Little Androscoggin River through a narrow channel in granite. The water has ground out interesting potholes and swirls in the rock.

Jockey Cap, a granite knob rising a couple of hundred feet above the surroundings near Fryeburg, provides a 360-degree view of peaks in western Maine and eastern New Hampshire. On top is a very interesting monument to Robert Peary, discoverer of the North Pole: a granite pedestal capped with a bronze model of the skyline. A sighting device enables you to identify all the prominent peaks.

Bibliography

The following publications were consulted in writing this book and are suggested for further reading.

Books
Blakemore, Jean. *We Walk on Jewels*. Rockland, Me.: Courier of Maine Books, 1976.

Bloom, Arthur L. *The Geology of Sebago Lake State Park* (State Park Series #1). Augusta: Maine Geological Survey, 1959.

Caldwell, Dabney W. *The Geology of Baxter State Park and Mount Katahdin* (State Park Series #2). Augusta: Maine Geological Survey, 1960.

Caswell, Bradford W. *Ground Water Handbook for the State of Maine*. Augusta: Maine Geological Survey, 1979.

Chapman, Carleton A. *The Geology of Acadia National Park*. N.Y.: Chatham Press (Viking), 1970.

Deis, Robert, ed. *The Geology of Maine's Coastline*. Augusta: Maine Geological Survey, 1983.

Hussey, Arthur M., II. *The Geology of Two Lights and Crescent Beach State Parks Area, Cape Elizabeth, Maine*, Bulletin 26. Augusta: Maine Geological Survey, 1982.

Monegain, Bernie. *Natural Sites*. Freeport, Me.: DeLorme Publishing Co., 1983.

Pankiwskyj, Kost A. *The Geology of Mount Blue State Park* (State Park Geologic Series #3). Augusta: Maine Geological Survey, 1965.

Thompson, Woodrow B. *Surficial Geology Handbook for Coastal Maine*. Augusta: Maine Geological Survey, 1979.

Maps
Maine Atlas and Gazetteer. Freeport, Me.: DeLorme Publishing Co., 1985.

Osberg, Philip A., Arthur M. Hussey, II, and Gary M. Boone, eds. *Bedrock Geologic Map of Maine*, Augusta: Maine Geological Survey, 1985.

Thompson, Woodrow B., and Harold W. Borns, Jr., eds. *Surficial Geologic Map of Maine*. Augusta: Maine Geological Survey, 1985.

State of Maine, 1:500,000, shaded relief map. Washington, D.C.: U.S.G.S., Dept of Interior, 1973.

The following additional publications also were consulted in writing this book.

From the Maine Critical Areas Program, State Planning Office, Augusta, planning reports as follows:

No. 37: Hussey, Arthur M., II. *Significant Geologic Localities in the Casco Bay Group, Southern Maine*. 1977.

No. 53: Borns, Harold W., Jr. *Emerged Glaciomarine Deltas in Maine*. 1981.

No. 56: Hussey, Arthur M., II. *Significant Geologic Localities in the York County Coastal Zone*. 1978.

No. 60: Brewer, Thomas. *Waterfalls in Maine*. 1978.

No. 64: Brewer, Thomas. *Gorges in Maine*. 1978.

No. 67: Borns, Harold W., Jr. *Eskers in Maine*. 1979.

Ackert, Robert P., Jr. *A quantitative study of an end moraine at Roque Bluffs, Maine*. Maine Geology Bulletin No. 2. Geological Society of Maine, Inc., 1982.

Caldwell, D.W. *Guidebook for Field Trips in the Mount Katahdin Region*. New England Intercollegiate Geological Conference, 1966.

Denny, Charles S. *Geomorphology of New England*, Professional Paper 1208. Washington, D.C.: United States Geological Survey, 1982.

Gates, Olcott. *The Silurian–Lower Devonian volcanic rocks of the Machias-Eastport area, Maine*, Maine Geology Bulletin No. 3. Geological Society of Maine, Inc., 1983.

Nelson, Bruce W., and L. Kenneth Fink. *Geological and Botanical Features of Sand Beach Systems in Maine*. Maine Sea Grant Publications, Bulletin 14.

Toppan, Frederick W. "The physiography of Maine." *Journal of Geology*, 43 (1935): 76–87.

Glossary

The authority for most of these terms is *Glossary of Geology*, Robert L. Bates and Julia A. Jackson, eds., published by the American Geological Institute, Falls Church, Va., 1980, although I have paraphrased many of the technical definitions.

absolute age—The geologic age of a rock or geologic event in units of time, usually years. Does not imply certainty; two radiometric ages calculated for the same pluton could differ by many millions of years.

anticline—An arch or tent-shaped fold in crustal beds, enclosing older rocks. Dimensions may be in feet or miles. Sides may be steep or very gentle.

anticlinorium—An anticline, regional in extent, that may contain numerous lesser folds, both anticlines and synclines.

aquifer—A layer or zone in unconsolidated materials or heavily fractured rock that contains and conducts significant quantities of water.

backdune—The area on the landward side of sand dunes and including the gently sloping backs of the dunes.

backshore—The upper, benchlike portion of the beach in front (seaward) of the dunes, above high water and covered only during storms or exceptionally high tides.

barrier spit—A sandbar with one end connected to the shore. It is built by longshore currents depositing sand out into a bay, cutting off access to the ocean.

basalt—Dark green to black, fine-grained igneous rock, high in magnesium and iron. Common in dikes and lava flows. Also called "traprock."

bedrock—Solid rock of the crust, underlying soil and other unconsolidated material. Often called "ledge."

cirque—Half-bowl shaped, steep-walled cut high on the mountainside at the head of a glacially carved valley. Locally called a "basin."

core—The central nucleus of the Earth, about 1800 miles below the surface. Also, a cylinder of rock obtained by drilling with a special hollow bit that retrieves a sample of the rock through which it is drilling.

crust—The outermost layer of the earth, four to six miles thick under the oceans and up to sixty miles thick under the continents.

crystal—A solid with a definite chemical composition and a unique repeating arrangement of its atoms, which may be revealed by flat faces. **Crystalline** rocks are those in which minerals formed from hot solutions and are visible to the unaided eye.

dike—A thin slab of igneous rock that, when molten, was intruded along a crack or fault cutting across other rocks.

drumlin—A smooth, elongated hill of compact glacial till, its long axis parallel to the direction the ice moved. The blunter end faces the direction from which the ice approached; the downstream end tapers off gradually.

erratic—A rock carried and then deposited by the glacier some distance from the outcrop of bedrock from which it was derived.

erosion—The removal and transport of soft rock, sand, soil, and the products of weathering.

esker—A long, narrow, steep-sided ridge of sand and gravel deposited by meltwater flowing in an ice tunnel under a glacier and left behind when the glacier melted away. Often called a "horseback" in Maine.

estuary—The bay where a river meets tidewater.

exfoliation—The process by which concentric shells of weathered rock are spalled, or stripped away, from the fresh rock. Occurs on any scale from hand specimen to mountainsides, generally as the result of physical stresses produced by weathering of minerals.

fault—A fracture in rock along which there was movement, as shown by displaced rock units on opposite sides of the break.

fjord—A glacial trough valley now flooded with seawater to create a steep-walled inlet. Somes Sound on Mount Desert Island is Maine's only fjord.

floodplain—Flat land adjacent to a stream, built of alluvium deposited by the stream during flood stage.

foliated—Rock in which flattened and platy minerals are lined up and arranged like leaves, giving it a distinct grain.

foreshore—The lower, seaward-sloping portion of a beach; the zone between normal high and low tide levels.

gabbro—An igneous, plutonic rock of the basalt family. Generally dark colored and medium- to coarse-grained, with a high iron and magnesium content.

gneiss—A foliated metamorphic rock with alternating bands of light, granular minerals and dark platy minerals, indicating a high level of metamorphism.

gorge—A narrow valley with steep rocky walls, often occupied by a cascading stream.

granite—A plutonic igneous rock, generally light in color (gray to white and shades of pink to red) with visible grains of quartz, feldspar, and mica.

groundwater—Subsurface water held in saturated unconsolidated rock materials and in fractured bedrock.

half-life—The time required for a radioactive substance to lose half its radioactivity by the "decay" of one-half its radioactive atoms.

headland—A rocky promontory jutting out from the coast, usually with steep cliff faces.

horseback—*See* esker.

hydrolysis—A chemical reaction involving water; important in the weathering of silicate minerals like feldspar.

igneous—A rock or mineral that crystallized from a molten or partly molten source material, i.e. magma. From Latin *ignis*, for fire. One of the three main classes into which rocks are classified, the others being sedimentary and metamorphic.

joint—A planar break or parting in a rock along which there has been no displacement. Joints usually ocur in *sets*, or groups of parallel breaks, and frequently separate sets intersect at a distinct angle.

lava—Molten (or hardened) igneous rock that has extruded onto the surface.

longshore current—A current in the ocean close to and parallel with the shore. Caused by surf striking the beach at an angle.

magma—Molten, mobile rock within the earth from which igneous rocks crystallize.

mantle—The layer of the earth between the crust and core.

massif—A topographic mass of rock more resistant or rigid than its surroundings, frequently (as in Chain Lakes Massif) formed during an earlier orogeny.

meander—One of a series of curves, bends, and loops developed by a stream flowing from side to side across its floodplain.

metamorphic—A rock derived from a preexisting rock by mineralogic or textural changes, essentially in the solid state, in response to marked changes in temperature, pressure, or chemical environment deep inside the earth.

mineral—A naturally occuring element or compound having a definite composition and physical properties and an orderly atomic structure.

moraine—A ridge, mound, or other landform of unsorted and unstratified glacial drift, predominantly till, deposited by the direct action of glacial ice.

ore—A natural deposit from which a mineral of economic value can be mined at a profit.

orogeny—The process—including folding, faulting, and thrusting—by which the underlying structures in fold-belt mountains are formed. Also, the period during which these processes acted, e.g., the Acadian Orogeny in Maine. (The development of "mountain topography," on the other hand, is the result of erosion.)

outcrop—An exposure of bedrock projecting above unconsolidated surficial material.

overburden—Loose, unconsolidated sediment overlying bedrock. Also, barren rock material overlying a mineral deposit.

oxbow—A tightly looping meander in which the stream channel is nearly closed back on itself. Eventually it may be cut off to form an **oxbow lake.**

phyllite—A metamorphic rock intermediate between slate and schist, often characterized by a silky sheen.

pillow lava—Volcanic rock structure formed by lava (usually basalt) flowing into water and forming pillow-shaped blobs that tuck together in closely nestled yet distinct masses as it cools.

plate tectonics—A concept dealing with global-sized slabs (plates) of Earth's crust, and their motions and interactions in forming continents and ocean basins.

plateau—A flat, upland region underlain by horizontal or very gently dipping rock layers.

pluton—A large body of igneous, crystalline rock that cooled at great depth and was subsequently exposed at the earth's surface by uplift and erosion of the overlying cover.

radioactive isotope—An atom that, unlike most atoms of a particular element, has the capacity to emit nuclear particles and radio-energy.

relative age—The geologic age of a rock or fossil or event defined relative to the age of other similar objects or events, rather than in terms of years.

remanent magnetism—Magnetization preserved in rocks. Generally refers to the orientation of magnetic minerals to the contemporary magnetic field of the earth during deposition of the rocks.

rhyolite—Fine-grained volcanic rock of the same general composition as granite.

schist—A well foliated metamorphic rock in which more than 50 percent of the platy minerals (especially mica) are aligned parallel, allowing splitting of the rock into thin slabs. It is coarser grained than slate or phyllite; minerals are readily seen.

sedimentary—Rock formed by compacting and cementing loose sediment, i.e., fragments of other rocks. Characterized by layers deposited by wind or water.

sheeting—In igneous rocks, jointing more or less parallel to the rock surface, produced by the release of internal pressure and sometimes giving the appearance of stratification.

slate—Dense, fine-grained metamorphic rock that can be cleaved into thin slabs. Derived from shale.

slickenside—A hard, polished, striated fault plane created by the friction of sliding blocks of rock.

spit—A small point of sand deposited by longshore currents, having one end anchored to the land but projecting out into deeper water.

subduction—The process by which one crustal plate descends beneath another. Subduction zones commonly border continents where ocean crust is forced down into the mantle.

surficial—Unconsolidated alluvial or glacial deposits overlying bedrock.

syncline—A sag or downfold in crustal rocks enclosing younger rocks. Dimensions may be in feet or miles. The slope of the limbs may be very gentle to nearly vertical.

synclinorium—A syncline of regional extent that is a composite of lesser folds, both anticlines and synclines.

talus—A sloping mass of angular fragments of any size beneath a rock cliff.

tarn—A small lake occupying a cirque, or ice-gouged basin, in a glaciated mountain.

texture—The relative grain size of minerals in rocks: fine, medium, coarse, etc.

thrust fault—A fault dipping into the earth at a low angle where an upper block of older, deeper rocks has been slid, or thrust, over younger rocks.

till—A heterogenous, unconsolidated mixture of clay, sand, pebbles, boulders, and rock debris of all descriptions deposited by and underneath a glacier without sorting and reworking by meltwater.

tombolo—A sandbar that connects an island with another island or the mainland.

weathering—A destructive process by which earth materials are altered in strength, composition, and color by atmospheric agents, primarily water. Weathering may proceed beneath the surface, especially along cracks and fissures in rock. (*Erosion* implies the transport of weathered material.)

Index

Abbott Village, 210
Abol Slide, 92
Acadia National Park, 35, 48, 64, 66-67, 222.
Addison, 71
Agamenticus, Mount, 15, 219
Agamenticus pluton, 189
Airline, the, 207
Allagash River, 18, 78, 101, 104
Allagash Falls, 110
Alton Bog, 99, 195
Amherst, 206
Androscoggin River, 39, 78, 105, 106, 213-14,
    227
Anemone Cave, 67
Appalachian Mountains, 21, 77, 80, 89, 165,
    171, 173, 217
Aroostook County, 184, 196, 198-99, 224
Aroostook River, 18, 102, 104, 198
Aroostook State Park, 80, 196
Arrowsic Island, 59
Ash Hill, 200, 224
Attean Pond, 166-67, 217
Auburn, 187, 193
Augusta, 18, 179
Aurora, 206
Avalonia, 166, 168, 171, 173, 192

Back Cove, 31
backshore, 46
Bailey Island, 59
Balanced Rock, 35
Bald Head Cliff, 15, 51
Bald Mountain deposit, 184, 200
Bangor: 18, 123, 195, 208; Basin, 195, 209
Bar Harbor, 66-67
Baring, 207
Bar Island, 67
Barred Island, 65, 115
basalt, 56, 70, 115-116, 150, 152-153, 203,
    222
Basin Ponds, 28
Bass Harbor Head, 68
Bath, 58, 187, 201
Battie, Mount, 62, 84, 120, 222
Baxter Peak, 17, 81
Baxter State Park, 92, 225
beach, 45, 46, 48-49, 54, 56, 58, 60, 61, 66,
    70, 72
beaches, 50-54, 57-61, 67, 71-72, 220
beachfront, 46
Beals Island, 71

Belfast, 19
Bethel, 98, 106, 214
Biddeford: 189; Point, 15; Pool, 56, 220
Big Ambejackmockamus Falls, 107, 225
Bigelow, Mount, 17, 78, 84, 90, 127, 226
Big Spencer Mountain, 80, 212
Big Squaw Mountain, 84, 127, 211
Big Wilson Stream, 107-9, 225
Bingham, 39, 215
biotite, 139
blowouts, 37
Blue Hill Bay, 16, 64, 65
Blue, Mount, 78, 84
Blue Ridge, 212
Boarstone Mountain, 16, 99, 226
bog, peat, 195-96
boudinage, 62
Brewer, 19
Bull Hill, 210, 224

Cadillac Mountain, 64, 65, 78, 89, 90
Calais, 19
calcite, 121,139, 200
Camden Hills State Park, 62-64, 84, 120, 201,
    222
Camp Ellis, 57
Cape Arundel, 15, 55
Cape Elizabeth, 50, 58, 166, 221
Cape Neddick, 50, 51, 118, 119, 220
Cape Neddick Harbor, 51
Cape Porpoise, 50, 55
Cape Rosier, 65
Cape Split, 71
Caribou, 179, 198
Carrabassett River, 100, 112, 223, 226
Carroll, 208
Casco Bay, 15, 50, 58
Caterpillar Hill, 65, 222
Central Upland region, 17-18, 100, 192-201
Chain Lakes massif, 165
Chamberlain Lake, 96
Champlain Mountain, 91
Charleston, 209
Chase, Mount, 184, 224
Chesuncook Lake, 96
Chimney Pond, 27, 98
Chiputneticook Lakes, 96, 205
chlorite, 139
cirque, 25, 28, 98, 201, 226
cliff-and-bench topography, 56
Clifton, 206
coast, 15, 16, 31, 38-41, 49, 50-63, 189-92,
    201-5, 219-21, 222-23
Coast Guard Beach, 59

Cobscook Bay, 75, 204
Coburn Gore, 166
continental drift. See plate tectonics, sea floor spreading
continents, collision of, 80-81, 124-25, 143, 150, 166-71, 192
Crawford, 207
Crescent Beach State Park, 58
Crocker Mountain, 27, 226
Crooked River, 98, 106
Crotch Island, 64
Crystal Bog, 99, 196, 224
crystals, 56
Cutler, 16

Daggett Rock, 35
Damariscotta, 58
Damariscotta Reversing Falls, 221
Damariscotta River, 59
Danforth, 19, 205
dating: by magnetic data, 152-53; by radioactivity, 161-64 ; radiocarbon, 54; relative, 71, 121-22, 158, 161
Deboullie Mountain, 18
Dedham Bald Mountain, 83, 205
Deer Isle, 64, 65
deltas, 39
Desert of Maine, 18, 38, 223
dike, basalt, 56, 70, 71, 72, 115-16, 203, 211
diorite, 200, 211
Dixfield, 213
Doubletop mountain, 225
Dover-Foxcroft, 16, 187
Downeast Coast, 50
Downeast Mountains, 19, 83, 100, 205-08
drainage pattern, 18, 20, 101-2
Drake's Island beach, 52, 54
drumlin, 31-32
Dyer Neck, 71

Eagle Lake, 67, 200
Earth, 143-45, 148
earthquakes, 144-45, 148, 153, 155, 186-87
East Grand Lake, 205, 224
East Musquash Lake, 208
East Point, 56
East Point Sanctuary, 220
Eastport, 118
East Wilton, 213
Echo Lake, 68
Edgecomb, 201
Ellsworth, 187, 202, 205
Englishman Bay, 64
Englishman River, 72
Enfield Horseback, 32
erosion, 13, 20, 75, 78, 80-81, 82, 85, 101-2, 119
erratic, 35, 67, 207
esker, 32, 206, 208, 223
Eustis, 115
Eustis Ridge, 226
Eyebrow, the, 215

exfoliation, 89, 206

Falmouth, 191, 192
Farmington, 16, 35
Farrar Hill, 207
fault: 56, 68, 86, 122, 168-70, 192, 205-06; Fundy, 72; Norumbega, 168, 192
feldspar, 82, 87-89, 138, 139, 204
Ferry Beach State Park, 57
Ferry—Old Orchard beaches, 50
Fish River, 104, 200
fjord, 27
Flagstaff Lake, 98, 127
floodplain, 102, 105, 199, 213
fold, rock, 56, 59, 62, 80, 86, 168-70, 194
foliation, definition of, 123
Fore River, 30
foreshore, 46
Forks, The, 216
Fort Fairfield, 179
Fort Kent, 199
Fort Knox State Park, 127
Fort Popham, 59
Fortunes Rocks, 56
fossils: 18, 72, 122, 148, 173, 201; dating by, 122, 158-60
Fox Island, 61
fractures, 68-70
Frenchman Bay, 16, 50, 64, 65, 203
Frenchville, 199
Friendship, 59
Fundy Fault, 72

gabbro, 51, 71, 83, 118-19, 203
Gardiner, 171
Gardner Mountain, 18
garnet, 48, 60, 84, 140
Georges Bank, 38, 48
glacial debris, 48, 56
glacial drift, 29
glaciation: 21-42; constructive processes of, 18, 29-35; continental, 20, 22, 175-76; destructive processes of, 13, 19, 23-27, 66, 195, 205, 210
glaciers: alpine, 21, 25, 98; flow of, 19, 25, 212; retreat of, 19, 31, 72, 175; sculpture by, 66, 68, 201, 205, 212, 215
gneiss, 84, 123, 171, 192-93
gold, 140
Goose Rocks Beach, 51, 55
gorge, 100, 107, 110-112, 223, 225, 227
Gorham, 18, 31, 93
Gouldsboro, 203
Grafton Notch State Park, 27, 107, 111, 214-15, 227
Grand Pitch, 110
granite: 78-83, 185; coastal, 16, 55, 61, 62, 70, 89; commercial, 64, 177-79; islands, 64-65, 68, 71, 223; Lucerne, 205-06
Gray, 187
Great Basin, 25, 201

Great Eddy, 213, 223
Great Heath, 99, 181
Great Hill (Eliot), 32
Great Hill (Kennebunk Beach), 54
Great Pond (Belgrade) 96
Great South Beach, 71
Great Wass Island, 71, 222
Greenville, 211
Greenville Junction, 211
Griffith Head, 61
Grindstone Falls, 110, 224
Grindstone Point, 222
groundwater, 93-96, 100, 184-185
Gulf Hagas, 111
Gulliver's Hole, 72-73, 223

hardpan, 31, 95
Half Mile Beach, 61-62
Hall Quarry, 68
Hallowell, 179
Harpswell Neck, 59
Haystack Mountain, 80, 118, 198, 200
Height of Land, 226
Hills Beach, 220
hornblende, 139
Horns Pond, 98
Horn, the, 83
Horse Mountain, 92, 225
horseback, 22, 32, 208
Houlton, 18
Hunnewell Beach, 59, 61

Iapetus Ocean, 166-67, 171
Ice Age, 20, 175-76. See also glaciation
Indian Hill, 211
intervale, 214
intrusions, 56, 59, 61, 84, 207, 208
Isle Au Haut, 64
Israels Head, 220

joints, 71, 82, 107
Jockey Cap, 22, 227
Jonesport, 71
Jordan Pond, 67

Katahdin Iron Works, 182-83
Katahdin, Mount: 17, 104, 195, 201, 224;
    erosion of, 81-82, 87-89, 119; glaciation
    of 25-28, 41, 77, 78, 225
Kenduskeag, 208
Kennebec River: 16, 17, 39, 59, 78, 105, 212,
    215, 223; Gorge, 110-11
Kennebunk Beach, 54-55
kettle lake, 39, 207
Kibby Stream, 141
Kineo, Mount, 80, 118, 212, 225
Kingsbury Stream, 210
Kittery, 50, 58
Knife-edge, the, 27
Knowles Corner, 200

lakes, 96-100
landslides, 31, 93
lava, 65, 72, 80, 115, 200
Lead Mountain, 19, 207
Ledge Falls, 225
Lee, 208
Limestone, 179
limestone, 121, 179, 196
Lincoln, 208
Little Peaked Mountain, 206
Little River, 61
Little Squaw Mountain, 211
Little Wilson Falls, 109
Livermore Falls, 39
Long Beach, 50
Long Lake, 68
Long Pond Stream, 99
longshore current, 45, 51
Lower South Branch Pond, 225
Lucerne, 19, 205

Machias Bay, 16, 64
Madawaska, 199
magnetism, 151-56
Maine Geological Survey, 183
mantle, 145, 150
maps, geologic, 180-83
marble, 124
Marginal Way, 51, 220
marsh, salt, 46, 47, 52, 54
Marshall Point, 15, 59, 62
Mars Hill, 196, 224
Massacre Pond, 58
Mattawamkeag, 18
Medway, 31, 39, 224
Megunticook, Mount, 84, 222
meltwater, glacial, 22, 29, 32, 35, 39, 72, 193
metamorphism: 122, 125; contact, 127, 194,
    196, 206, 207, 208; regional, 125, 160-
    61, 194. See also rocks, metamorphic
mica, 48, 113, 139, 193
Midcoast region, 50, 84
Milbridge, 203
Mile Beach, 61
Millinocket, 16
Milo, 187
minerals, 48, 60, 87-89, 113, 116-17, 122, 128-
    39, 194. See also individual names.
mining, 181, 182, 183-84, 200
Monson, 122, 180, 210
Moody Point, 51, 54
Moose Cave, 214
Moosehead Plateau, 17
Moosehead Lake, 17, 96, 127, 158, 211, 212
Mooselookmeguntic Lake, 78, 96, 226
Moose River, 212
moraine, 27, 29, 39, 72
Morse River, 59
Moscow, 215
Mother Walker Falls, 214

mountain building, *80, 81, 84, 150*
Mountain Upland region, 16, 77-84, 85-86, 100, 210-17
Mount Blue State Park, 226
Mount Desert Island, 27, 50, 64, 65-70, 85, 127, 222
mountains, 19, 25, 80-83, 84
Moxie Falls Park, 109, 216, 226
mudstone, 84
muscovite, 139
Musquash Mountain, 19

Newcastle, 58, 201
Newport, 195
New Sharon, 213
Newry, 213, 214
Norridgewock, 213
North Anson Gorge, 112, 223
North Basin, 25, 201
North Haven Island, 65
Northern region, 18-19, 25, 101-02, 104
Norton Hill, 210, 224
Norumbega Fault zone, 168, 192
Nubble, the, 51, 220

O-J-I Mountain, 92
Ogunquit-Moody beaches, 15, 48, 49, 50, 51, 220
Old Orchard beach, 15, 49, 50, 57
Old Speck, 17, 215
olivine, 139
Onawa, Lake, 99
orogeny, 171, 192
Orland, 201
Orrs Island, 59
orthoclase, 138
Ossipee River, 106
Ovens, the, 68-70
Owls Head, 50

Pamola Peak, 27
Pangaea, 172
Paris, 184
Parlin Pond, 216
Passadumkeag Mountain, 19
Passamaquoddy Bay, 75
Patten, 200
Peaked Mountain, 83, 89, 195, 206
peat, 54, 99, 181-82, 195-96
pegmatite, 138, 192, 193, 213
Pemaquid Point, 15, 59, 62, 221
Penobscot Bay, 16, 50, 58, 62, 64, 201
Penobscot River: 78, 105; East Branch, 18, 104, 110, 224; West Branch, 83, 104, 107, 225
peninsulas, 58-59
Perry, 204
Petit Manan Point, 71
phyllite, 122, 194, 195, 201, 210
Pineo Ridge, 39
Pine Point, 57

Pinnacle Ridge, 225
Piscataquis Valley, 224
plagioclase, 138
plate tectonics, 150-51, 166-75, 176
Pleasant Bay, 16
pluton, 82, 118, 127, 204
Popham Beach State Park, 16, 47, 48, 59, 221
Popham, Fort, 59, 105
Porcupines (islands), 25
Portage Lake, 199, 200
Portland, 58, 171, 189, 190, 191
Presidential Range, 17
Presque Isle, 158, 198
Presumpscot River, 31
Prouts Neck, 57, 58
pyrite, 89, 139, 194
pyroxene, 139

Quaggy Joe Mountain, 80, 118
quarry: granite, 64, 68, 177-79; limestone, 121, 179; slate, 122, 180, 194, 210
quartz, 48, 51, 56, 113, 120, 124, 137-38
quartzite, 124, 192, 210
Quoddy Head State Park, 50, 223

radioactive wastes, 185
Rangeley Lake, 96
rebound, crustal, 38
Red Beach, 204, 223
Reed Mountain, 18
Reid State Park, 61
reversing falls, 75, 204, 221
rhyolite, 118, 198, 203, 212, 216
Richmond, 123
Ripley Neck, 71
Ripogenus Gorge, 110, 225
rock cycle, 85-86, 140-42
Rockland, 31, 93, 179
rocks: 113, 118, 121, 138; age of, 161-64, 165; basalt family, 115-16, 141, 166, 203; granite family, 115, 118, 142, 200, 203; igneous, 113-19; metamorphic, 51, 58, 62-64, 84, 122-27, 171, 193, 194; plutonic, 82, 118, 127, 171, 189, 201, 204, 205; sedimentary, 119-22, 158, 171, 196, 204; volcanic, 65, 68, 70, 75, 118, 121, 183, 196, 203
rock slides, 92
Rockwood, 212, 225
Roque Bluffs, 175
Roque Bluffs Beach State Park, 72
Roque Island, 71
Rumford, 16, 213
Rumford Falls, 227

Sabbattus River, 193
Saco, 190
Saco River, 102, 105-6
Saddleback Mountain, 83
St. Croix River, 187
St. George River, 59

St. John River, 18, 78, 101, 104, 199
St. Lawrence Valley, 25
Salt Bay, 221
sand, 47, 48-49, 51-52, 54, 56, 59-62
sandbar, 45, 102
Sand Beach, 67
sand dunes, 35-38, 46-47, 48, 54, 61, 62, 215
Sand Point, 68
sandstone, 47, 84, 120
Sandy River, 102, 109
Scarborough: Beach, 57; River, 57, 58
schist, 84, 123, 192
Schoodic Peninsula, 70, 89, 116, 203, 222
Screw Auger Gorge, 111
sea arch, 68
sea cave, 67, 68
sea cliff, 55, 67
sea floor spreading, 149-50
Seal Cove, 68
seawall, 49, 55, 68
Seawall Beach, 61
Seawall picnic area, 68
Sebago Lake, 78, 96, 98, 99, 106, 223
Sebago State Park, 106
Sedgwick, 65
Settlement Quarry, 64
shale, 84, 121
Shatter Zone, the, 68, 127
sheeting, 71, 189, 194, 204, 205
Sherman, 195
shingle, beach, 70
Shin Pond, 158
Shoppee Point, 72
Sidney, 194
silt, marine, 30, 31, 39, 93, 121, 191
Skowhegan, 213, 223
slate, 84, 121, 122, 180, 194, 210
slickensides, 56, 205, 210
Smalls Falls, 109, 226
Smyrna Mills, 18
Snow Falls Gorge, 100, 111-12, 227
Soldier Pond, 200
Solon, 215
Somes Sound, 27, 66, 67
South Basin, 25, 27, 98, 201
South Bubble, 35, 67
South Peak, 27
spit, barrier, 51, 52, 61
Springfield, 208
Spruce Meadow Picnic Area, 215
Squire Point, 71
Step Falls, 107
Stillwater River, 105
Stonington, 95
striations, glacial, 23, 25
subduction, 150, 153, 171
subsidence, coastal, 41
Sugarloaf Mountain, 83
Sunkhaze Bog, 99
Swift River: 141; Falls, 107

Tablelands, the, 81, 90
talus, 91-92
tarn, 27, 28, 98
Tarn, the, 67
Telos Lake, 104
Thomaston, 121, 173, 179, 201
till, 31, 72, 175
timberline, 84-85
Tobey Falls, 109
Todd's Head, 61
Togue Pond, 225
tombolo, 61, 65, 67, 221
Topsfield, 204
Topsham, 123
tourmaline, 139
traprock, 118
Traveler Mountain, 80, 118, 158, 224, 225
Trout Brook, 158
tuff, 69-70, 121, 203
Tumbledown Cliffs, 226
Tumbledown Pond, 98
Tumbledown Range, 226
Tunk Mountain, 203
Two Lights State Park, 58, 221

uplift, crustal, 19, 38, 39, 41, 54, 80, 119
U-shaped valley, 27, 66, 68, 215

Van Buren, 199
Vinalhaven, 64, 179
volcano, 80, 68, 153. See also rock, volcanic

Waldo, Mount, 127
waterfalls, 107-10
Waterville, 19
Wayne, 223
weathering, 13, 19, 27, 56, 78, 87-91, 193,
   194, 195, 196, 211-12
Webster Stream, 105
Wells Beach, 15, 51, 52, 54, 220
Wesley, 207
Western Beach, 57, 58
West Bath, 201
West Gardiner, 194
West Grand Lake, 78, 96
West Kennebago Mountain, 83
Weston, 205, 224
West Pembroke, 204
West Quoddy Head, 16, 50, 72, 118
West Sullivan, 203
Whalesback, the, 32, 206, 223
Willard Mountain, 18
Winterville, 115, 200
Wiscassett, 58, 187
Wood Island, 61
Woolwich, 58
Wyman Lake, 215

Yarmouth, 192